PUBLIC LIBRARY
ASSOCIATION
A division of the American Library Association

THE GUIDE TO
❧INTERNET❧
JOB
SEARCHING

Margaret Riley Dikel
Frances Roehm   Steve Oserman

Job and Career Information Services Committee of the Adult Lifelong Learning Section

Public Library Association
American Library Association

VGM Career Horizons
NTC/Contemporary Publishing Group

Library of Congress Cataloging-in-Publication Data

Riley Dikel, Margaret.
      The guide to internet job searching, 1998–99 edition / Margaret Riley Dikel, Frances
Roehm, and Steve Oserman.
      p.   cm.
    Includes index.
    ISBN 0-8442-8199-9
     1. Job hunting—Computer network resources.   2. Internet (Computer
network)   3. World Wide Web (Information retrieval system)
I. Roehm, Frances.   II. Oserman, Steve.   III. Title.
HF5382.7.R557   1998
025.06′65014—dc21   98-16128
                                           CIP

HF
5382.7
. D54
1998

Interior design by Precision Graphics

Published by VGM Career Horizons
A division of NTC/Contemporary Publishing Group, Inc.
4255 West Touhy Avenue, Lincolnwood (Chicago), Illinois 60646-1975 U.S.A.
Printed in the United States of America
International Standard Book Number: 0-8442-8199-9

18   17   16   15   14   13   12   11   10   9   8   7   6   5   4   3   2   1

Contents

FOREWORD   v

INTRODUCTION   vii

ACKNOWLEDGMENTS AND DEDICATIONS   ix

CHAPTER 1   Using the Internet in Your Search for Employment   1

CHAPTER 2   The Internet Job Application   11

CHAPTER 3   Pounding the Virtual Pavement: Beginning Your   17
              Internet Job Search

CHAPTER 4   The Great Job Listing Sites   35

CHAPTER 5   Jobs in Business, Marketing, and Personal or   49
              Commercial Services

CHAPTER 6   Jobs in the Social Sciences and the World of Nonprofits   57

CHAPTER 7   Jobs in the Humanities, Recreation, Hospitality,   71
              and Transportation

CHAPTER 8   Jobs in Science, Health, and Medicine   81

CHAPTER 9   Jobs in Engineering, Mathematics, and Technology   91

CHAPTER 10   Opportunities in Government, Public Policy, and   109
              Public Service

CHAPTER 11   Entry-Level and Summer Employment, Internships,   123
              and Co-ops

CHAPTER 12   State and Local Resources for the United States   133

CHAPTER 13   International Opportunities   209

CHAPTER 14   Career Resources Online   233

APPENDIX A   Services for the Experienced Job Seeker   245

APPENDIX B   Networking on the Net   255

              INDEXES   265

Foreword

Whenever I speak to a job search club or workshop, I ask for a show of hands from those who are using the Internet actively to uncover opportunities. To my amazement, only a few hands typically go up (unless I'm addressing a college audience, where almost everyone is connected). Yet, when I ask how many have access to the Internet at home or work, most say they do.

So, why aren't people who can surf the Net doing so to find new jobs? The most common reply is that they've tried looking electronically, but have quit after a few hours of frustration. They say there are just too many places to search for job leads, and that there's no directory to guide them effectively.

But, there is. In fact, there are many, both online and in print. And the leader in directing job-search traffic online is Margaret Riley Dikel. *The Riley Guide,* which she created while a librarian at Worcester Polytechnic Institute, is the foremost resource online for job hunters (*http://www.dbm.com/jobguide/*). It combines tremendous research and thoughtful analysis in an easy-to-review format. Fortunately, that formula has translated well into this print guide to Internet search sites.

Of course, writing about any aspect of job hunting can be tricky. While much of the advice offered by career advisers is evergreen (it doesn't change much), really good guidance changes almost daily to reflect the volatile job market. When you add the Internet into the equation, uncovering techniques for job hunting effectively becomes a daunting task. But Margaret has built her career on reviewing all of the advice on the Net and distilling the best and most useful from the rest.

To succeed in your search, you should learn to do the same. For example, when scanning job listings in a particular site, look for tools that will help you refine your efforts. You should be able to search job databases by industry and function, title, geographic location, company name, salary level, and years of experience. It also helps to find sites that offer direct access to each company's recruiters, as well as that employer's home page on the Net. Then, as companies are reviewing you as a candidate, you can research them as well to select those where you would enjoy working most.

This directory is organized in a similar format. Each chapter focuses on different Internet databases, ranging from jobs in business and science in the United States and abroad, to opportunities in the nonprofit world and federal government. It goes beyond job hunting to identify sites where you can better define and develop your career objectives. But to use this directory effectively—and to thoroughly tap into the resources of the Internet—you must abandon your inhibitions. If you are new to the Net, consider this guide your training wheels as you gain confidence in your ability to navigate among thousands of sites. If you're already a savvy surfer, you'll learn more about job hunting on the Internet than you ever imagined.

Tony Lee,
Editor in Chief/General Manager
Careers.wsj.com
The Wall Street Journal Interactive Edition

Introduction

Our local communities are adapting to the rapid changes in communication technology. Schools, local governments, libraries, businesses, and other groups are receiving and distributing information via the Internet. Today's public libraries are playing a vital role in the development of these local initiatives, and many of them are offering a connection with the information sources on the Internet along with their more traditional services.

The World Wide Web, with its easy-to-use browsing and searching features, has encouraged this rapid adaptation to Internet information services. Traditional information providers are finding that these services are not only "user friendly," but also cost-effective—they save paper, staff time, and long-distance charges—essentially, getting more bang for the buck.

Job and career information is perfectly suited to the trend toward online services, and the growth in Internet resources and services in this area is skyrocketing. In electronic format, information can be accessed from anywhere and by anyone on the planet! Job postings can be keyed or scanned in very quickly, making the information available almost as soon as a position is open. Resumes can be matched to companies or suitable job listings. Potential employees can obtain information about a company prior to the interview.

Public libraries have traditionally played a vital role in the job search, providing local and national newspapers, career guides, and knowledge of the community and its agencies to direct individuals to the information they need. With the changing job scene and the increasing number of electronic career services online and on CD-ROM, your public library is more important than ever!

This PLA guide will show you how to access the information you need and where to look for it. It will also give you the guidelines you need to manage this new, increasingly active environment. Your public library can help point the way with books about job searching, writing resumes, and other career guides, as well as the new materials on using the Internet. It should soon, if it does not now, also provide you with access to the Internet. If you live in a community whose public library doesn't provide these services yet, try the local community college or high school. In any event, we hope it's just a matter of time until you can be surfing with the best of them, adding a new dimension to your job search with great results.

You will notice some changes in this edition of the guide. Our chapter on local resources has expanded tremendously with the growth of smaller, more regional services to help you. The international chapter has expanded into new countries with recruiting needs. And we have included resources for many occupations and industries that were not online when the first edition went to press, but are now adding their electronic voices and resources to the Internet. The more we progress, the more this virtual environment grows to meet the needs of the many rather than just the needs of a few.

Use the guide with our best wishes for success in your job search!

Margaret Riley Dikel	Frances E. Roehm	Steve Oserman
Rockville, MD	Skokie, IL	Skokie, IL

Acknowledgments and Dedications

From Steve:

My deepest appreciation goes to the Skokie Public Library staff, the Public Library Association, and all of the Job and Career Information Services Committee members. My greatest thanks to those who have given me vision and encouragement when I needed it most: Jean Patterson, Joan Durrance, Vera Green, Carolyn Anthony, Marilyn Moats Kennedy, George Needham, and Dick Bolles.

Margaret, Frances, and Betsy are the most inspirational and enjoyable people in the world to work with.

And thank you, Danielle, for your most special friendship and support.

From Frances:

In memory of my parents, Louis B. and Mary Kathryn Sutton, and my aunts, Frankie, Jane, Lillian, and Margaret.

Thank you to Carolyn Anthony and the staff and volunteers of the Skokie Public Library for lending their support, encouragement, and resources to this project.

And my thanks to all those who have, each in his or her own way, contributed to my professional and personal development, especially:

Leonard J. Cotter, Christopher Roehm, Larry (Charlie) Faber, Elaine Hershbarger, Barbara Roberts, and Harriet Wallace.

Professors Robert Sutton, Lachlan Blair, Kathryn Luther Henderson, Maynard Brichford, and Terry Weech.

Barbara Stuart, Mildred and Jack Bates.

The staff and volunteers of the Champaign County Historical Archives.

All of my colleagues and friends from Urbana-Champaign, the History Department, Archives, and Graduate School of Library and Information Science at the University of Illinois, and the great libraries of Illinois.

And Wulfy too.

From Margaret:

I owe a debt of gratitude to many, many people, including:

The staff of the Kensington Park Library for providing access to sources and services above and beyond the call, and the Washington, D.C., chapter of the International Association of Career Management Professionals for their encouragement, information, and support.

David Bacharach, Bob Stirling, and Steve Hoffman, all of whom have been wonderful resources and strong supporters of *The Riley Guide*.

Drake Beam Morin, Inc., for providing support for *The Riley Guide* while letting me continue to work it as I wish.

Tony Lee, Gabrielle Solomon, and everyone else I have worked with at the *National Business Employment Weekly*.

Dick Bolles, in whom I find tremendous inspiration.

But my work in this book is dedicated to my parents, Stewart and Marian Finkler; to my husband, David Dikel; and to the memory of my grandmother, Florence Neu.

1

Using the Internet in Your Search for Employment

What Is the Internet Job Search?

You can find any number of books about job hunting and about the Internet. Why is the Internet so important to your job search, and why do you need a book about it? You can just get on the Web, connect to a site like The Monster Board or the Online Career Center, and get to everything easily, right? *Wrong!* Job hunting on the Internet uses a broad variety of resources and services. No single list, site, or resource will contain all of the information you want or need. To use the Internet effectively in your job search, you must be prepared to look at every piece of it—not just the Web, but also Usenet newsgroups and mailing lists. You have to know what types of resources are there to guide you, like virtual libraries, online resource guides, and search engines, and how to use them. You need to know how to use online recruiting sites, resume databases, electronic journals and newspapers, and other services and resources to help you find leads and win jobs. And most importantly, you need to be aware that the Internet is much more than the world's largest database of job listings. It's the world's largest information database, just waiting for you to get out there and find what you need to get you in the door and behind the desk. You can pick and choose among all of these services and resources to better customize your search, but they are all essential pieces of your strategy.

Why Use the Internet as a Part of Your Job Search?

Many of you are sitting out there wondering why you picked up this book. The job search is already tough. Why do you want to make it any harder by looking at something as vast as the Internet? There are several reasons why the Internet can be an asset to your job search.

1. Networking! Experts suggest that 80 percent of available jobs are never advertised. They are filled by a friend or acquaintance of someone already in the organization or by a person already known to the organization. All of the job-search gurus say that networking is an important part of making the job search a success. The Internet is the world's largest network, so use its reach to your advantage. Get to know people both locally and internationally, because sometimes those distant contacts can be much closer than you think. Use the Internet's e-mail and Usenet newsgroup resources to help break the ice when meeting new people, so when you have the chance for a face-to-face meeting, your stress will be reduced. After all, you already know this person, so it's no big deal!

2. Current growth of the Internet. As the Internet grows and expands, so do the number of participants and the available resources for finding jobs. Profit and nonprofit organizations are coming online, and they are finding it not only easy, but also inexpensive, to add their available job openings to their public servers. Even better, these companies are posting information about themselves, giving you access to press releases, product information, and annual reports. To gain access to all of these opportunities, you need to be online too.

3. Round-the-clock availability. Many job seekers cannot search for work during regular business hours because of current work schedules or other responsibilities. The Internet is available to you when you are ready to use it, 24 hours a day, seven days a week, regardless of time zones. Employers aren't concerned that you are looking at the job opportunities at 2 A.M., they are only concerned with finding the best person to fill the position. If your letter and resume will be accepted via e-mail, they can be sent at any time and will calmly wait in the company e-mail box for the first person who comes in.

4. Free access to information and resources. Once you have gotten access to the Internet, you can use hundreds of free resources with job listings, find help for writing resumes and constructing cover letters, and even plan your career path online. Although several agencies in your community can help you in the same ways, many of them are limited in their hours of operation. Consult your local agencies and use their support and feedback, but also use the good resources you find online, again with that 24-hour access!

5. Broad geographic reach. Current employment trends in the United States and abroad are making us a more mobile society. Perhaps your spouse, partner, or family has been transferred, or you just want to move elsewhere to try for better or different work. You can begin investigating that move now on the Internet. Check out various cities and regions online. You can even look at other countries, find out what opportunities for employment exist there, and begin contacting employers. You may be able to set up interviews by phone or have them scheduled for shortly after your arrival. Whether you are moving across the state, across the country, or out of the country, there is no need to wait until you actually arrive in your new location to begin your search for employment.

6. Opportunity to demonstrate leading-edge skills. Organizations, especially businesses, are rushing to get onto the Internet. They see opportunities for advertising, possible commercial markets, and a vast wealth of information they can tap. Using the Internet as a tool in your job search demonstrates to an employer your familiarity and skill with this new market area, and that could set you apart from other candidates in his or her eyes. If you found the information on the Internet, make sure you let the employer know this.

7. Keyword search capability. How many newspapers do you read to look for employment? Think of each newspaper as a separate database of information. You read the classified ads of each one looking for job titles, lists of required skills, and position responsibilities that match your own interests and experiences. Even if your newspaper uses keywords to bring all job listings in a field together, you still have to read the entire help wanted section to find all of the possible listings in your field—and even then you may miss some. Any given job may be listed under several different job titles, but the skills and responsibilities are consistent. Keyword searching in the various Internet databases and resources allows you to pull up similar listings much more quickly and efficiently, cutting down on the amount of time and effort you need for each separate database.

8. Tips on companies that are hiring.* If you see a company posting a lot of jobs online, that's a clue that it might be expanding operations or even starting something new. Check the company webserver, but also begin researching it in the online newspapers and electronic journals. Try to find out what the company is working on, and even if it is not recruiting for someone with your skills right now, get your resume and cover letter ready and get it in there. Be a step ahead and the first in line with a resume when attention turns toward your field.

9. Resume posting at no cost.* There are several databases and newsgroups that allow you to post your resume at no charge once you have Internet access. Although this raises some questions about the control and confidentiality of your resume (more about this in Chapter 2), it is an effective way to get your resume seen by recruiters and employers who use these databases regularly.

Job Search Tip: Finding Your Niche. The Internet is not just for techies! As the number of participants grows, so does the diversity of the online information and the online job listings. Move away from the **misc.jobs.offered** newsgroup and follow the smaller newsgroups discussing topics in your field. Look for links to more specific information resources for other good starting points.

Getting Started on the Internet: Connectivity and the Basics

Before we take you onto the Internet to begin your job search, we'll take a few minutes to talk about what you are about to get into. Almost every general Internet book gives you an overview of the Internet and a bit of its history, so we aren't going to discuss that. You can also pick up any number of good books on how to use the Internet at your local public library. At the end of this chapter we have listed some we find most useful, along with some magazines with good information to help you online. What we will address in this chapter is how you can connect to the Internet, the places where you might be able to hook up, and the equipment you will need to use the whole Internet.

You see, the Internet is a mix of networks and computers with different ways of connecting and communicating, called *protocols*. To use the Internet effectively for your job search means learning enough about these networks and the various ways of communicating to be sure you can connect and find the information you need.

---

* Goldsborough, Reid. *Straight Talk About the Information Superhighway.* New York: Alpha Books, 1994, p. 48.

What do you need to learn in order to use the Internet? You need to know how to access and navigate the World Wide Web. You also need to learn how to access electronic mail (e-mail) and Usenet newsgroups and how to communicate with others using these and mailing lists. If you are connecting from home, you'll need to know how to use the dial-up program provided by your Internet service. There are different software programs used to access each piece, and there are numerous vendors marketing different packages, so you may find yourself looking at one program at home but a different one at work or at the library. The thing to remember is that all of these programs have the same basic functions. If you can't find a book that discusses the program you are using, take the ideas and functions outlined in another book and look for similar features in your program. The most common features will always be present, no matter which software program you use.

Internet Tips: Reading the Net. Although there are several programs to access the various parts of the Internet, they are grouped into basic categories.

- *Mailers* are those programs you use to read and send e-mail and to access mailing lists.
- *Newsreaders* are used to read the Usenet newsgroups.
- *Web browsers* are used to access the World Wide Web. Some of these are text based, but most will display graphics.

Equipment Needed to Use the Internet

Do you have a computer with a hard drive, a 9200-baud modem, and a communication program? Then you are all set to go online. That really is all you need to access the Internet. You don't need 56K modems, Windows, graphics capability, or color monitors unless you want to use a graphical browser to access the World Wide Web. You just need something reliable to dial into the provider's service and display the text. You'll want a printer too, so you can print the things you find online, especially the job listings, but even this doesn't have to be fancy. It just all needs to be reliable.

What if you don't have a computer but are willing to buy one? You can decide for yourself between a PC and a Macintosh system—either will work. Regardless of the system you decide to buy, keep these few ideas in mind when you are computer shopping to help you choose wisely.

1. Speed. Get the fastest processor and the fastest modem you can afford. Processor speeds are measured in *megahertz* (MHz) and modem speeds are measured in *bits per second* (bps), also referred to as *baud rates*. The higher the numbers, the faster the equipment, and on the Internet, faster is always better. The standard for modems right now is 28800 bps, but that is rising.

2. Memory. Get the biggest hard drive and the most *random access memory* (RAM) you can. Memory is measured in *bytes,* and the amounts found in personal computers are stated in terms of *kilobytes* (K) or *megabytes* (MB). If you get a new computer, look for a 500MB hard drive and at least 8MB of RAM; 16 to 32MB of RAM is even better.

3. A good monitor. Your eyes are important, and using a computer can be strenuous on your eyes, especially after a long day at work. Get the best monitor you can afford. Ask about the *resolution* or clarity. The higher the numbers, the better the monitor. Also ask about the *pitch,* the space between the letters. The smaller the numbers, the better. And if you can find a 17-inch monitor for a reasonable price, you might want to buy it and enlarge your viewable space.

You can probably get a used computer at a great bargain. Check the newspaper for people selling their old computers, watch for "computer swap" meets, or see if there is a computer-user club in your area. They might be able to help you get set up for a low price. At the minimum, you should look for a 486 PC with Windows 3.1 or a Macintosh with System 7 software or better. Then you will be ready to surf the Internet with the rest of the world! Oh, wait. There is one more thing. You'll need access to the Internet.

Internet Tip: Graphics and Browsers. In order to view the graphics on the World Wide Web, you will need a 486 PC with Windows 3.1 or Windows 95 and a modem that connects at 14400 bps or faster. For Macintosh users, you should have a Mac with System 7 or later.

When you call providers about access through their services, ask them what software you need in order to use their *graphical browser* for the Web.

Just a Thought: If you are buying a new computer for yourself, why not donate your old one to a shelter, church, or food bank in your area? Many of these organizations are in need of computers, and they certainly don't have to be the biggest, fastest, most colorful machines available. They just have to be working computers that can be used for simple record keeping and resume preparation. Your local public library can probably help you find a list of organizations in your area that would love to have your old equipment.

Connecting to the Internet

There are several places that make it possible for you to access the Internet. Some of these places will charge you a fee, but it's possible that you are lucky enough to live near someone who provides free access. Here is a list of the places to check for Internet access, starting with some free sources.

1. Your local public library. Many public libraries are getting funding from government agencies as well as nonprofit foundations established to help them set up public terminals with Internet access. If your local library doesn't yet offer this service, ask if they can refer you to another library that does.

2. Community Freenets. Many local networks out there are providing information on local communities, their government, and local businesses, and these networks are also connecting to the Internet. Check with your public library or a local computer user group to see if one is available in your area.

3. Your place of work. More organizations and businesses are joining the Internet, and many permit their employees to access it also. If they do, there may be in-house regulations for use and security precautions. Check with your employer before you begin any personal surfing on the company system.

4. Cybercafés. If you don't need access that often but you just have to have your coffee with you when you're online, these businesses give you a place to go for a sandwich, a cup of coffee, and the Internet. Most require that you buy a card with cash credit on it and pay for the amount of time you are connected.

5. A commercial provider. America Online and similar services all offer access to the Internet. You can send e-mail to the Internet, read Usenet newsgroups, and use a *web browser* to access the World Wide Web. You also have access to private information sites available from the network providers.

6. Internet service providers (ISPS). Like the commercial providers, you pay a monthly fee and are given a software package to use when connecting, but these services connect you directly to the Internet without any detours through the private networks.

Internet Tip: Distinguishing Between Providers. What is the difference between using a commercial provider like America Online and an Internet service provider? It depends on what you want. America Online and the other commercial providers have a great deal of information within their private networks that Internet users cannot get to. These private networks are usually well organized and the information is easy to find, something of which the Internet cannot boast. On the other hand, some commercial providers have slow and somewhat problematic connections to the Internet, and some of their private information is now available through the Internet. The final decision is yours.

If you are one of those lucky people with several options for Internet access, how do you select the best one for you? Is it always best to use a free service? No, not always. Your local public library will probably not give you an e-mail account, and cybercafés can't provide this either. Your community Freenet might be so busy you can't get connected. Many employers are limiting Internet access to certain employees or restricting use to work-related issues only. You may already be thinking about buying an account, so how do you go about finding out which service has the best deal for you? Use **The List** of ISPS available at *http://thelist.internet.com/* to search for services in your area code or state, and then read over **Jay Barker's Online Connection** at *http://www.barkers.org/online/* for comparisons between the major commercial online services and national ISPs. Draw up a list of several that serve your area, and then call and speak with them about their services. What should you ask them?

1. How much will it cost? If there is a fee, what is the *set-up fee* (the original cost to get you started) and the *usage fee* (the monthly base charge)? What do these include? Is there a *fee for connect time* (the actual amount of time you spend online)? How are these charges *collected?* Most companies want to bill your credit card. Is there a *discount* for paying for one year in advance? Many will offer you a discount on your monthly fee if you pay for a whole year in advance.

2. Is there a local number you can dial to access the service? You don't want to pay long-distance charges for access. Ask for a complete list of their dial-in numbers and check them yourself.

3. What Internet services will you have access to? You want access to e-mail, Usenet newsgroups, and the Web.

4. What computers and operating systems do they support? Can you get software that runs on DOS or Macintosh? Do you need Windows 95 or will Windows 3.1 be okay? Can you get a package that works with your OS/2 system? Tell them what you have and make sure they will support it.

5. Do they provide the software you need to connect with and use the Internet? Most Internet service providers have a standard software package they send you to set up your access to their services, including the dialer software your modem will need. This should come with a note on how to configure all of the software to work properly, or instructions on calling technical support to complete the setup.

6. Do the mailer and newsreader programs they use let you read and respond to messages offline? If you are paying for your connect time, this feature can save you a lot of money.

7. What are their minimum and maximum baud rates for connecting? At the very least, they should offer connectivity from *9200 to 28800 bps.* Some services support up to 57200 bps connections, but this capability is limited.

8. What is their modem-to-user ratio? You want to know how easy it is to connect when you want to. A ratio of *30-to-1* may mean you get a lot of busy signals. A ratio of *15-to-1* is much more reasonable.

9. How do you get help if you get stuck? Does the provider have a local or 800 number to call, and will they respond to your calls? At what times can you get support—during working hours only, or can you talk to someone late evenings and weekends too? Also, ask how large their support staff is. Only one person, even during low-use periods, is not enough.

10. Can you get some free time just to try their service? Most providers will let you try them out for five hours or so at no cost. Go ahead and ask!

11. How many years have they been in business? It's fast-paced and furious, and many ISPS have come and gone very quickly.

Once you have collected information from several providers, compare their answers. Online access is a very competitive business, so shop around for the best rates, the best deals, and the package that best fits your needs.

Recommended Reading to Learn More About the Internet

Check your local library for these titles. If they are not in the collection, ask the librarians if they can get them for you through an interlibrary loan or if they might recommend other helpful titles.

BOOKS

- Ellsworth, Jill. *The Internet 1997 Unleashed.* Indianapolis: Sams, 1996. (A well-written reference to the whole Internet.)
- Gilster, Paul. *The Web Navigator.* New York: John Wiley & Sons, 1997. (Gilster is an excellent author, giving easy instructions for new users but never ignoring the more advanced surfer.)
- Grimes, Galen A. *10-Minute Guide to the Internet and the World Wide Web.* New York: Que Education & Training, 1996. (Quick pointers to getting online.)
- Hahn, Harley. *Harley Hahn's Internet & Web Yellow Pages 1997.* Berkeley, CA: Osborne McGraw-Hill, 1996. (Renowned for its simple yet amusing look at the online world.)
- Levine, John R., et al. *The Internet for Dummies,* 4th ed. Chicago: IDG Books Worldwide, 1997. (The favored text of the computer fearful!)

MAGAZINES (SUBSCRIPTION INFORMATION)

Computer Currents
Computer Currents Publishing, Inc.
5720 Hollis St., Emeryville, CA 94608
Phone: (510) 547-6800

Internet World

U.S. and Canada:

MecklerMedia Corp.

P.O. Box 713

Mount Morris, IL 61054-9965

Phone: (800) 573-3062

Elsewhere:

Mecklermedia Ltd.

Artillery House, Artillery Row

London SWIP 1RT, England

Phone: (0) 71 976-0405

NetGuide

CMP Media

P.O. Box 420355

Palm Coast, FL 32142-9371

Phone: (800) 829-0421

2

The Internet
Job Application

You know why you want to go online, you know how to get online, you think you know what you are getting yourself into, so let's go! *Wait a second!* First things first. How do you *respond* to the job listings you find on the Internet? Do you just send e-mail back to the poster and say, "Hi, I want that job you advertised on the Internet?" *No! No! No!* Your electronic application for employment has to be just as good online as it is off, so let's take a minute to go over a few more things before you begin your electronic job search.

Applying to Positions Advertised on the Internet

The fastest way to respond to Internet job listings is by e-mailing your cover letter and resume to the person or organization indicated. You still need that great resume and fantastic cover letter, but there are a few things you need to do a little differently.

1. You need a resume in plain text, sometimes called ASCII or DOS text, for sending via e-mail. (See "Preparing Your Resume for E-mail.") Check it and make sure it looks good! You don't want your text to wrap and look bad on a different size screen, so keep the width to *65 columns (characters) wide*. Absolutely no word processing files! These will not e-mail well, and the person on the receiving end will not take the time to reassemble your resume.

2. Send your resume in the text of the e-mail message. You have only about 30 seconds to catch the eye of recruiters and get them to read your resume. If you send your resume as an attachment, recruiters have to go looking for it and try to decipher it. Zip! Your 30 seconds are over before they even start. Put the resume right in the message so they will see it immediately upon opening the mail. You should also be aware that many e-mail systems cannot handle attachments well, and many attachments are lost in transmission.

> **Internet Tip: Using Attachments.** An *attachment* is a file or message that travels along with an e-mail but is not a part of it, like a photo clipped to the front of a report circulating around the office. E-mail can only transmit plain text, but you can paper clip or attach other types of files to the messages to travel with and be delivered to the same place as the e-mail.

3. Include a cover letter and be sure to note where you found the ad. Make sure recruiters know you are an Internet user and that their online recruiting has been successful so they will do it again. You can create and store a "standard" cover letter in text, but remember to customize it for each job listing you are applying for. Again, check the format and width before you send it.

4. Send your resume and cover letter in one file. Would you mail a letter and resume in separate envelopes? *Never!* You may think your resume is too long because it covers many screens, but if you have written a one- or two-page resume and merely transferred it to plain text, it is the proper length. Catch the employer's eye with a good objective statement and a summary of your skills at the top.

5. Use the advertised job title as the Subject of your e-mail message, citing any relevant job numbers as noted in the ad. This makes it easy to route your resume and letter to the appropriate person. If you are "cold calling" to get your resume into someone's hands without an advertised position to reference, put a few words stating your objective in the "Subject" line. If you use one Internet job service frequently and have had good luck finding positions advertised there, consider registering your resume with that service. Then you can send a message with the reference number of your resume to apply for any position that service advertises. The same recruiters will also find you when they search the database.

6. *Warning:* **Some organizations advertise online but do not accept resumes via e-mail!** Sometimes employers want the materials sent to a different e-mail address, but sometimes they will only accept resumes via fax or regular mail. Be sure to read a listing carefully before you respond to it! Follow the application instructions as the company has given them. You don't want to send your resume to the wrong address or the wrong person. Always cite the job title advertised and any code numbers requested.

Job Search Tip: Responding to Internet Job Postings. It is very important that you read the *entire* posting and respond according to the directions given. It only takes a second and a couple of keystrokes to delete a message that wasn't sent properly, and you don't want that to happen to you. *Read and think before you respond!*

Preparing Your Resume for E-Mail

This is really an easy process, and anyone who is preparing a resume should take a few extra minutes to create a plain text version while they are still on the computer. Most word processors and resume-writing programs will let you save a file to plain text; then altering the format is simple.

1. Create your resume with the formatting and display style recommended by the people helping you or the guides you are reading. Check it for spelling and grammar, and read it over carefully to be sure you catch any mistakes the computer didn't. Since this is the resume you'll send to employers through the mail, let's call it your *mail resume*.

2. Print a copy of the mail resume and then make a copy of the computer file. Name the copy "resume.txt" and tell the program to save it to text only. You will probably get a message saying that you will lose the formatting, which is what you want. Say "Yes."

3. Using any text editor, edit the resume.txt file to resemble your printed resume. Notepad in the Windows program and Appletext in the Macintosh program are examples of text editors. Redo the spacing using the space bar, and add some characters to highlight your skills and so on, as you did in your mail resume. You must alter the margins for e-mail, so count 65 characters across the screen and end the line with a carriage return. (Yes, you may have to sit there and count each letter and space to 65.) Again, save this copy as text. This is your *Internet resume.*

Internet Tip: Using a Text Editor. Why use a text editor? So you can see the real plain text resume. A word processor will take your text file and try to make it look nice on the screen, wrapping the lines and such. In order to prepare your resume for e-mail, you have to see the real formatting so you can make all the necessary changes.

4. Save both of the files on a diskette. Keep that resume ready to edit, print, or e-mail on demand. If you make changes to your mail resume, make the same changes to your Internet resume. If you create a new mail resume, take a few minutes to set up the companion Internet resume at the same time.

Internet Tip: Highlighting Your Resume. Since you cannot use boldface, underlining, or bullets in a plain text document, consider using the following characters as substitutes:

- **Bullets.** Use *asterisks* (*) or *plus signs* (+) at the beginning of lines.
- **Underscoring.** Use a *series of dashes* to separate sections. Don't try to underline text.
- **Boldface.** Consider using *capital letters* or use *asterisks* to surround the text. Don't try to highlight text within your resume, but highlight the headers or titles of each section.

Once you have redone your resume in the text format, send it to yourself or to a friend to see how it looks after being e-mailed. This will help you identify any more formatting problems before you start sending it out to possible employers.

There are several places on the Internet where you can examine text resumes to see what other job seekers have done to present their information. The **misc.jobs.resumes** Usenet newsgroup is one good place to view resumes. **CareerMosaic** (*http://www.careermosaic.com*) has a public resume database that you can search, as does **Career Magazine** (*http://www.careermag.com/*). You will find some very good and some not so good resumes out there, so note the problems and don't copy them.

Posting Your Resume—Some Points to Consider

For some people, posting a resume has been a great way to get work. For others, there is the fear that someone will get their home address and phone number; still others don't want some people or organizations looking at their resumes. Control and confidentiality might be a concern for you, so here are some things to think about before posting.

1. Do you want your resume made public? Once you have posted it, consider your resume a public document and out of your control. Anyone can look in the public databases and see what is there. Even the closed resume databanks do not let you dictate who can and cannot look at your resume. If possible, consider posting your *skill set,* a summary of your areas of interest and expertise. Instead of putting a home address on the resume, some people list merely a phone number and e-mail address, but a mailing address of some kind is still preferable. Many employers and recruiters prefer to contact you by phone, so if you don't include a phone number, you might not be considered for a position. If you don't want to put your home address and phone number on your resume, consider renting a post office box and contracting for a voice-mail service. List the box address and service phone number on your resume, and when your search is over, cancel both. Just remember to check for mail and messages!

2. Check the confidentiality of the database or service where you are placing your resume. Who can get access to this database? How is that access granted? Will you be notified if your resume is forwarded to an employer? Is it possible your boss will see your resume? If the answers to these questions make you the least bit uncomfortable, consider another service or consider not posting online.

3. Once your resume is listed, can it be updated *at no cost?* Some services on the Internet will let you post your resume free, but they will charge you for updates. You don't want an old resume out there, and you don't want to pay for updates. You want an unlimited number of updates, even if it is only to correct a typo or to word something a little better. Skip any service that limits or charges for updates.

4. Will your resume be deleted from the databank if you don't update it? You don't want an old resume out there, and, once you are successfully reemployed, you don't necessarily want to be getting calls from other employers. A good database will delete your resume after three months if it is not updated.

You see, it's not all that simple. In fact, it's just as hard as a traditional job search. You have to prepare your resume, your letter, and even yourself for this new online environment. Once you've thought this all over and worked everything out, you are ready to step onto the virtual pavement to begin looking for work.

> **Internet Tip: Updating Resume Postings.** When searched, many resume databases sort the results from newest to oldest, so the most recent resumes appear first in the list. If you are posting in an Internet resume database, consider updating your resume every *30 days* to make sure it's always near the beginning of the list.

Recommended Sites for Posting Your Resume

The following are a few well-established Internet sites that are frequently visited by the many employers and recruiters using the Internet as a part of *their* hunt for new talent. More information and sites can be found using the resources in this book.

Online Career Center
http://www.occ.com

CareerMosaic
http://www.careermosaic.com/cm/

The Monster Board
http://www.monster.com/

E-Span
http://www.espan.com

America's Talent Bank
http://www.atb.org

A list of resume databases with notes to help guide you in selecting those that might be useful to your search is available in *The Riley Guide* at *http://www.dbm.com/jobguide/resumes.html.*

3

Pounding the Virtual Pavement: Beginning Your Internet Job Search

You have the resume, you have the equipment, and you are ready to go online and begin your job search. Where do you start and how do you find the jobs—and not just any jobs, but those in your field? Here lies the difficulty of the Internet, namely *finding the information you want*. What is the best way to search for information, and where can you begin? Let's look at some ideas for finding Internet information, strategies for locating employment opportunities and other good information, and some resources at your beck and call to help you in your search.

Before Going Online, Decide . . .

One of the biggest problems people encounter in trying to search the Internet for information is *they don't know what they are really searching for*. Think about it—do you really know how to describe what you are looking for? To use the Internet in your search, you must know how to describe what you want using the same words that the employers and recruiters do. Without these words, you will not be able to find that job that speaks to you as a great opportunity, nor will you be able to find the job listings and potential employers themselves. You won't know where to look or how to look. So, before you can go online, you have to make some decisions.

1. *What do you want to do?*

   What skills do you have, what interests, and so on? Identify general occupations that interest you, like chemist, bricklayer, and airline attendant, not job titles like head of research or shift supervisor.

2. *Who do you want to work for?*

   What industry interests you, what type of employer? Are you interested in a Fortune 500 company, an organization that is known as being family friendly, or one that is very small?

3. *Where do you want to live and work?*

   What city, state, region, or country are you interested in?

Job Search Tip: Narrowing the Field. If you are saying to yourself, "I'll go any place I can find a job," you need to stop and find out where the jobs are so you can target employers in that area. There are too many employers and too many newspapers to read for you to look everywhere. You can use *labor market information* available from each state to help. Information on this, along with other resources, can be found in Chapter 14.

Focus your search on *skills and occupations* applied to *industries and employers,* and then finally *geographic location.* This will form the *keyword list* you need for searching the Internet. Without this list, you can't search in the many databases out there. And your list will change as you search. You'll cross out the words that do not work at all and add more which not only work but also get you to more information about what you are really interested in.

Job Search Tip: Finding Out What You Want. If you can't think of words for skills and occupations, search the **Online Career Center** (*http://www.occ.com*) or **America's Job Bank** (*http://www.ajb.dni.us*) and look for jobs that interest you. Read the descriptions, note the skills and kinds of experience the employers are seeking, and then use these words in your search. *What Color Is Your Parachute?* is a great book to read for ideas and ways to identify your skills and interests, and your employment service center has more resources you can use. You can even look at some information from this book online at *http://www.washingtonpost.com/parachute/.*

If you have a lot of trouble figuring out what you really want to do, you might want to seek out a *career counselor.* Information to help you locate a counselor can be found in Chapter 14.

Breaking Out of the Job Banks! a.k.a. The Real Job Search

The real job search includes researching employers and opportunities, networking, distributing your resume, and reading job ads. And yes, you are doing a real job search on the Internet! It's more than just reading the job ads! You need to take some time to find out what else is out there. No single list, job bank, or resource will contain all of the information you want for an effective online job search.

The *total Internet job search* includes: researching employers and opportunities, networking, finding job listings and recruiting sites, and posting your resume. The *total job search* includes all of these activities—both online and off!

To begin your Internet Job Search, you need to know only three methods for finding information: *browsing, searching,* and *inquiring.*

Browsing: I just want to take a little look around and see what is available. I'm not really ready to jump in yet, or I'm not fully focused on what I want to search for.

Think of this as walking the mall and looking in the store windows, or sitting in front of the TV flipping the channels with your remote. You know you want something, you just aren't sure what, but you'll know it when you see it. Browsing is a great way to look at your options and see what might be possible.

Searching: I have the resume and letter ready in plain text, my objectives identified, my search terms prepared, and I am ready to job hunt!

You know what you want right down to the color, size, and number of buttons. Now you just have to find what store carries it or what magazine it was published in. Browsing will get you to the point where you can search by allowing you to look at many things that interest you and help you identify the right fit. To really search, you have to have specific things to search for, like a list of employers or some unique skills you have identified as being in demand.

Inquiring: Where do I begin? How do I use this? Can anyone help me locate the information I need?

All you have to do is ask. Ask a friend or colleague. Ask a librarian or an Internet volunteer for help.

But alongside these simple *methods,* you need to know what *type* of resource you need or are looking at right now—a *virtual library,* an *online resource guide,* or a *search engine.*

Virtual libraries. Large collections of information arranged by broad topics. Many feature a searchable catalog of their holdings just like the catalog in the library. Use the search feature, but also take some time to "browse" the shelves.

Examples: Yahoo!, (*http://www.yahoo.com*), The Galaxy (*http://galaxy.tradewave.com*)

Online resource guides. Sites or resources that are generally dedicated to a specific topic or industry and have been compiled by organizations or specialists in each field represented.

Examples: The Riley Guide (*http://www.dbm.com/jobguide*), Hoovers Online (*http://www.hoovers.com*)

Search engines. Services that maintain searchable databases of keywords retrieved from Internet documents and then link you to the original resource. Each search engine is different in how it is searched and the documents indexed, so you might want to try several and regularly use two or three.

Examples: AltaVista (*http://www.altavista.digital.com*), InfoSeek (*http://www.infoseek.com*)

What you are doing is looking at the Internet by *types of resource* and how each can help you in your search. When you can figure out what type of resource you are looking at, you can choose the *best method* to survey this resource and find all the useful information it contains very quickly. This makes your time online much more effective, since no one ever has enough time to really do everything they want to, including find work!

Browsing. We suggest you start with a *virtual library* and look around using very broad terms in your field or industry, like "engineering" or "education," to start finding information. Follow links that look interesting. You'll start learning the words that are used to describe the work you want or the employers you are seeking, so add these to your keyword list. You'll also begin identifying *online resource guides* to use in your search.

Searching. Using very specific ideas and terms found in the *online resource guides,* you can turn your attention to the *search engines.*

Inquiring. You can ask on a *Usenet newsgroup* or a *mailing list,* but because so many people ask the same questions all the time, *this is a last resort online!* Before you ask online, check the FAQ (list of *Frequently Asked Questions*). Not every group or list has a FAQ, but it is better to look at the archives and see if one exists before you ask your question. A great collection of FAQs can be found at *http://www.cis.ohio-state.edu/hypertext/faq/usenet/top.html.*

Internet Tip: More Pointers for You. You can learn more about Usenet newsgroups and mailing lists and how they can help in your online job search by reviewing the articles in Appendix B.

The Total Internet Job Search

We are now going to take you step-by-step through the total job search online. We'll look at ways to research employers, find and review job listings, network online, and even post your resume. With each step, you'll find places to go and sample exercises to try. Most importantly, you'll see the variety of resources and methods available to you, and you can choose those that work best for you. If you have any problems along the way, ask for help from the librarians and Internet volunteers in your local library or from the many guides you'll find as you tour the online world.

Internet Tip: Figuring Out Internet Addresses: Internet addresses are given in the form of a *uniform resource locator* (URL). The URL consists of two pieces of information—how to connect and the address to connect to—separated by a colon and two slash marks. Additional information on the directory and file name might be included, and these pieces are separated from each other by slash marks.

how to connect://where to connect/directory path to follow/what to get
http://www.dbm.com/jobguide/index.html

Internet Tip: URLs. If you have trouble connecting to a site, try cutting the URL back one slash mark. The file or directory you are seeking may have moved, and by backing up one level at a time you may be able to find the new location easily.

Part I: Researching Employers, Opportunities, Occupations, and Industries

The Internet is a huge collection of databases just waiting to be discovered. Tap the resources provided by the thousands of companies, colleges and universities, governments, and news and information services to do extended research into your target occupations, industries, and employers. By being proactive and contacting them about possibilities, you have more control over your job search. You know what they are all about before you even apply. You even know what kind of opportunities might exist for you or ways you can benefit them, even if they don't know it yet.

RESEARCH 101: LOOKING FOR INFORMATION ON THE INTERNET

Remember our methods of browsing and searching. Now you are going to use them to start finding information you can use.

Begin with a virtual library. Use very broad terms in your field or industry to start finding information. Move toward online resource guides.

Step 1: Visit Virtual Libraries. These are the large collections of information arranged by broad topics used to identify terms and resources. The virtual libraries will help you to discover how your topic fits in the general scheme of things, where it expands into more ideas and subtopics, how it relates across subjects and industries, and what terms are used to describe it and the various functions or services within it. You can also use virtual libraries to quickly begin identifying potential employers, as well as online resource guides and very specific resources for your areas of interest.

Example: Search "education" or "finance" to find information on these topics in each library.

Yahoo	http://www.yahoo.com
Galaxy	http://galaxy.tradewave.com
Looksmart	http://www.looksmart.com
Virtual Library (W30)	http://vlib.stanford.edu/Overview.html
Librarian's Index to the Internet	http://sunsite.berkeley.edu/InternetIndex/
Search.Com	http://www.search.com
Magellan Internet Guide	http://www.mckinley.com/
The Mining Company	http://www.miningco.com/
New Rider's Official World Wide Web Yellow Pages	http://www.mcp.com/newriders/wwwyp/index.html
WebScout	http://www.webscout.com/
The Scout Report	http://wwwscout.cs.wisc.edu/scout/report/
Net Happenings	http://scout.cs.wisc.edu/scout/net-hap/
YPN: Your Personal Net	http://www.ypn.com/

Step 2: Read Online Resource Guides. These are those sites or online documents dedicated to a specific topic or industry. While the virtual libraries will get you started in finding resources and services of interest to you, resource guides go into much more depth in any given topic and are much more up-to-date. You will begin finding even more information on your field and its specialties, as well as more employer lists. And within many online resource guides you will find lists of employment opportunities or links to good employment resources.

Example: Look under "education" or "finance" to find websites dedicated to these topics.

The Clearinghouse (*a library of resource guides*)	http://www.clearinghouse.net
Hoover's Online (*companies*)	http://www.hoovers.com
ComFind (*companies*)	http://www.comfind.com
Scholarly Societies Project (*professional and scholarly societies*)	http://www.lib.uwaterloo.ca/society/overview.html
The Riley Guide (*jobs*)	http://www.dbm.com/jobguide/
Editor & Publisher Interactive (*newspapers*)	http://www.mediainfo.com/
Enews (*newspapers*)	http://www.enews.com
NewJour Archive (*journals*)	http://gort.ucsd.edu/newjour/

You can also search the virtual libraries for *indices* or *directories* in the various subject areas.

Job Search Tip: Check Electronic Journals and Newspapers. Read the trade and industry journals, society publications, and local news for your target occupation, industry, or region. You can watch industry trends, look for possible networking contacts, and find out who is doing what and how they will need your skills in order to succeed. Many of these electronic publications are free and include job listings.

Step 3: Tap Search Engines. Use these searchable databases of keywords retrieved from Internet documents to locate hidden information on any topic or employer. Each is different in how it works and what it indexes, so choose one or two you are comfortable with and learn every trick they offer to make your search more complete and less complex.

Example: Search any *employers* found in your previous searches here.

Alta Vista	http://www.altavista.digital.com
HotBot	http://www.hotbot.com
WebCrawler	http://webcrawler.com
Excite	http://www.excite.com
InfoSeek	http://www.infoseek.com
Lycos	http://www.lycos.com
Northern Lights	http://www.nlsearch.com

Internet Tip: Searching Online. Still having trouble figuring out how to find things online? Check out **Search Insider** (*http://www.searchinsider.com*) from Librarians and Educators Online (LEO). This site offers excellent tips, articles, pointers, and a glossary so you can understand what we librarians mean when we say, "Use a proximity delineator."

RESEARCH 102: READING AN EMPLOYER'S HOME PAGE

You can't just walk into an employer's office and say, "So, what is this job you are interviewing me for and how do I fit into your scheme?" Employers expect you to know who they are, what they do, what the job entails, and how you fit into the company structure and culture before you come in. Think of your job interview as the sales call where you get to sell your product. You've already sent your marketing brochure (the resume and cover letter), and they're interested. The interview is your chance to make the final pitch to sell yourself to the hiring manager. Like any good sales professional, you have to know what the company is buying in order to make the right pitch.

An employer's web page is like a custom-made book about that employer! Read it "cover to cover" and print pages that interest you or that have information you want to double-check either through *search engines* or a search of more *traditional resources* in a library.

1. Look at anything that says "News" or "What's New." This will give you the latest information on what is happening and possible clues on new areas you might fit into.

2. Read any *mission statements* or *description of services* to see how the organization describes itself. Use this information to fashion your cover letter to the company's interests.

3. Look for an *annual report* or *strategic plan* and read it carefully.

4. Check out the *career opportunities, jobs, and/or human resource* area. Read over the opportunities to see if the company is recruiting in a specific area, but realize that there will be many job openings not posted here. Use this as a guide to the organization's application procedures, and look for information on benefits and career advancement opportunities.

5. Look over the *whole site*. What does the design of these pages say to you about this organization? Is it conservative or funky? Is it well organized or difficult to follow? Do you feel that this is the kind of place you want to work for?

Don't be afraid to print pages that interest you or that have information you want to double-check either through search engines or in the many reference books found in your local library. And don't be afraid to refer to those pages when you are in your interview. Many employers don't know what their pages say or haven't seen them before. It will reinforce your Internet knowledge and skills. Bring a clean set of the pages with you, but don't point out their spelling errors!

RESEARCH 103: ADDITIONAL RESEARCH RESOURCES FOR YOUR SEARCH

While you are working to identify employers and reviewing job listings, you will want to know things like how does a certain salary offer compare to the average for this region. These sources can help you in your search for that kind of information along with other resources for learning about your employer.

JobSmart Salary Surveys (*salary guides*)   http://jobsmart.org/tools/salary/

EDGAR 10K Reports (*employer financials*)   http://edgar.stern.nyu.edu

CityNet (*location information*)   http://www.city.net

State & Local Government on the Net   http://www.piperinfo.com/state/states.html
(*information from official state and local government organizations*)

The Riley Guide has an entire section dedicated to researching employers and other information on your career and job prospects. You will find it at *http://www.dbm.com/jobguide/research.html.*

Part II: Job Listings and Recruiting Sites

While searching for employers and opportunities, check the hundreds of large recruiting sites on the Web, as well as employer websites for any postings on their own pages. You can read the many online journals and newspapers, scan through the professional and trade association websites and journals, and even scan several Usenet newsgroups and mailing lists that carry job postings. Many recruiters are now dedicating their websites to a particular industry, occupation, or group, so target these in your search.

JOB LISTINGS 101: LARGE STARTING POINTS

These contain links to hundreds of Internet employment resources and link you to more guides like themselves. You can find more of these guides in Chapter 4, but these will help you quickly find some places to search for jobs.

The Riley Guide   http://www.dbm.com/jobguide/

Job Hunt   http://www.job-hunt.org

JOB LISTINGS 102: THE MAJOR JOB BANKS

These are the large online job-listing services carrying thousands of job listings in hundreds of occupations and industries. Again, we have a much larger list in Chapter 4, but this is a sample to get you started.

America's Job Bank   http://www.ajb.dni.us

The Online Career Center   http://www.occ.com

JOB LISTINGS 103: SPECIAL SERVICES

These are employment services designed to serve a particular industry, occupation, or group of people. They can be sites maintained by a recruiter, a professional society, a trade journal, or any number of other participants. Examples include:

Disability Services Careers Online (*disabled*)	http://disserv3.stu.umn.edu
Info-Mine (*mining industry*)	http://www.info-mine.com
Asianet (*Asian-language specialists*)	http://www.asia-net.com
SaludosWeb (*persons of Hispanic descent*)	http://www.saludos.com

You can locate even more sites like these through the virtual libraries and online resource guides and by looking at the large starting points for your job search.

Part III: Networking

Yes, you can use the communication capabilities of the Internet to connect with others, either for information or networking purposes. Many professionals use mailing lists and Usenet newsgroups as networking tools, discussing recent developments in their occupation or industry and asking questions of each other. Anyone involved in career exploration or a job search can benefit from following these online public discussions, learning about current trends and developments and the interests and concerns of those involved.

Usenet newsgroups. These are discussion groups carried on the Usenet network. The jobs groups have job listings, resume postings, and discussions on job hunting. But, if you go to the newsgroups dedicated to various subjects or topics like **sci.engineering**, you'll find networking contacts, industry trends, current information, and better job listings. Active public participation is necessary to get networking contacts. To read and participate in Usenet newsgroups, you need a *newsreader* (the software used to access this information), access to a *newsfeed* (the network that carries the newsgroups), and access to the *particular newsgroups* you are interested in because each site has the ability to select which groups it will carry. Another feature of Usenet newsgroups is you must go to them to read the messages, they do not come to you.

Mailing lists. These are discussion groups operating through electronic mail. A central computer called the *listserv, listproc,* or *majordomo* runs the list. You send a message to the computer asking to be added to the mailing list you are interested in, and the computer responds to let you know your status. Once it says you are successfully added, you will automatically begin receiving the messages from that mailing list in your e-mail. You must have a personal e-mail account to use mailing lists. For help with the commands needed to operate the mailing list, read *Discussion Lists: Mail List Manager Commands,* written by Jim Milles at the Saint Louis University School of Law (*http://lawlib.slu.edu/training/mailser.htm*).

Internet Tip: Joining a Mailing List. To join a mailing list, send an e-mail message to the listserv, listproc, or majordomo—whichever is the computer operating the distribution of the list. Leave the "Subject" line blank and, in the body of the mail, type *subscribe listname yourfirstname yourlastname.* For example,

TO: *listproc@harold.lemon.com*

SUBJECT: *subscribe moneybags Emily Dickinson*

is the message Emily Dickinson would send to join the mailing list **Moneybags** at the computer site *harold.lemon.com.* To send messages to the other readers of this list, she sends her e-mail to *moneybags@harold.lemon.com.*

There are some real advantages to networking online. You can "break the ice" before meeting someone in person. You can also make contact with people who are not in your local area, thereby expanding your network geographically. You can listen, engage, or be engaged as you wish, choosing when and where you will speak and to whom. But, most importantly, no one can see you sweat.

To start networking, you need to identify the Usenet newsgroups and mailing lists that discuss the field or discipline you are interested in investigating. Search these lists using keywords describing your industry or employment field, and see what kind of discussion groups you find.

Example: Search these lists for "education" or "finance" to locate Usenet newsgroups and mailing lists that discuss these areas.

The Liszt	http://www.liszt.com
The Kovacs List	http://www.n2h2.com/KOVACS/

Internet Tip: Free E-Mail Accounts. There are several places on the Web that will give you a private e-mail account at no cost. You will have to read a lot of advertisements once you join, but that is all you pay for this service. Three places to check out are **HotMail** (*http://www.hotmail.com*), **Juno** (*http://www.juno.com*), and **Yahoo! Mail** (*http://www.yahoo.com*). If you get your Internet access through your local public library and other free services, consider registering with one of these groups to get e-mail through the Web.

If you don't have access to the Usenet, you can still participate to a limited extent through Usenet Archives on the Web. You can search these collections of Usenet postings for discussion groups that interest you, or search for messages on topics that interest you. Although you cannot post directly to the discussion groups, you can send an e-mail message to the person who posted the message you are reading and establish a relationship with him or her.

Example: Search these archives for "education" or "finance" to find messages about these topics.

AltaVista   http://www.altavista.digital.com (select Usenet)

DejaNews   http://www.dejanews.com

Along with all the advantages of online networking come a few disadvantages. Your online behavior is very important! You don't get a second chance to make a first impression, and no one can see that you don't mean to be impolite, so your first words and how they are delivered make all the difference in the world. You want to be sure to speak in the language and manner acceptable to the group. Stepping right up there and sending a message to everyone that says, "Hi, I need a job; here's my resume, call me if you hear of anything" is not networking and will do nothing except get you noticed and disliked by everyone on the list. So, before you do anything wrong, take a few minutes to learn the basics of online etiquette, also know as *Netiquette.*

ONLINE NETWORK ETIQUETTE: NETIQUETTE

The basic rule: *Do not go boldly where you have never gone before!*

1. *Stop* and learn the rules of netiquette for each discussion group.

2. *Look* for a list of Frequently Asked Questions (the FAQ) for the group before joining in.

3. *Listen* patiently to the lists or newsgroups you have joined until you know the culture of the group.

Suggested Reading

The Net: User Guidelines and Netiquette, Arlene H. Rinaldi
http://www.fau.edu/rinaldi/net/index.html

Newsgroup FAQs, Ohio State University
http://www.cis.ohio-state.edu/hypertext/faq/usenet/top.html

Internet Tip: Looking Before You Leap. You should *monitor* your chosen newsgroups and mailing lists, following the discussions and looking for information on the field or discipline. Do *not* participate in the discussions until you are quite comfortable with the group, how the participants address each other, and the topics that are acceptable for discussion.

While you are monitoring Usenet newsgroups and mailing lists, look for postings by someone who seems to be knowledgeable about the topic being discussed. Note his or her e-mail address at the top, and look for signature information citing his or her organizational affiliation, position in the organization, and more complete contact information like a phone number, address, and perhaps web page.

MAKING THAT FIRST CONTACT VIA THE INTERNET

Once you have identified some mailing list or newsgroup participants you want to contact, prepare your e-mail letter as carefully as you do your standard mail letter. Be especially polite, apologizing immediately for taking their time.

1. Be sure to contact each person *directly* and not through the list or newsgroup. Do not post a general message to the list or newsgroup asking if anyone is willing to talk to you.

2. Be *concise*, identify yourself, and state why you are contacting this person. List some of your interests and where you noticed some correlation with his or her postings.

3. Request a *follow-up* to your e-mail, via phone or e-mail. Give your contact the choice of how to continue.

The *National Business Employment Weekly* along with other publications is including more information on the Internet in their coverage. These articles usually include tips on contacting prospective employers with cover letters and resumes. We have included a couple of these tips in Appendix B, but we suggest you also look at the articles for additional information.

Margaret Riley Dikel, "Newsgroup Knowhow." *National Business Employment Weekly* 16 (45) pp. 17–19: (November 9–15, 1997).

Phil Agre, *Networking on the Network*. http://communication.ucsd.edu/pagre/network.html (Although intended for advanced graduate students, the principles discussed apply widely and can easily be adapted for various audiences.)

Internet Tip: Flaming. Make sure you know what you are doing before you post so you do not become the victim of those nasty messages called *flames*. These can be particularly degrading and insulting messages, and can make many veterans of the Internet turn off the computer for months. Think of each newsgroup as a meeting or an office party where you are the new person in the office and must introduce yourself. You want to make a good impression your first time out there, so don't get burned!

Part IV: Posting Your Resume Online

For some people, posting a resume online has been a great way to get work. For others, there is the fear that someone will get their home address and phone number or that certain people or organizations, like their current employer, might find their resume. You are the only one who can say how comfortable you are with this decision and how you want to approach the idea of posting your resume. Before you begin, think about these things.

1. Do you want your resume public? Once you have posted your resume, consider it a public document and out of your control. Anyone can look in the public databases to see what is there. Even the private resume databanks do not always let you dictate who can and cannot look at your resume. If making your address and phone number public is a concern, consider renting a post office box and contracting a voice-mail account during your job search. When you are done, cancel both. *Don't leave this information off your resume and figure the employer will contact you by e-mail!* Many employers and recruiters still prefer to contact you by phone, so if you don't include a phone number, you may be overlooked. Don't use your office address and phone either unless you have the permission of your employer.

2. How confidential is the database or service where you are placing your resume? Who can get access to this database? How is that access granted? Will you be notified if your resume is forwarded to an employer? Will you be contacted *before* your resume is released? Is it possible your boss will see your resume? If the answers to these questions make you the least bit uncomfortable, consider another service or consider not posting at all. If the answers to these questions are not easily found on the website of the resume service, look for a phone number and call them.

3. Once your resume is listed, can it be updated at no cost? Some Internet services will let you post your resume free, but they charge you for updates or they don't permit them at all. You don't want an old resume out there, and you don't want to pay for updates. Look for services offering an unlimited number of updates, even if it is only to correct a typo or to word something a little better. Skip any service that limits or charges for your updates. The online market is huge, and you can get better service elsewhere.

4. Will your resume be deleted from the databank if you don't update it, and if so, when? You don't want an old resume out there, and once you are successfully employed in a new job, you don't want to be getting calls from other employers. A good database will delete your resume within three months if it is not updated; a better one will give you a passcode and allow you to delete your own resume whenever you choose.

For more information on how to prepare your resume for the Internet along with a short list of places you might post online, refer to Chapter 2.

Time Management for Your Internet Job Search

Every day or evening, many people start their Internet search in the same place and, gee, they spend so much time in those pages that they never get anywhere else. So, why are they doing that? We don't know, but we have a suggestion to help combat it.

Every time you connect, start someplace new. Pick out a select list of general resources, use them to find more specific resources, and keep moving. Things change, but not so rapidly that you will miss something important if you check there only twice a week. So, try this schedule to establish a routine in your job search that keeps you moving forward all the time.

1. **Visit the large information databases first.** These include virtual libraries and large recruiting sites with employer profiles. Looks for links to information in your chosen field or industry. Repeat this search every few days, perhaps on Monday and Thursday.

2. **Move on to the smaller, more exclusive resources and services,** including online resource guides and sites dedicated to your field or industry. You want to find links to employers or collected information in your field that can give you leads or networking contacts. Repeat this search every few days, maybe on Tuesday and Friday.

3. **Use search engines to locate new and hidden resources specific to your occupation and field.** If you have a company you are interested in, search on the company name, any variations or nicknames it is known by, and names of its major products. Repeat this search every few days, most likely Wednesday and Saturday.

4. **And, on the seventh day, take some time for yourself and rebuild your attitude.** The job search is a stressful process, and the best thing you can do for yourself at this time is take some time for yourself. You have to maintain a winning attitude and a healthy body. Take one day a week and spend some time with your friends, your family, the dog or cat or whatever other pets you may have. Go for a walk or a swim or just go window-shopping. But shut down the computer and enjoy life a little, and reenergize yourself for the next week ahead.

Job Search Tip: Really, Truly, the Most Important Notice in This Entire Book. The Internet *cannot* be the only resource you use for your job search! You must continue to utilize all contacts, information resources, and services available to you for the most effective and efficient search for employment. Limit your time online to *one quarter* of the total time you can dedicate to your job search.

What this means is if you can dedicate 10 hours a week to your job search, you can spend 2.5 hours online. It's not that we are saying this isn't important, but more we are saying you have to balance yourself. Don't put all your eggs in the online basket and ignore the offline basket. Put some in each, dividing them between the four corners of research, job listings, networking, and distributing your resume. As you become better at searching, you'll find the best way to balance yourself, noting what things work better for you and which don't work as well. But never leave any basket empty.

Questions on Getting Started with Your Search

1. *I'm just starting out and I'd like to see what is available out there in terms of job listings. Where do I begin?*

> A good way to get a broad overview is to look at the major recruiting services like the **Online Career Center** or **America's Job Bank** and the many job guides on the Internet. We've covered these in Chapter 4, but you can also link to these through the large employment sites like *The Riley Guide* (*http://www.dbm.com/jobguide/index.html*). This online resource guide includes over 800 links to job listings and information resources on the Internet, all of which are useful for your job search. Use it as a starting point for your browsing and searching and to double-check sites that are not responding. And *The Riley Guide* will take you to more sites like itself, other large employment guides that can help you do the search you want the way you want.

2. *I'm looking for work in a specific field. Where do I look for information and job listings in that field?*

> One of the best ways to find employment information in a specific field is to find a good site dedicated to that field. Colleges and universities frequently collect information for their own use in many subjects, and they put it on their public webservers. These sites usually include information on finding employment, research resources, and links to similar sites elsewhere. Many professional societies are now on the Internet, and, even if you are not a member, you can use their public information to help with your search. The many virtual libraries on the Internet can also be used in this way, and we've included several in the list of resources in the next section. The online resource guides for employment information will also help you to find specific resources for your chosen field or industry.

3. *I'm going to be moving and I'd like to begin my job search now. Is there any way I can do it?*

> Absolutely! The Web has lists of registered servers that are arranged by geographic location, and many of the virtual libraries have collections for local regions. Choose where you want to be and begin examining the servers in that area for information and opportunities. Many of the ***.jobs newsgroups** on the Usenet are also specific to a geographic region, so you can read newsgroups for the area you are moving to and begin contacting employers now. And don't forget about the hundreds of local newspapers on the Internet and the many public libraries. These organizations have collected information about their areas and made it freely available to you through the Web.

4. I really want to work for XYZ company. How can I find information about it and see if it has any positions available?

Use a search engine like AltaVista, Excite, or Lycos to search a company's name as a keyword. Check the **ComFind** (*http://www.comfind.com*) and **Hoovers Online** (*http://www.hoovers.com*) business directories to see if it is included in their listings. Check the virtual libraries for links to the company under a variety of headings such as "business" or "commerce." Once you connect to the company's site, look for "Personnel" or "Human Resources." Many organizations are now putting a link to their job listings right on the front page or within a section called "About Us," so you shouldn't have to look very far.

Suggested Reading for Your Internet Job Search

- Bolles, Richard Nelson. *Job Hunting on the Internet (Parachute Library)*. Ten Speed Press, 1997.
- Criscito, Pat. *Resumes in Cyberspace: Your Complete Guide to a Computerized Job Search*. Barrons Educational Series, 1997.
- Crispin, Gerry, and Mark Mehler. *CareerXroads: The 1998 Directory to the 500 Best Job, Resume and Career Management Sites on the World Wide Web*. MMC Group, 1998.
- Karl, Shannon, and Arthur Karl. *How to Get Your Dream Job Using the Web*. Coriolis Group, 1997.
- Lauber, Daniel. *Professional's Job Finder: 1997–2000*. Planning Communications, 1997.
- Swartz, Mark. *Get Wired, You're Hired: The Canadian Guide to Job Hunting Online*. Prentice Hall Canada, 1997.

You should also regularly check the *National Business Employment Weekly* for articles on how the Internet fits into the job search and career management processes (*http://www.nbew.com*) as well as the new **Careers, Not Just Jobs** section of the **Wall Street Interactive** website (*http://careers.wsj.com*).

The Great Job Listing Sites

The Internet sites and services listed in this chapter are known for their collected job listings. They cover multiple fields, industries, and occupations, providing leads for almost every job you can think of. Most of them are based in the United States, but do not necessarily limit themselves to U.S. job listings. What has been included here?

1. Usenet newsgroups. These include primarily the **misc.jobs.*** collection of newsgroups. Many other newsgroups are included with the local or international listings in Chapters 12 and 13.

2. Online recruiting services. These are recruiters and other organizations posting job announcements on the Internet.

3. Online guides to the job hunt. These give you tips and pointers along with their lists of resources. Most, but not all, of them cover Internet resources exclusively.

Usenet Newsgroups

These newsgroups are specifically for posting jobs unless otherwise indicated in their descriptions. Please do not post resumes or begin discussions in newsgroups that are not specifically set up for these things. See the note on "flaming" in Chapter 3 if you do not understand this warning.

biz.jobs.offered

Commercial postings of jobs available all over.

misc.jobs.offered

General positions available, although jobs in technology (computing and software) tend to dominate this group. This group sometimes sees as many as 500 new listings a day, so read it frequently if you want to include it in your search.

misc.jobs.offered.entry

Entry-level positions available; one to two years experience sometimes preferred.

misc.jobs.contract

Contract positions; usually short-term and with minimal benefits. This could be a good way to find employment when you are between other jobs.

misc.jobs.resumes

The place to post your resume, in ASCII or text format only. Recruiters and employers scan this newsgroup regularly looking for potential employees. Read it for ideas on your own resume. *Please do not post jobs here.*

misc.jobs.wanted

People looking for jobs. You can post your "dream job" and see if anyone has something like it to offer you.

Online Recruiting Services

These services offer job listings in multiple fields, industries, and occupations. Job banks primarily serving non–U.S. audiences are included in Chapter 13. This section is arranged alphabetically by the title of the service.

AdOne

http://www.adone.com

This is a compilation of searchable classifieds from hundreds of newspapers around the United States. Select a region (or all regions) and then narrow your search by state, city, area code, or job area. A nice touch is that the job area list tells you how many current listings are included. All announcements are dated, but some have very sketchy contact info.

AdSearch

http://www.adsearch.com

All kinds of classified ads, including employment opportunities. You can either select the appropriate heading for your occupation or try a free-form search. Dates are not posted on the job announcements, and not all of them have contact names, phone numbers, and addresses for applying.

America's Employers

http://www.americasemployers.com/

This site features a searchable company database, job listings, recruiter listings, and other interesting information.

America's Job Bank

http://www.ajb.dni.us/

This is a joint effort of the 2,000 offices of the state employment services. They have a variety of ways for you to search this site, including by military specialty codes so those leaving the military might be able to match their skills to jobs in the nonmilitary marketplace. It is one of the largest job sources online, and it is not limited to the continental United States. It also links to the many state employment services with

Internet job databases available. Keep watching this site as many improvements are in the works.

Asianet

http://www.asia-net.com/

Asianet is a clearinghouse for jobs that require a knowledge of Asian languages, specifically Japanese, Korean, and Chinese.

Best Jobs in the USA Today

http://www.bestjobsusa.com/

This site includes listings from *Employment Review,* a publication of Recourse Communications, Inc. Employers can also post jobs directly to this site.

The Black Collegian

http://www.black-collegian.com/

The online site of the magazine dedicated to college students and professionals of color. This has one of the fastest job search engines we have ever seen and some wonderful position announcements. Search by keywords and target a location, or scan the list of employers. Great stuff for all levels and backgrounds.

Career Blazers

http://www.cblazers.com/

A staffing and recruiting agency with locations all over the United States. Resumes can be submitted through this web page, and you can obtain the contact information for local offices to check on possible temporary or permanent employment opportunities. Unfortunately, many pages on this site use frames, so those with browsers that do not support frames may be frustrated. No fees are charged to the job seeker.

CareerBuilder

http://www.careerbuilder.com/

A source for jobs from all over the place on a unique site set up to work directly with the human resource professionals of its member companies. Check out the search and interview tips also.

CareerCity

http://www.careercity.com

A revamped version of the Adams Online site from Adams Publishing, the job-search experts. It includes links to hundreds of company pages, an executive search directory, and an index of Usenet newsgroups. Job-search tips included from the Adams publications.

Career Expo

http://www.careerexpo.com

This site features career tips, job listings, and a virtual job fair.

Career Magazine

http://www.careermag.com

This online magazine includes job listings, employer profiles, and news and articles related to the job hunt today. Career Magazine also scans and archives job announcements from several Usenet newsgroups to permit easy access. The Jobnet Forum allows "discussions" with others about job hunting. This is a great resource for jobs and information.

CareerMart

http://www.careermart.com

A service of BSA Advertising, this site offers you the option of viewing jobs by location and then job category (you must select a location), or by employers and what jobs they have listed. Some interesting articles appear in the Advice area. It also offers an e-mail option to send you announcements of new openings as they become available.

CareerMosaic

http://www.careermosaic.com

Job listings can be searched by keyword, or you can choose a listed company and view its available positions. Information about each company is included. There is also a tremendous amount of additional job hunting information here, along with a searchable archive of several of the Usenet *.jobs newsgroups. Resumes are accepted for inclusion in the resume bank at no charge. One of the original online recruiting sites, this is also one of the biggest.

CareerPath.com

http://www.careerpath.com

This service includes job advertisements placed in several newspapers across the United States. The database is searchable by a combination of keywords and categories. Choose one newspaper or all of them and then select your major field. Hint—the *New York Times* has ads for all over the United States, and we bet the others do too. Includes two weeks of classifieds from the many participating newspapers, over 200,000 at any given time. This is definitely a must-see online.

Careers, Not Just Jobs, from the *Wall Street Journal* Interactive

http://careers.wsj.com

This free site features articles and information from the *Wall Street Journal* and the *National Business Employment Weekly* (*NBEW*) as well as jobs. The job listings here are not from the print publications, but are drawn from new resources. Scan by employers to see everything they are listing or search by employment field. The articles are the best things available from the *Wall Street Journal* and *NBEW,* updated almost immediately. Absolutely wonderful stuff, and free!

Careersite

http://www.careersite.com

This site has a lot of job listings, but searching takes some getting used to because it gives you many options. Read the help files for ideas. Full registration entitles you to many advanced features, including registration of your search profile. The list of featured employers includes links to their current job openings.

CareerWeb

http://www.cweb.com

CareerWeb is a subsidiary of Landmark Communications, owner of such broadcasting operations as the Weather Channel. This site not only has job listings and information on the employers, but a unique Career Fitness Guide, which helps you make the decision as to where you are going and whether you are ready to take the next step.

The Huntington Group's Career Network

http://www.hgllc.com

The Huntington Group, a professional search firm for the high-tech industry, maintains this site. Resumes are accepted via e-mail or can be submitted online using a forms-capable browser. Even though the recruiting company is a high-tech specialist, jobs in many other areas are included here along with information for the Internet job search.

Contract Employment Weekly, Jobs Online

http://www.ceweekly.wa.com

This site has two sets of job listings—one for members and one for nonmembers. Even with that restriction, there is a lot of information here and several listings. If you have never worked on contract before, you should read the information on contract work.

The EPages Classifieds

http://ep.com/

Although you see a full list of occupational areas, only the ones with jobs are active. You can contact the poster through the service page. The listings are from all over the United States.

E-Span, The Interactive Employment Network

http://www.espan.com

E-Span provides a searchable database of job openings as well as a wide variety of resources for the job seeker. There is lots of great information here. One of the original online recruiting sites, and still a leader of the pack.

Experience on Demand

http://www.experienceondemand.com

Sponsored by Source Services, this site includes work opportunities through Source Staffing along with several articles on career, transition, and work. It is particularly strong in finance and accounting, but other specialties are available.

4Work

http://www.4work.com

4Work is a searchable source of job listings from all over the United States, including volunteer opportunities.

HeadHunter.Net

http://www.headhunter.net/

This is a tremendous source for all kinds of jobs in all fields, and no listing is more than 45 days old. Use the form provided to set your search parameters, but you can leave keyword, salary, and location boxes empty.

Heart Advertising's Career.com

http://www.career.com/

One of the oldest commercial recruiters on the Internet, you can search this site by company name, category of employment, location, or keywords. Entry-level and international jobs are easily searched in their own lists. You can also elect to view the list of participating employers and see every opening advertised in the system along with an employer profile.

Help Wanted.Com
Yss Inc.

http://www.helpwanted.com/

This company specializes in career opportunity development and support, and it offers recruiting services in the university arena, data management, market research, and management. This is a service of Your Software Solutions, Inc., in Marlborough, Massachusetts.

Hire Quality

http://www.hire-quality.com/

This recruiter is providing career opportunities for individuals departing from the American armed forces. All kinds of positions from part-time to senior management can be found through these job listings. Access to job listings requires registration with the organization. Numerous articles about this organization have been very complimentary.

Imcor

http://www.imcor.com/

Imcor is "America's Leading Supplier of Portable Executives," with short- to mid-term placement in senior management positions. Current assignments are posted on the web page with date, title, and location information. They do request mailed or faxed resumes, but hope to have e-mail access in the future.

Internet Career Connection

http://www.iccweb.com/

The Internet Career Connection is a service from Gonyea and Assoc., the developers of Help Wanted USA. This site includes listings from that service as well, and information on careers. For a fee you can request an evaluation of your skills and what careers might be best for you through a form you download and mail in.

The Job Market

http://www.thejobmarket.com/

The Job Market is operated by Tri-Logix of Miami, Florida, and wants to be a comprehensive source for employment information as well as employment opportunities. Offering both free and fee-based services, you can search through thousands of employment listings in several fields, build your resume using their Online Resume builder, and review sources of correspondence samples, relocation information, and entrepreneurial information. A very nice feature of this site is the ability to quickly move from a job announcement to a profile for the employer and back again. Registration is not required to access the free areas of this site.

Recruiters OnLine Network

http://www.ipa.com/

"An association of executive recruiters, search firms and employment professionals around the world who have created a virtual organization on the Internet." The association has a website that offers a database of users, resources for recruiters as well as those in a career search, and an area for individuals to post resumes for review by the members. This site also includes tips on job hunting and articles on using recruiters in the job search.

JobBank USA

http://www.jobbankusa.com/

A good site for many jobs in all kinds of fields. It has information organized and accessible through a variety of means. You can use keyword searching, search by company name, or search by a specific field. If your browser can handle news and these sites are available to you, click on the Usenet news search and read the newsgroups included there. *Jobs MetaSEARCH @ JobBank USA* allows you to access the searchable databases of several of the major job resources.

JobCenter

http://www.jobcenter.com

This extensive site has listings in all fields searchable by keyword. A resume database is also available for employers to scan resumes online. Job seekers will have to pay a fee for registering a resume, but doing this means the daily listings are e-mailed to you so there's no need to search the database yourself.

JobTrak

http://www.jobtrak.com

Notice—your college or university must be a member for you to gain access to the job listings! Now, having said that, see if your institution is listed and then call and ask for the password. Those who cannot access the job listings can use the other great information provided to aid in the job search. Employers can easily target entry-level employees through this service, along with the alumni of the member institutions.

Home Page of Malachy

http://www.execpc.com/~maltoal/

This is a service of Mal Toal in Wisconsin. The company is recruiting in all locations and industries.

Manpower

http://www.manpower.com

Manpower is the largest employer in the United States today, and not just because it is placing secretaries and receptionists in offices. The world of the temp has opened up all the way to the chief executive's office. Assignments are searchable by location, and you can submit resumes by e-mail, fax, or the online form.

The Monster Board

http://www.monster.com/

The Monster Board offers an overview of employers and several interfaces for job hunting. You can search by company name, location, discipline, industry, job title, or combinations of these. The employer overview gives some background information on the company selected, the products and services, and employee benefits. The site also has a tremendous database of information for the job seeker and the employer.

NationJob Online Job Database

http://www.nationjob.com

This site features an impressive collection of job openings, company info, and a variety of ways to find what you are looking for. It divides into many sources of occupational and/or industry-related resources, creating an excellent source of information for all.

Online Career Center

http://www.occ.com/

This is the granddaddy of the Internet recruiting market. You can opt for a keyword or geographic search through this enormous database of job listings. There is a resume bank you can submit your resume to at no cost via e-mail. The site also has a number of additional information resources for the job hunter.

Priority Search.Com

http://prioritysearch.com/career.htm

A service of two recruiting firms in Orlando, Florida, this site comprises several different areas, including Agriculture/Horticulture, Educational Publishing, Manufacturing, and Financial Publishing. Resumes can be submitted online to the appropriate account manager noted on each page.

PursuitNet

http://www.tiac.net/users/jobs/index.html

This recruiter matches your resume and skills against a database of jobs to match you to an employer. The job seeker submits a standard resume into the database. The database is then searched against job requirements, and appropriate matches are coordinated with the potential employer and employee.

Recruitinglinks.Com

http://www.recruiting-links.com/index.html

This site allows you to search the human resources pages of several companies for jobs in all industries and fields.

Saludos Web Site

http://www.saludos.com

A website dedicated exclusively to promoting Hispanic careers and education, supported by *Saludos Hispanos* magazine. Information here includes a Career Center with job listings and other good career information; an Education Center with announcements of internships, mentoring programs, and scholarship opportunities. In addition, you can access the Resume Pool where Hispanic job seekers can post their resumes, the Article Archive with recent articles from *Saludos Hispanos,* and the Hispanic Resource Index with links to additional Internet resources of interest to the Hispanic community. Very, very nice resource!

Topjobs USA

http://www.topjobsusa.com/

This focuses only on information about professional, managerial, or technical specialist job opportunities. Updated weekly! Excellent!

The Virtual Job Fair

http://www.vjf.com

The Virtual Job Fair has sophisticated layout and graphics but is easy to use. Users can store and send resumes as well as search job listings and articles. Lots of stuff in a variety of fields. Plug in your keywords and select the month of listings to search.

Work-Web

http://www.work-web.com

This site includes links to listings from all over the United States. A project of the Private Industry Council of Columbus and Franklin Counties, Ohio, it is not limited to that area.

The World Wide Web Employment Office

http://www.harbornet.com/biz/office/annex.html

This site includes links to other sites; places to post classified ads within this site. Lots of categories shown, but not all have listings available.

Yahoo's Classifieds

http://classifieds.yahoo.com

Job postings from all over the United States. Many cities are represented separately, and you can choose the state you want to target.

Online Guides to the Job Hunt

These Internet guides for the online job search gather information and resources to help you use the Internet to find employment. Some will give you notes about the resources, some will give you articles on the job search, but all will take you to more online information for your search.

The Riley Guide: Employment Opportunities and Job Resources on the Internet
Margaret Riley Dikel

http://www.dbm.com/jobguide/index.html

The first guide to the Internet as a tool for finding new employment, this resource started in January 1994 and has been going strong ever since. With the support of Drake Beam Morin, Inc., one of the largest career management and outplacement firms in the world, *The Riley Guide* links you to hundreds of sources of information for job leads, career exploration, and potential employers. It even has information to help you make a decision about moving.

CareerNET, Career Resource Center

http://www.careers.org

Over 7,500 links to employers, recruiters, magazines and newspapers, and other resources for your job search. It has even linked in travel and hobby sites to provide some relief from all the work.

Career Paradise

http://www.emory.edu/CAREER/

Supported by the career center at Emory University, this is a fun site to surf for your employment and career information needs.

The Career Resource Homepage
RPI

http://www.eng.rpi.edu/dept/cdc/homepage.html

Started by Jasmit Singh Kochhar, this site at Rensselaer Polytechnic Institute (RPI) is a megalist of resources for the online job search. All categories are arranged alphabetically, be they titles or topics, but you can browse and hit hundreds of interesting sites online.

The Catapult, Career Service Professionals Homepage

http://www.jobweb.org/catapult/catapult.htm

Originally developed by Leo Charette to guide career counselors in the use of the Internet, this service is now supported by the National Association of Colleges and Employers and provides numerous quality links to information and resources that can help anyone in their search.

College Grad Job Hunter

http://www.collegegrad.com/

Don't let that title fool you! This website, based on the book of the same title, is a cornucopia of resources and information to guide you through a complete job search.

College of William and Mary Career Services Center

http://www.wm.edu/csrv/career/index.html

When Leo Charette gave up The Catapult, he began working on a new site for the students at William and Mary. Once again, he has created an absolutely fantastic guide to the employment and career information resources online, and you don't even have to be a college graduate to benefit from this.

JobHunt: A Meta-List of On-Line Job Search Resources and Services

http://www.job-hunt.org

One of the earliest guides to the Internet job search, Dane Spearing works to bring together numerous resources on where to look for employment online.

JobSmart

http://jobsmart.org

It says "The California Job Search Guide," but don't let that stop you from using this resource. JobSmart is one of the best places online to find out how and where to look for employment both online and offline. Articles on the hidden job market, negotiating salaries, and numerous other topics enhance the choice resources here, selected because they are the best.

Purdue University Center for Career Opportunities

http://www.ups.purdue.edu/Student/jobsites.htm

Purdue's award-winning site has more than a thousand resources divided into categories. Some of the pages are quite large and take a long time to fully download, so you will have to be patient in order to use them. However, it is a huge resource and worth looking at.

Weddle's Web Guide

http://www.nbew.com/weddle.html

The Web Guide, part of the *National Business Employment Weekly,* publishes a review a week of the online recruiting hubs. You will learn some very interesting facts about the sites when you read these.

What Color Is Your Parachute: The Net Guide

http://www.washingtonpost.com/parachute/

The online guide from the dean of career counseling himself, Richard Bolles! The Net Guide is based on Bolles's information on the Internet job search and is spiced with his comments and observations on the job search and your decision-making process. Only the best sites online get his stamp of approval.

Yahoo's Listings of Employment Information

http://www.yahoo.com/Business/Employment

Yahoo links to over 1,500 sites for job leads and other sources of employment information. Don't limit yourself to just this list. Almost every category on Yahoo has a separate employment category, so browse frequently.

5

Jobs in Business, Marketing, and Personal or Commercial Services

The resources covered in this chapter point to job information in business fields followed by personal and commercial services. Personal and commercial services are those services provided to you, the individual, or to your company, such as child care, janitorial services, and equipment leasing.

We have not included names of specific companies or organizations that are recruiting in these fields, although many of the links listed will take you to the companies. Use the resources given in Chapter 3 to look for prospective employers on your own. For example, if you are interested in working for a medical firm, use search terms or follow links that relate to the medical field. You can use the virtual libraries to identify organizations or employers of interest. Keep in mind that even high-tech companies cannot do business without a team of accountants, sales representatives, and managers to help them run efficiently. The opportunities are endless, and this list is just the beginning!

Great Business Starting Points

Business Job Finder

http://www.cob.ohio-state.edu/dept/fin/osujobs.htm

Maintained by Tim Opler, a member of the faculty at Ohio State University, Job Finder is a fantastic collection of links to job listings, information, and recruiting resources for the business or finance specialist, or for someone considering work in these fields.

MIT Sloan School of Management

http://web.mit.edu/cdo/www

MIT's Sloan School manages this informative site for its students. Included in the publicly accessible resources are a list of employers who have hired Sloan students and/or graduates in the past two years, with links to their organizational home pages and a guide to online resources for your job search, including several informational links you can use to find leads.

The Online MBA

http://www.columbia.edu/cu/business/career/links/

Created by the Career Services office at the Columbia Business School, this is a good guide to online resources for job and industry information for the MBA.

Accounting and Finance

AAFA—The American Association of Finance and Accounting

http://www.aafa.com

The AAFA has recruiting specialists in accounting and finance. They recruit in the United States as well as internationally. Select a location to view openings in that area.

AccountingNet

http://www.accountingnet.com

AccountingNet includes all kinds of positions in accounting and finance for all levels of experience. It also provides great links to industry and professional information.

Bloomberg Online: Career Opportunities

http://www.bloomberg.com/fun/jobs.html

Bloomberg Online is by far the most extensive site on the Internet for broker, trader, and analyst jobs in the United States as well as internationally.

Cross Staffing Services

http://www.snelling.com/cross

Cross has been serving the New York banking, brokerage, and financial community for many years. This site has an impressive list of openings for sales, marketing, financial, accounting, banking, and information technology personnel.

CareerMosaic's Accounting and Finance Jobs

http://www.accountingjobs.com/

You can search through thousands of jobs or post your resume free at this great new partnership site from AccountingNet and CareerMosaic.

Nationjob Network Financial/Accounting/Insurance Jobs Page

http://www.nationjob.com/financial

These positions are listed by category but can also be searched by location, keyword, or position type.

National Banking Network

http://www.banking-financejobs.com

National Banking Network (NBN) is a very large association of recruiting firms with nation-wide job listings. This site includes jobs in finance, banking, credit, and many more opportunities within this industry.

RJ Pascale & Company

http://www.ct-jobs.com/pascale/

RJ Pascale & Company is a professional search-and-recruiting firm located in southwestern Connecticut. The firm specializes in placement and staff fulfillment for accounting and electronic data processing (EDP) professionals. Online listings are updated daily. Accounting and EDP professionals who wish to post to the candidate section must first submit their resumes for approval.

FinancialJobs.com

http://www.FINANCIALjobs.com/

These are jobs for accounting and financial professionals primarily located in Southern California.

Rutgers Accounting Web

http://www.rutgers.edu/Accounting/raw.html

The Accounting Research Center at Rutgers University supports RAW to promote and facilitate moving the accounting profession into the electronic age. Within this enormous site you will find links to information on taxation, finance, auditing, professional associations, accounting firms in the United States, publishers, and a special page dedicated to the Big 6 accounting firms, including links to their recruiting information.

Robert Half

http://www.roberthalf.com/jobsRH/

Robert Half is a major recruiter specializing in finance, accounting, treasury, and information systems.

Fund-Raising

Philanthropy Journal Online

http://www.philanthropy-journal.org

Are you interested in work as a development officer, nonprofit account manager, or director of planned giving? This is the source for you. The listings are from the current month only. This site also hosts two major guides to philanthropy and nonprofit organizations on the Internet, which might yield even more information for your job search.

Human Resources and Training

Society for Human Resource Management

http://www.shrm.org/jobs

The Society for Human Resource Management (SHRM) is posting over 100 new job listings each week. You can also find a very well-organized collection of human resources links at this noteworthy site.

NationJob Network Human Resources Jobs Page

http://www.nationjob.com/hr

This is a very significant specialty page from a large network of employers.

HR Careers

http://www.tcm.com/hr-careers/career

Concentrating on opportunities in training, this site has job listings and numerous other resources. You are able to search for jobs or post your resume at this promising new site.

Job Postings for Benefits & HR Professionals

http://www.ifebp.org/jobs/index.html

The International Foundation of Employee Benefit Plans, the largest association for employee benefit plans, provides a forum for 34,000 members to post employment listings.

Instructional Systems Technology Jobs

http://education.indiana.edu/ist/students/jobs/joblink.html

This site lists opportunities in all areas of training, including academic faculty and corporate trainers.

Insurance

Insurance Career Center

http://www.connectyou.com/talent/

This is a specialized recruiting site for insurance professionals. It is part of the CareerMosaic Career Network and can also be accessed from that site.

Rollins Search Group

http://www.rollinssearch.com/

Rollins specializes in jobs in the insurance industry, especially for actuaries.

MBA–Specific Resources

Management Consulting Online

http://www.cob.ohio-state.edu/~fin/jobs/mco/mco.html

This site, operated by Tim Opler, covers four topics—careers, thought, trends, and firms. Although intended for the new MBA, this site has some interesting articles and a list of firms to contact.

MBAJob

http://www.mbajob.com

This is obviously a source of jobs for MBAS. The site is new, and you have to scroll the listings, but it has promise. Many of the jobs posted here require 10 or more years experience.

Management Recruiters International

http://www.mrinet.com/

Management Recruiters International is one of the world's largest search and recruitment firms. Its recruiters look for the best executive, managerial, and professional talent for their clients. From this site you can review the job openings posted through all of the firm's regional offices, submit your resume for review, and review some good career advice from these recruiting experts.

Office Support Services

Champion Personnel System

http://www.championjobs.com

Champion is a Cleveland, Ohio–based staffing agency. Its site offers limited job postings for temporary and permanent office support and is updated weekly. It also includes useful information on job searching, resume preparation, and interview techniques, along with a salary guide for this level of employment.

Real Estate

RealBank

http://www.realbank.com

RealBank recruits executives and others for the real estate industry in 12 different occupational areas.

Sales and Marketing

American Marketing Association

http://www.ama.org

This site offers a couple of different placement and referral services for a fee. It does not have a menu structure of any kind, so use the search engine to find resources.

Advertising Age's Online JobBank

http://adage.com/job_bank/index.html

Advertising Age is placing its classified ads online with the help of The Monster Board.

Marketing Classifieds

http://www.marketingjobs.com

This site posts professional marketing, sales, and advertising employment opportunities.

NationJob Network Marketing and Sales Jobs Page

http://www.nationjob.com/marketing

NationJob's specialty pages bring together jobs from nearly 1,000 employers.

Retail JobNet

http://www.retailjobnet.com/cf/main.cfm

This is a database of jobs in the retail industry, from deli managers in supermarkets to chief operating officers. You must select a location and a title to activate the search.

Quality Control

American Society for Quality

http: //www.asqc.org/

The American Society for Quality (ASQ) is the leading quality improvement organization in the United States, with more than 130,000 individual and 1,000 sustaining members worldwide. The ASQ's *Personnel Listing Service*—a monthly publication in which companies and recruiters advertise position openings—is free to all members who request it, but you must be a member.

Personal Care

BeautyVision

http://www.beautyvision.com/

This site includes industry news, lists of schools, state certification programs, links to salons, and jobs, all in a very chatty kind of way. It also includes tips on building your own clientele.

Funeral Directors

National Funeral Directors Association

http://www.nfda.org/

The National Funeral Directors Association (NFDA) has an excellent site with good information on education and licensing requirements for this field. Scholarships for people interested in this area are available, as well as job listings.

FuneralNet

http://www.funeralnet.com

FuneralNet links to extensive information on funeral homes nationwide, as well as information on funeral services. Employment opportunities are posted in the Classified Ads with the most recent ads at the end of the list.

Child and Elder Care

CareGuide

http://www.careguide.net

This directory contains thousands of listings for child and elder care providers all over the United States. Although it does not contain job listings, you can use this information to contact potential employers.

Equipment Leasing

Equipment Leasing Association Online

http://www.elaonline.com

The Equipment Leasing Association (ELA) provides information on the industry, searchable corporate directories, and jobs.

Packaging

Food and Drug Packaging

http://www.fdp.com

You must register to use this site, but it is free and worth it! This site includes searchable product information, industry news, and, of course, jobs (under What's New).

Packinfo-World

http://www.packinfo-world.com/WPO/

PackInfo-World gives you news and events from all over the world and includes a worldwide list of packaging institutions. Jobs in the United States can be found here, along with lists of placement agencies and recruiters.

6

Jobs in the Social Sciences and the World of Nonprofits

The social sciences and nonprofit organizations have been grouped together for their interest in society and the public. The social sciences cover many fields, including education and academe, and many of these organizations cross into the nonprofit field. Opportunities with the many nonprofit organizations are not easy to locate. We have provided you with a few job databases for this area as well as information to help you locate and contact these organizations.

Archaeology

Archaeological Fieldwork Server

http://www.cincpac.com/afs/testpit.html

Individuals seeking archaeology fieldwork opportunities can browse through postings, including positions for volunteers, full-time jobs, positions in field schools, contract jobs, and other archaeological postings that are submitted or found on mailing lists and in newsgroups. This service does not contain position announcements for professional academic and staff archaeologists. Positions are categorized by the geographic location of the site or school.

Career Counseling

JOBPLACE Mailing List

LISTSERV@news.jobweb.org

The National Association of Colleges and Employers (NACE) provides this mailing list as a network for professionals interested in discussing career development and employment strategies. Job announcements for career services professionals are included. The association maintains archives of postings on its webserver at *http://www.jobweb.org/*.

JobWire

http://www.jobweb.org/jobwire.htm

Jobs for college career services and human resources professionals from *The Spotlight*, NACE's biweekly newsletter, are available from the two most recent issues. Contact the employers for more information and to apply for advertised listings.

Economics

JOE—Job Opportunities for Economists

http://www.eco.utexas.edu/joe/

This is the electronic version of *Job Opportunities for Economists* (JOE) and is now published by the University of Texas. These are job listings reported by the members of the American

Economic Association. Updates are published about every two months, and only the current file is available. The listings are arranged alphabetically by institution (note that "University of" is ignored in this arrangement), with U.S. academic positions first.

E-JOE

http://maynard.ww.tu-berlin.de/e-joe/

This European *Job Openings for Economists* is loaded with links and international jobs.

Education and Academe

Academe This Week

http://chronicle.merit.edu/.ads/.links.html

The current job listings from *The Chronicle of Higher Education,* the weekly newspaper of higher education, are online every Tuesday afternoon, a day before the print publication is released. Listings can be searched by geographic location, the *Chronicle*'s list of job terms, or keywords of your own choosing. Only the current week's listings are maintained, and all old listings are deleted. This is the best source for academic and research positions with U.S. colleges and universities, and many international institutions and companies with research divisions advertise here also.

Academic Position Network (APN)

http://www.umn.edu/apn/

The Academic Position Network is an online position announcement service for academic institutions all over the world. Job listings include faculty, administration, and staff positions, as well as announcements for research fellowships and graduate assistantships.

AERA Job Openings

http://tikkun.ed.asu.edu/~jobs/joblinks.html

The American Educational Research Association (AERA) has a long list of job openings taken from its mailing list.

Job Search Tip: Looking for Work in Academe. If you are interested in teaching at a college or university, you can check an institution's webserver to look for job listings, including assistantships, fellowships, and postdoctoral opportunities. Use The Master List of Servers (see Chapter 3) and directories like Petersons (*http://www.petersons.com*) to look for institutions in various areas, and then look for their human resources departments and even the specific department you are interested in. Professional societies may also carry good announcements. If you are looking for an institution with a particular specialty, use virtual libraries to target departments.

Cause Job Posting Service

http://cause-www.colorado.edu/pd/jobpost/jobpost.html

Cause is the association for managing and using information resources in higher education. Its membership includes network administrators, librarians, and chief information officers (CIOs) for academic institutions all over the world. The Cause Job Posting Service allows member organizations to post job openings. Positions for information managers, CIOs, directors of information systems, technical support personnel, and even some librarians were included at the time of review. Positions are removed on the date of closing.

Council for Advancement and Support of Education (CASE) Job Classifieds

http://www.case.org/

Specializing in administrative positions in academe and education, these jobs might be listed elsewhere, such as in *The Chronicle of Higher Education*.

Jobs in Higher Education—Geographical Listings

http://volvo.gslis.utexas.edu/~acadres/jobs/index.html

This site provides an extremely comprehensive set of links to faculty and staff job listings in the United States, Canada, Australia, and the United Kingdom. It is highly recommended!

Niss, National Information Services and Systems

http://www.niss.ac.uk/noticeboard/index.html

This list includes employment opportunities at the many universities in the Commonwealth countries (the United Kingdom, Canada, Australia, India, etc.). There are several fields listed, and links to additional job resources for these areas are also included.

Thesis: The Times Higher Education Supplement InterView Service

http://www.thesis.co.uk/

The Thesis service is the fastest way to find jobs in higher education. Jobs are updated every Tuesday at 3 P.M., with the ads booked to appear in the following Friday's print edition of *The Times Higher Education Supplement*. Thesis carries lists from all categories of higher education job vacancies worldwide as advertised in *The Times*. Jobs are sorted into U.K. or international groups and then sorted by their classification type, that is, lecturers and tutors, principal/senior lecturers, professors, and readers and chairs. Listings are retained for about one month or until filled, whichever comes first. This is a great resource for U.K. educational postings. You do not need to be a subscriber to the print version of *The Times Higher Education Supplement* to register to access the new Thesis site.

University of Minnesota's College of Education Job Search Bulletin Board

http://www.cis.umn.edu:11119/

gopher://rodent.cis.umn.edu:11119/

Administrative, K–12, and higher education jobs of all kinds are arranged by broad areas. The location of the positions is included in the menu, so you can look for those in specific areas.

AIR-L, Electronic Newsletter of the Association for Institutional Research

http://www.fsu.edu/~air

The Association for Institutional Research is dedicated to the professional growth of all who participate in decision making related to higher education via management research, policy analysis, and planning. Association members work in many different postsecondary areas—finance, academic affairs, instruction, student services, and institutional development—and in offices at the international, state, system, or campus levels. The Job Bulletin contains the full text of job announcements noted in the Electronic AIR, part B.

Independent School Management

http://www.isminc.com/mm.html

This site posts opportunities for principals and other administrators in private schools around the United States.

English as a Second or a Foreign Language (ESL/EFL)

TESLJB-L

listserv@cunyvm.cunyedu.

This is a sublist of TESL-L, which is found at the same listserv address. Participants must be members of the TESL-L main list to join this list, which announces and discusses job opportunities in the field of teaching English as a second language.

EFLWEB

http://www.u-net.com/eflweb/home.htm

This is an online magazine for those teaching and learning English as a foreign language. It is an excellent resource for those interested in this profession and includes a resume bank.

The EsL Job Center

http://www.pacificnet.net/~sperling/jobcenter.html

This site, presented by Dane Sperling, provides a wonderful list of resources for ESL educators.

Law

The Seamless Web Legal Job Center

http://www.seamless.com/jobs/

The Seamless Web is a great resource for those in the law profession. On the job page, you can post an opportunity or a "position wanted" announcement at no cost. Only job listings that directly relate to the legal profession will be posted. Such listings are defined as those messages that seek or offer employment for lawyers, barristers, solicitors, legal assistants, paralegals, legal secretaries, and so on. Freelance legal or computer consultants, and/or law-related consulting companies are encouraged to contact the owners for information on their standard rates for promoting services.

Hieros Gamos Legal Employment Classified

http://www.cgsg.com/hg/employ.html

Hieros Gamos is the most comprehensive source of legal information on the Internet. Job listings can be searched by position or location. A great set of links to other sources of legal jobs is provided.

The Legal Employment Search Site

http://www.legalemploy.com/

The Legal Employment Search Site has compiled a large set of links that deal strictly with legal-related employment.

The National Federation of Paralegal Associations

http://www.paralegals.org/Center/home.html

A limited number of national positions for paralegals, combined with employment resources and some recruiters, can be found at this promising new site.

You will also want to look at the U.S. Department of Justice listing in Chapter 10.

Library and Information Sciences

American Association of Law Libraries Job Placement Hotline

http://www.aallnet.org/services/hotline.html

Law librarians can find an assortment of university law schools to choose from at this site.

ALA Library Education and Employment Menu Page

http://www.ala.org/education/

The American Library Association Employment Page has the latest job listings from American Libraries and C&RL NewsNet combined with impressive links to other library job postings on the Internet.

Ann's Place—Library Job Hunting

http://tigger.cc.uic.edu/~aerobin/libjob.html

Go to Ann's Place to begin your search for library positions or links to organizations with valuable career resources for librarians.

BUBL Employment Bulletin Board

http://bubl.ac.uk

This site includes extensive information resources for librarians and international employment opportunities for librarians in Britain and other European countries and in the United States.

C. Berger and Company: Library Consultants

http://www.cberger.com/

Carol Berger's temporary placement agency is a well-known place for librarians and paraprofessionals seeking employment in the Midwest.

College and Research Libraries News Classified Advertising Archives

http://www.ala.org/acrl/advert3.html

These are primarily the academic job listings from the monthly *C&RL News* published by the Association of College and Research Libraries, a division of the American Library Association. The listings are updated monthly and are available two to three weeks before the print version.

LIBJOB-L

listserv@ubvm.cc.buffalo.edu

This mailing list features entry-level library positions in New York State.

Library Jobs and Employment: A Guide to Internet Resources by Jeff Lee

http://www.zoots.com/libjob/jefflee.htm

In a professional paper compiled to fulfill the requirements for his master of library science degree, Jeff has created a new listing of Internet resources to assist librarians with their online job searches. Information on searching the Internet and basic guides to Telnet, news, and so on are included.

The Networked Librarian: Job Search Guide

http://www.netcom.com/~feridun/libjobs.htm

The Networked Librarian is a new collection of links to employment resources for librarians.

Library and Information Specialists' Jobs

http://www.palinet.org/stecem/

Drexel University information science students produced this long list of job resources for librarians. Check the last category at the end of the document, "Related Employment," for links to information-industry businesses employing librarians.

North Suburban Library System Blue Sheets

http://nsls1.nslsilus.org/SERVICES/BlueSheets/bsinfo.html

Positions for librarians in Chicago and suburbs north of Chicago can be found here.

LIS-JOBLIST

mailserv@ac.dal.ca

Lori Small at Dalhousie University is the moderator of this Internet mailing list discussing entry-level jobs in library and information studies. All postings are announcements for such positions within Atlantic Canada. Contact Lori for more information at *lsmall@ac.dal.ca.*

SLAJOB

listserv@iubvm.ucs.indiana.edu

The Special Libraries Association mailing list discusses international opportunities for librarians. Contact Spencer Anspach *(SANSPACH@ucs.indiana.edu)* or Roger Beckman *(BEC@ucs.indiana.edu)* for more information.

Southern Connecticut State University Library

http://scsu.ctstateu.edu/~jobline/

A must for librarians seeking jobs! Southern Connecticut State University provides links to its own Library Jobline, Lee's Library Jobs and Employment, and numerous other great resources.

University of Illinois at Urbana-Champaign, Graduate School of Library and Information Science Placement Online—Library Job Service

http://carousel.lis.uiuc.edu/~jobs/

Library positions nationwide are listed with the University of Illinois GSLIS. This is probably the single largest source of position announcements for librarians available online and can be searched in many ways.

University of Michigan ILSL Library Job Postings

http://www.lib.umich.edu/libhome/ILSL.lib/ILSLjobs.html

The Information and Library Studies Library (ILSL) has produced an impressive collection of sources of library jobs by region or specific type of position.

Library Job Postings on the Internet

http://www.sils.umich.edu/~nesbeitt/libraryjobs.html

This is a very comprehensive list of resources. The descriptions include the update schedule for each site, scope of jobs included, and instructions for navigating each site.

Music Library Association Joblist

http://www.music.indiana.edu/tech_s/mla/joblist/joblist.htm

This is the monthly newsletter of the MLA with the job announcements.

ARLIS/NA JobNet

http://afalib.uflib.ufl.edu/arlis/jobs.html

The Art Libraries Society of North America (ARLIS/NA) provides these vacancy announcements for art librarians, visual resources professionals, and related positions.

Job Search from Library Journal Digital

http://www.bookwire.com/ljdigital/job.htm

Library Journal, the trade journal of the library and information sciences profession, is now online, complete with the classified ads.

See also the listing for the Library of Congress in Chapter 10.

Linguistics

Jobs in Linguistics

http://www.linguistlist.org/jobsindex.html

This site is updated almost daily with mostly, but not exclusively, academic openings. The main page (*http://www.linguistlist.org/*) has excellent resources for linguists.

Nonprofit

Impact Online

http://www.impactonline.org

Impact Online is a new nonprofit organization that helps people get involved with nonprofits nationwide through the use of technology. Impact educates, informs, and provides guidance to those interested in volunteering.

International Service Agencies

http://www.charity.org/

The International Service Agencies' (ISA's) stated mission is "to help millions of people overseas and in the United States who suffer from hunger, poverty, and disease or from the ravages of war, oppression, and natural disasters." The ISA is made up of 55 diverse member agencies ranging from African medical relief funds to the Boy Scouts (overseas) and Catholic Charities. Information about each is provided.

Good Works

http://www.tripod.com/work/goodworks/search.html

This is a good source for those seeking nontraditional employment in social change organizations.

Internet Non-Profit Center: Home to Donors and Volunteers

http://www.nonprofits.org/

The Internet Non-Profit Center has no paid staff. The center does not list jobs, but it does provide documents describing hundreds of voluntary and nonprofit organizations, including financial data about these organizations.

The National Civic League

http://www.ncl.org/ncl

Founded in 1894 by Theodore Roosevelt, Louis Brandeis, and other turn-of-the-century Progressives, the National Civic League (NCL) is a community-focused advocacy organization.

The site highlights grassroots efforts from around the United States and covers every field, from prenatal care to parent education, from job training to school-based health clinics, from affordable housing to community-oriented policing.

Philanthropy Journal **Online**

http://www.philanthropy-journal.org

All kinds of resources for nonprofit jobs and careers are featured in *Philanthropy Journal Online*. Check out the link to the Meta-Index of Nonprofits for a wide range of potential employers.

soc.org.nonprofit

This newsgroup covers all topics related to nonprofits: funding, technology, programming, and so forth. It is one of the primary Internet resources for nonprofit administrators.

Opportunity Nocs

http://www.opnocs.org

This is a biweekly publication published by Executive Services Corp. The site contains all levels of jobs in the nonprofit sector of the New England area, as well as links to other nonprofit sites and job sites. Job leads appear on this site a week after appearing in the newsletter. Subscription to the newsletter is definitely stressed, but this site would be useful to someone seeking employment or just general information in this area.

Community Career Center

http://www.nonprofitjobs.org/

This site lists nonprofit jobs all over the United States and ranking from support staff to chief toxicologist to executive director.

Psychology

American Psychological Society (APS) *Observer* **Job Listings**

http://psych.hanover.edu/APS/job.html

The APS site has job listings in the social sciences and psychology, most of which are college and university postings. It also includes job listings from the APS, news about the organization, and related psychology resources.

APA Monitor **Classified Advertising**

http://apa.org/ads/

The last two months of the *American Psychological Association Monitor* are searchable by state at this location.

Mental Health Net Joblink: Openings

http://cmhc.com/joblink/

Employers of all types can post their mental health positions free of charge at this site. Resumes can also be posted here at no charge.

Tip: The Industrial and Organizational Psychologist Home Page

http://www.siop.org/positions.html

The Society for Industrial and Organizational Psychology publishes this newsletter containing jobs, internships, and grant resources.

Psych-Web List of Scholarly Psychology Resources on the Web

http://www.psych-web.com/resource/bytopic.htm

In addition to a massive set of psychology-related links, this site contains great sources of job and career information.

Positions in Psychology: The First Worldwide Register

http://psy.anu.edu.au/academia/psy.htm

The Australian National University maintains this free international service for posting academic psychology positions.

Social Work

NASW Jobs Bulletin

http://naswca.org/jobbulletin.html

The National Association of Social Workers (NASW), California Chapter, publishes a large list of social work positions on the fifth and twentieth of each month.

Socialservice.com

http://socialservice.com

Any social service organization that has a website and a job openings page on that website can get a free link here, increasing its visibility.

Social Work and Social Services Jobs Online

http://128.252.132.4/jobs/

The George Warren Brown School of Social Work has created this promising forum for job listings by location. There are also links to job-related resources.

Women's Studies

Employment Opportunities in Women's Studies and Feminism

http://www.inform.umd.edu/EdRes/Topic/WomensStudies/

This directory is part of the Women's Studies Database at inforM, the University of Maryland, College Park Campus's online information system. Job postings include the closing date on the menu so you can easily see application deadlines.

7

Jobs in the Humanities, Recreation, Hospitality, and Transportation

We have grouped the humanities, recreation, and hospitality together for their creativity and the enjoyment that they bring the participants as well as others. Because transportation is important to travel, recreation, and hospitality, it has been placed here also.

Opportunities for employment in the arts and humanities or in sports and recreation are not easily found on the Internet, but they are there. As a job seeker, you should first discover what your options are based on what you like to do and what interests you, and then use your training to help you find the career path that will best fit these criteria. Remember that job listings might not come right out and state that a degree in English or art is necessary. You need to know where the skills and training you have will fit in along with your interests! Examine the job-listing sites in Chapter 4 for more leads and use your creativity to explore the options.

General Arts Sources

The Arts Deadlines List Information

http://www.xensei.com/adl

This server lists "competitions, contests, calls for entries/papers, grants, scholarships, fellowships, jobs, internships, etc. in the arts or related areas (painting, drawing, photography, etc.)." The list is also available by mail with a subscription.

Arts Wire Current

http://www.artswire.org

Arts Wire is a national computer-based communications network for the arts community. It is designed to enable artists, individuals, and organizations in arts communities across the country to better communicate, share information, and coordinate their activities. Arts Wire has several job listings in every issue. The "Arts Wire Current" (formerly Hotwire) section is accessible free and lists a few jobs.

Acting and Entertainment Jobs

Playbill On-Line

http://www1.playbill.com/playbill/

Playbill On-Line is a great source for listings of acting and theatrical support positions on and off Broadway and throughout the United States, London, Canada, and Brazil.

Auditions Online

http://www.auditions.com/

Have you always wanted to make that big break? This site lists casting calls, including nonunion calls, for Los Angeles and San Francisco.

Showbizjobs.com

http://www.showbizjobs.com

Showbizjobs.com includes opportunities in all occupations in the film, television, recording, and attractions industry job markets.

Culinary and Baking Arts

Escoffier Online

http://www.escoffier.com/nonscape/index.shtml

Food service professionals can look for jobs here or participate in various forums to discuss the industry.

Bakery-Net

http://www.bakery-net.com

Are you interested in baking or the baking industry? Check out these links to equipment, suppliers, associations, and (of course) jobs.

Graphic Arts

3DSite

http://www.3dsite.com

The 3DSite is a server dedicated to three-dimensional computer graphics. The job list contains information on opportunities all over the world. These are arranged alphabetically by country, with the organization that is recruiting clearly noted. Postings are e-mailed to the owner every 30 days for updates. Note that not all of these positions require you to know programming languages! Many organizations are looking for talented artists who can use computers. A resume database is available to which you can add your information.

GWeb, An Electronic Trade Journal for Computer Animators

http://www.gweb.org/lists.html

GWeb has a great listing for those seeking work in computer animation. The company that is hiring lists jobs, and they look great. Announcements are dated so you know when they were posted, and contact information is included.

Design Sphere Online Job Hunt

http://www.dsphere.net/b2b/directory.html#browse

Jobs for graphic artists can be found on Design Sphere. This is also a good place to link to your resume on your personal home page.

Hospitality

Hospitality Net Virtual Job Exchange

http://www.hospitalitynet.nl/job/

This is a great source for jobs in hotels and restaurants as well as the food and beverage industry.

Executive Placement Services

http://www.execplacement.com

An executive recruiting service specializing in the retail, gaming, and hospitality industries nationwide.

Journalism and Broadcast Media

Airwaves Job Services

http://www.airwaves.com

Airwaves Media Page began as an outgrowth of Airwaves Radio Journal (ARJ) an interactive "Cyberzine" dedicated to domestic radio broadcasting. The journal has been serving the Internet with professional-level radio discussion since 1991, as an e-mail reflector of the Usenet newsgroup rec.radiobroadcasting, which continues to be the place for radio professionals and serious nonprofessionals to meet and talk in a friendly and noise-free environment. The job site is a great addition to the webserver and is a varied listing of all kinds of work in the radio broadcast industry. You can also post positions wanted at this site.

Job Openings in Newspaper New Media (and Related Fields)

http://www.mediainfo.com/ephome/class/classhtm/class.htm

Editor and Publisher Classifieds provides positions listed in "new media," including journalism and online journalism-related positions. There are some technical jobs as well.

Media Links

http://www.bctv.net/telcom/pub/links/marks.html

This site is loaded with links to media jobs and organizations where media instruction is used.

Mediaweek Help Wanted: Miscellaneous

http://www.mediaweek.com/classifieds/multi.asp

All kinds of media, publishing, and advertising jobs are listed here every Monday morning (9 A.M. EST). You can also access *Adweek*, *Brandweek*, and *Marketing Computers* from this site!

National Writers Union Job Hotline

http://www.nwu.org/nwu/hotline/hotwrite.htm

The National Writers Union (NWU) Hotline lists writing, authoring, and multimedia jobs in the United States. The employers who list the jobs are only given out to members of NWU who agree to pay the Hotline 10 percent of their first month's earnings.

Newspaper Mania Job Center

http://www.club.innet.be/~year0230/jobs.htm

Newspaper Mania contains a very large collection of links to news- and media-related jobs.

Journalism-Related Job Openings

http://eb.journ.latech.edu/jobs/jobs_home.html

These listings are collected from various listservs, and the site also links to several good journalism job sites.

National Diversity Journalism Job Bank

http://www.newsjobs.com/jobs.html

These are jobs in all facets of the journalism industry. Although it is targeted to minority populations, it is open to all users.

TV Jobs

http://www.tvjobs.com

This is a fantastic site with jobs and information for the entire broadcast industry in all fields.

The Inkspot: Resources for Writers

http://www.inkspot.com/

This is a fantastic site with lots of information for all kinds of writers. The resources include upcoming events, a place to advertise yourself, a place to find others who want you to write for them, and links to resources for literary agents.

The Write Jobs from The Writers Write

http://www.writerswrite.com/jobs/jobs.htm

These are listings for all kinds of writing work, including technical writing. Many of the solicitations are openings for writers with electronic journals.

Multimedia and Web Design

HotWired's Dream Jobs

http://www.hotwired.com/dreamjobs/

This listing includes jobs for designers, multimedia specialists, and even surfers for Yahoo! It's quirky but definitely interesting.

Silicon Alley Connections

http://www.salley.com

Job listings for specialists in Internet/www technology, multimedia, networking, PC programming, and technical support. They even include opportunities for art directors, Web programmers and developers, and copywriters.

Museums and Archives

Museum Employment Resource Center (MERC)

http://199.190.151.4:80/~MERC/

The Museum Employment Resource Center (MERC) has listed jobs for hundreds of museums in eight countries at no charge. There is a minimal charge for posting resumes.

Music

Yahoo! Symphony Orchestra

http://www.yahoo.com/Entertainment/Music/Artists/Orchestras/Symphony_Orchestras/

Still regarded as the premier directory of Internet information, Yahoo! has a wonderful list of links and resources for symphonies all over the world. For those seeking employment in this field, you can find contact information for all of these groups, personnel lists including the administrative staff, and notices of job openings as well as current auditions.

ORCHESTRALIST

To subscribe: listproc@hubcap.clemson.edu

Message: subscribe orchestralist

ORCHESTRALIST is an unmoderated mailing list devoted to matters orchestral, and specifically designed for the orchestra professional. It serves as a forum to discuss such matters as orchestral repertoire, performance questions, conducting techniques, auditions, job opportunities (both professional and academic), marketing, organization, and other subjects. Note: This list is not a forum for discussion of recordings, anecdotes about conductors, and so on. There are other forums devoted to these topics. Although there are not many job listings, this list is a very active discussion group and a good way for orchestra professionals to network.

Philosophy

Jobs in Philosophy

http://www.sozialwiss.uni-hamburg.de/phil/ag/jobs/main_english.html

PhilNet in Hamburg, Germany, is to be commended for this excellent worldwide list of jobs in philosophy, which may be posted in any language.

Printing and Bookbinding

PressTemps

http://www.presstemps.com

This agency offers temporary and contract services for all areas of the printing industry. Jobs listed here include customer service representatives, drivers, press operators, silk screen supervisors, and numerous other opportunities.

The Bookbinders Guild of New York Job Bank

http://www.bbgny.com/guild/jb.html

These are employment opportunities in all areas concerned with the publishing, printing, and purchasing of books.

Sports and Recreation

Cool Works

http://www.coolworks.com/showme

The major source for jobs in our national parks, ski resorts nationwide, and other similar opportunities organized by state. The listings range from summer/seasonal to year-round permanent, and go from the person who points out where to park your car up to the manager of the resort.

Online Sports Career Center

http://www.onlinesports.com/pages/CareerCenter.html

These are job opportunities in all areas of the sports and recreation industry.

SportLink

http://www.sportlink.com

SportLink includes a variety of jobs all in the sports equipment industry, from marketing to manufacturing and beyond.

Transportation

Find a Pilot

http://www.findapilot.com/

This is a source of job announcements as well as a resume database for pilots and flight trainers.

Natca, the National Air Traffic Controllers Association

http://home.natca.org/natca/default.html

The National Air Traffic Controllers Association is the collective bargaining unit for the 14,000-plus air traffic controllers serving the Federal Aviation Administration, Department of Defense, and private sector. This site includes information on the organization and about the career of air traffic controller as well as links to related information and organizations.

The Airline Employment Assistance Corps

http://www.avjobs.com

You can view all kinds of good information for this industry here, but access to the ads requires a paid membership.

Aviation Employee Placement Service

http://www.aeps.com/aeps/aepshm.html

The Aviation Employee Placement Service (AEPS) is a source of jobs for all occupations and fields in the aviation industry from executives down to mechanics and including both general and corporate opportunities. The current jobs require a paid subscription, but you can sample the old listings (over 30 days old) in the "New Members" area. For good links to industry information, select the "Other Aviation Information Menu." The Aviation Net is a great resource for news.

JobXchange

http://www.jobxchange.com

Dedicated exclusively to the global cruise and maritime industry, the International Seafarers Exchange sets up a direct connection among cruise and maritime companies, crewing agents, maritime schools, universities, and prospective crew members.

Truckers.com

http://www.truckers.com/

This is a source of links to all kinds of information for the trucking and transportation industry. It includes a great list of online sources for road conditions and traffic cameras.

TruckNet

http://www.truck.net/

Like Truckers.com, TruckNet has many links to resources for the trucking industry, including jobs.

Video Production

VideoPro Classifieds

http://www.txdirect.net/videopro/default.html

VideoPro is a directory of video production professionals and services. The opportunities in video production range from graphics designer to videographer to equipment maintenance engineer. Postings can be added for freelance work in any area of video production.

8

Jobs in Science,
Health, and Medicine

This chapter focuses on the natural sciences, including physics, chemistry, and the earth sciences, as well as the many health and medical fields. You may also want to review the sections on health and medicine for related areas of interest as well as cross-disciplinary fields.

General Resources

Science Professional Network

http://recruit.sciencemag.org/

From the American Association for the Advancement of Science comes *Science,* a global weekly magazine. *Science* is now online, and its many job listings are included. These cover academic, government, and private industry jobs in all scientific fields.

sci.research.careers

A Usenet newsgroup for discussions about careers for those in the sciences. It also carries job postings.

sci.research.postdoc

This is a Usenet newsgroup for discussions among postdoctoral candidates about careers in the sciences, including opportunities for employment and continued postdoctoral work.

Agriculture and Forestry

AgriCareers

http://www.agricareers.com

A source for jobs in all areas of agriculture, including animal health, turf specialists, and administration/sales. The listings are primarily Canadian at this time, but the site offers several links to additional resources.

College of Food, Agricultural, and Environmental Sciences Career Information, Ohio State University

http://hortwww-2.ag.ohio-state.edu/faes/career/career.html

This college offers a searchable database of positions listed for its alumni and graduating students.

Career Resources in Agronomy

http://www.agronomy.org/career/career.html

This is a joint project of the American Society of Agronomy (ASA), the Crop Science Society of America (CSSA), and the Soil Science Society of America (SSSA). You can browse the listings from *Agronomy News* or check the other links and services available.

WeedJobs, Positions in Weed Science

http://www.nrcan.gc.ca/~bcampbel/

These are permanent, term, and postdoctoral and graduate student positions in weed science. Links to related pages are also provided.

AAEA Employment Service, American Agricultural Economic Association

http://www.aaea.org/employment.html

These are M.S./Ph.D. employment opportunities in the agricultural field. Most have application deadlines, with the later postings being further down the page. The jobs are primarily academic, but there are some nonprofit opportunities also.

International Agribusiness Internship Center

http://www.usu.edu/~iaic/

Utah State University lists these internships which focus on agribusiness. The internship openings are sorted by fields, then position titles.

Astronomy

American Astronomical Society Job Register

http://www.aas.org/JobRegister/aasjobs.html

This professional society will not publish a job announcement without an accompanying statement assuring that the vacancy is bona fide and the position has not been promised to anyone. The listings are updated monthly.

Biology/Biotechnology/Physiology

bionet.jobs.offered
bionet.jobs.wanted

These Usenet newsgroups list resumes and requests from persons looking for work and research opportunities in biology fields.

BioNet Employment Opportunities

http://www.bio.net:80/hypermail/EMPLOYMENT

BioNet Employment Wanted

http://www.bio.net:80/hypermail/EMPLOYMENT-WANTED/

These sites offer archives for the bionet.jobs.offered and bionet.jobs.wanted newsgroups, easily accessed through the Web.

Cell Press Online

http://www.cellpress.com

Cell Press is a publisher of several major journals for various fields, including *Cell, Immunity,* and *Neuron.* The most recent classified ads are posted on this site.

More biotechnology opportunities can be found in Chapter 9.

Chemistry

Chemistry and Industry

http://chemistry.mond.org

This site lists jobs in chemistry from all over the world and in all employment sectors (private industry, academe, government, etc.).

Ensign Bickford Industries

http://pages.prodigy.com/CT/aspire/

This employer has been operating in the specialty chemical business areas since 1836.

Environment/Geographic Information Systems/Earth Sciences

Environmental Careers Organization

http://www.eco.org/

This group lists internships in environmental areas.

EE-Link: The Environmental Education Web Server

http://www.nceet.snre.umich.edu/jobs.html

This site is a great source for internships, postdoctoral opportunities, and other job openings in environmental work. Several listings also request volunteers.

Environmental Careers World

http://environmental-jobs.com/

A source of positions in environmental work, primarily for entry- to mid-level job seekers.

Job.com

http://www.job.com/main.html

This is a recruiting service for architects, consulting engineers, and environmental consultants provided by Hall & Company.

Ecological Society of America NewSource

http://www.sdsc.edu/~esa/newspage.htm

This is the monthly newsletter from the association, including very good job announcements. Select a newsletter and scan to the bottom of the page to view these.

Environmental Sites on the Internet

http://www.lib.kth.se/~lg/envsite.htm

Developed and designed by Larsgöran Strandberg, Environmental Technology and Work Science at KTH—Royal Institute of Technology—Stockholm, Sweden, this is a huge site with links to information on all areas of environmental work.

Gis Jobs Clearinghouse

http://www.gis.umn.edu/rsgisinfo/jobs.html

This is a great source for position announcements in geographic information systems (GIS), image processing (IP), and global positioning systems (GPS).

Employment Opportunities in Water Resources

http://www.uwin.siu.edu/announce/jobs/

This site includes academic, government, nonprofit, and private industry opportunities.

GeoWeb

http://www.ggrweb.com/job.html

GeoWeb includes free and fee-based listings for jobs in academic and private industry.

Ores—Online Resources for Earth Scientists

http://www.calweb.com/~tcsmith/ores/

This is a great site with lots of information for this profession, including links to employment resources.

Geosci—Jobs Mailing List Archives

http://www.eskimo.com/~tcsmith/mail/geoscij.html

This is the archive of the free mailing list carrying employment opportunities for geologists, mine engineers, and all other earth scientists in academe, government, or private industry.

MET—Jobs Mailing List Archives

http://www.eskimo.com/~tcsmith/mail/met-jobs.html

This is the archive of the free mailing list carrying meteorology and atmospheric sciences employment opportunities.

Soil and Water Conservation Society Jobs Database

http://www.swcs.org/

This is a collection of announcements for soil management jobs in the United States posted with this professional society.

Health Care

Allied Health Opportunities

http://www.gvpub.com

This site includes jobs in many medical fields all over the country as well as job lines for many of the participating institutions.

Call24 Online

http://www.call24online.com/

This site includes jobs in the health care industry as well as links to licensing boards and professional associations.

Experimental Medicine Job Listings

http://www.medcor.mcgill.ca/EXPMED/DOCS/jobs.html

This is the official job board of the Canadian Society of Biochemistry and Molecular and Cellular Biologists (CSBMCB) and includes jobs from all around the world. The listings are primarily, but not exclusively, academic and government research facilities.

Global Health Network

http://info.pitt.edu/HOME/GHNet/GHNet.html

This is an alliance of experts in health and telecommunications and includes lists of organizations and available positions from all over the world.

Health Careers Online

http://www.healthcareers-online.com

This is a source for jobs in all areas of health care, including administration and management.

Interim Services

http://www.interim.com

This agency offers flexible-staffing and full-time placement for the health care industry.

JobSpan

http://www.jobspan.com

JobSpan is a service used to screen and recruit health care professionals. Clients of EthoSolutions' JobSpan service are primarily human resources departments seeking to fill executive, management, and professional positions in the health and managed care industry.

National Network for HealthCare Professionals

http://www.treknet.net/hcroaz/

The National Network recruits for all types of work in the health care industry. A partial list of current searches is available, and resumes are accepted in Word for Windows, WordPerfect, or ASCII text. This is a service of HealthCare Recruiters of Arizona.

Mental Health

Mental Health Net

http://www.cmhc.com

This is an excellent resource for information on all topics related to mental health. Job opportunities are available under the "Professional resources" category.

Midwives

Professional Information from the American College of Nurse-Midwives

http://www.midwife.org/prof/

This site includes employment opportunities as well as excellent information on certification, clinical practice, and other important issues for this profession.

Nursing

Nightingale

http://nightingale.con.utk.edu

Nursing positions and pointers to more information from the school at the University of Tennessee, Knoxville.

Physical and Occupational Therapy

RehabJobs

http://www.rehabjobs.com

This includes employment opportunities and career information for specialists in all therapy areas.

Physicians

Physican Recruitment Ads from *JAMA*, the *Journal of the American Medical Association*

http://www.ama-assn.org/sci-pubs/md_recr/md_recr.htm

These are the current month's openings as listed in *JAMA* and available at no charge.

Physicians Employment

http://www.fairfield.com/physemp/

This is a source of job listings for physicians in all specialties. The listings are arranged by specialty, and notes show the last time a file was updated. Military positions are included, and if your specialty is not listed, you can send in a form requesting referrals. Great site!

Academic Physician and Scientist

http://www.acphysci.com/

This site is a joint effort of *Academic Physician and Scientist* and the Association of American Medical Colleges (AAMC). It lists open academic medical teaching positions for the 126 U.S. medical schools and their affiliated institutions.

Physics

Career Services, American Institute of Physics

http://www.aps.org/industry.html

Job in the academic, industry, and business worlds updated every two to three days. You should also review the great links to related sites for more employment information.

Physics Jobs On-Line

http://www.tp.umu.se/TIPTOP/FORUM/JOBS/

This is a dynamic list of job opportunities around the world.

Physics Job Announcements by Thread

http://XXX.lanl.gov/Announce/Jobs/date.html#end

This site is a constantly updated list of jobs. You will be placed at the bottom of the list where the latest announcements have been added, so page up to see slightly older listings.

JobLinks

http://cip.physik.uni-wuerzburg.de/Job/job.html

This site lists jobs in physics from all over the world. It includes links to many organizations hiring physicists.

9 Jobs in Engineering, Mathematics, and Technology

This chapter covers all the fields and occupations with any relation to engineering and technology. These include all of the engineering specialties, mathematics, construction, mining, and manufacturing. You may want to look at Chapter 8 for some related areas. Transportation jobs are included in Chapter 7.

Multiple Fields

Alpha Systems

http://www.jobbs.com

This is a contingency recruiter for technical, industrial, and engineering fields and industries. Top jobs are posted and resumes can be submitted for a specific job or for future consideration. Read over the preferred method of receiving your information.

Engineering Job Source

http://www.engineerjobs.com/

Free web pages and weekly newsletters concentrating on jobs in Indiana, Illinois, and Michigan.

EngineeringJobs.com

http://www.engineeringjobs.com

A listing of jobs for engineers, this includes links to employers who maintain job listings on their company pages.

IndustryNet

http://www.monster.com/inet/inet.srch.html

A source for technical and industrial jobs hosted by The Monster Board. More great information can be found on the main page (*http://www.industry.net*).

National Society of Professional Engineers

http://www.nspe.org

This society page includes links to *Engineering Times* as well as a national list of firms offering engineering services. The society provides excellent career information for anyone interested in an engineering specialty.

Olsten Professional Technical Services

http://www.olstenpts.com

This is a Southern California recruiting and contract agency. Several technical and engineering areas are included along with technical writing and project management.

Sanford Rose Associates

http://www.sanfordrose.com

This executive search firm has a large number of engineering searches in process at any given time.

Superior Group of Companies

http://www.supdes.com

Three corporations—Superior Design Co., Inc.; SDC Computer Services, Inc.; and Superior Temporary Services Inc.—have banded together to form this site. Superior Design specializes in engineering and design/drafting, and SDC in technical areas; each has its own job listings. Superior Temporary gives you a list of its representatives all over the United States and contact information for each.

Aeronautics/Aviation

Aeronautics/Aviation Career Search Resources

http://24.1.77.43/career.html

The San Francisco chapter of the American Institute of Aeronautics and Astronautics (AIAA) maintains this directory of career and job resources.

Space Jobs

http://www.spacejobs.com

These are employment opportunities worldwide in the aerospace industry.

AeroJobs

http://www.aerojobs.com

Employment opportunities in the aeronautics industry.

Mooney Aircraft Corporation Employment Opportunities

http://www.mooney.com/EMPLOY.HTM

These are employment opportunities with Mooney, an aircraft manufacturer in Texas. Resumes are not accepted through e-mail, but the phone number to call is given on the page.

Employment Opportunities from *The Mechanic*

http://www.the-mechanic.com/jobs.html

This is the website for the Aircraft Mechanics Fraternal Association, and this resource includes several good articles on the need for aircraft mechanics, industry and union news, and direct links to the major airlines online.

Other opportunities in the transportation industry can be found in Chapter 7.

Architecture

Job Hunting in Planning, Architecture, and Landscape Architecture

http://www.lib.berkeley.edu/ENVI/jobs.html

Created by the Environmental Design Library at the University of California, Berkeley, this is a selectively annotated guide to help job seekers in the professions of architecture, landscape architecture, and city/regional planning. This is not a resource for job listings, but a guide to the job search process with cited resources for these fields.

AIA Online

http://www.aia.org

This is the home of The American Institute of Architects. This site includes many resources for professional development, connecting with others in this field, and a soon-to-be-added area for classified ads.

Automotive

Automotive Employment Connection

http://www.autocareers.com

This is a source of job opportunities for everyone from mechanics to general managers. You will need to register to view the database, so have a current resume ready to make this process easier.

Biomedicine/Biotechnology

Medical Device Link

http://www.devicelink.com/index.html

This site recruits the people who build and manage the equipment. It includes an excellent salary survey and salary estimator worksheet along with extensive links to suppliers, consultants, and industry news.

Medzilla/Fsg Online

http://www.chemistry.com/

This is a great recruiting site for the biotechnology, health, and medical industries. Medzilla gives a great salary survey and private resume postings, all at no cost to you.

MedSearch

http://www.medsearch.com

This is a major online site for jobs in the medical, biomedical, and health care fields.

You should also review Chapter 8 for more areas of interest.

Camera Repair

Fargo Enterprise Gateway to the Camera Repair Industry

http://www.fargo-ent.com/index.html

You can search for repair shops, connect to manufacturers, check repair manuals, and even view a few employment opportunities at this site.

Civil Engineering

CIVENG-JOBS

http://www.eskimo.com/~ltcsmith/mail/civengj.html

This is a free mailing list for job announcements in civil engineering. The link will take you to a website with information about the free mailing list (*CIVENG-JOBS-REQUEST@eskimo.com*) or the fee-based Web archive.

You should also review resources for the earth sciences, as well as the sections on construction, mining, and several other areas in this chapter, that may interest you.

Computer-Aided Design (CAD), Manufacturing (CAM), and Engineering (CAE)

UG Job Network

http://www.ugjn.com

Job listings involving Unigraphics CAD/CAM/CAE skills.

Pro/E Job Network

http://www.pejn.com

Job listings involving Pro/ENGINEER CAD/CAM/CAE skills.

IDEAS Job Network

http://www.ideasjn.com

Job listings involving Structural Dynamics Research Corporation (SDRC) CAD/CAM/CAE skills.

Computer-Aided Three-Dimensional Interactive Application (CATIA) Job Network

http://www.catjn.com

Job listings involving CATIA CAD/CAM/CAE skills.

Computing and Technology

Because this is a very established area online, it is broken into several sections.

GENERAL RESOURCES

Career Information from the ACM

http://www.acm.org/member_services/career

The Association for Computing Machinery (ACM) provides this free resource for announcements placed in some of its journals and articles. Some services here are limited to ACM members and require a member ID to access them.

The Ada Project (TAP)

http://www.cs.yale.edu/HTML/YALE/CS/HyPlans/tap/positions.html

This is a clearinghouse for information and links to employment resources. It was developed for women in computing and technology but is certainly not limited to this group alone.

comp.jobs.offered

A Usenet newsgroup offering jobs in computing and technology.

RECRUITERS AND RECRUITING SITES

AD&A Software Jobs Home Page

http://www.softwarejobs.com

This is the home of Allen Davis & Associates, a respected search firm specializing in software and information technology (IT) search and placement. Jobs listed here are divided by technical specialty.

The Beardsley Group

http://www.beardsleygroup.com

A recruiting and placement firm looking for those with expertise in routers, hubs, network management, network operations, and LAN/WAN. The "Hot Jobs" is an excellent list of opportunities for all over the United States.

Chancellor & Chancellor

http://www.chancellor.com

This recruiter has listings for contract and full-time openings.

Comforce Corporation

http://www.comforce.com

Comforce is a leading provider of staffing, consulting, and outsourcing solutions focused on the high-tech needs of the growing telecommunications, information technologies, and technical market sectors. The jobs can be searched by industry or location.

D.I.C.E., Data Processing Independent Consultant's Exchange

http://www.dice.com

Probably the best site online for data processing (DP), information services (IS), and information technology (IT) consultants. Go ahead and post a skill set for yourself. This site was highly rated by recruiters in the 1997 Internet Recruitment Survey from Austin Knight, which means that company is using this site for recruiting and liking it!

HotJobs!

http://www.hotjobs.com

A source for computing and technology jobs with Fortune 500 and other high-profile companies. You can search the regular database, the International database, or the entry-level database. Keyword and company searches are available, and a resume database is free for you to post in.

The Information Professional's Career Page

http://www.brint.com/jobs.htm

This is an excellent guide to career information for IS/IT professionals, including articles on how the jobs are changing.

MacTemps

http://www.mactemps.com

An agency matching candidates talented in both Macintosh and Windows programs with companies who need the right person with the right skills. MacTemps has been highly rated by the talent working with them.

Mindsource Software

http://www.mindsrc.com

A staffing firm located in Mountain View, California, owned and operated by Unix Software Engineers. It specializes in recruiting technical talent in the fields of Unix systems and network administration, Web engineering, quality assurance, and support for both contract and full-time staffing needs. Jobs focus on Silicon Valley.

New Dimensions in Technology, Inc.

http://www.ndt.com

This is a fairly good job resource for engineering, marketing, sales management, consulting, and IT at all levels, and all in the national and international technology and computing industry (although most of the jobs found were in Massachusetts). Job searching is easy, recruiter profiles are available, resumes can be submitted online, and everything is free.

Provident Search Group

http://www.dpjobs.com

The Provident Search Group (PSG) is working in the permanent placement of technical data processing professionals. Current job openings are listed by main specialty.

Transaction Information Systems

http://www.tkointl.com/

A systems integration and technology consulting firm, TKO was ranked 55 on the *Inc.* 500 list for 1997.

Winter, Wyman, and Co.

http://www.winterwyman.com

This is one of the largest recruitment firms in New England, now working in Atlanta too.

Daley Consulting & Search and Daley Technical Search

http://www.dpsearch.com

This group is made up of recruiting and search consultants specializing in the placement of experienced data processing professionals with client companies in the San Francisco Bay area and in Sacramento County and its surrounding communities.

Computer Jobs

http://www.computerjobs.com

This is an Internet-based advertising service that posts technical job and career information for the computer professional. Postings are for Atlanta, Carolina, Chicago, and Texas.

Computing and Technology Companies Online

http://www.cmpcmm.com/cc/companies.html

Are you trying to find an employer? Check out this list of links to almost every computing company with a presence on the Internet. Search by keywords or browse the alphabetical listings.

Seek Consulting

http://www.seek-consulting.com/

Seek is offering contract opportunities, its contract consulting guide, and other interesting information for the IS professional.

Virtual Job Fair

http://www.vjf.com

The Virtual Job Fair (VJF) hosts over 500 companies with thousands of listings for the high-tech industry.

Volt Services Group

http://www.volteast.com

Volt is a leading supplier of contract personnel in information technology and business process consulting. Jobs are listed for the United States as well as Europe, and you can locate local offices.

TRADE PUBLICATIONS AND PROFESSIONAL SOCIETIES

Computing Research Association

http://cra.org/jobs

The Computing Research Association (CRA) is made up of more than 180 North American academic departments of computer science and computer engineering, industrial and government laboratories engaging in basic computing research, and affiliated professional societies.

Communications Week Classifieds

http://techweb.cmp.com/cw/ccareers

Career and job information from this information networking trade journal.

ComputerWorld Careers

http://careers.computerworld.com

These are the classified ads and career columns from the leading weekly IS trade journal.

ComputerWorld's CareerAgent

http://careeragent.computerworld.com

This is for IT professionals and others thinking about additional training or investigating the new programming and computing skills needed to remain competitive. It includes searchable skill interests, training opportunities, and other interesting topics. You must register to establish a profile, but it's all free!

ACM SIGMOD's Database Jobs Listings

http://www1.acm.org.81/sigmod

Jobs posted with this special interest group (Association for Computing Machinery's Special Interest Group on Management of Data) are in data management. Search the hypertext dbworld archives to find jobs and research positions for experts in this area.

NACCB Online Job Board & Resume Bank

http://www.computerwork.com

The National Association of Computer Consultant Businesses (NACCB) posts jobs as well as information on computer consulting careers.

AECT Placement Center

http://www.aect.org/Employment/Employment.htm

The Association for Educational Communications and Technology (AECT) posts jobs on its site.

Women in Technology International (WITI)

http://www.witi.com/

The resources are geared for women, but this site offers some excellent advice to all. Under the "Areas" category you can access career advice, while under "Hot Spots" you'll find job opportunities.

Construction and Public Works

American Public Works Association

http://www.pubworks.org

The American Public Works Association (APWA) is a tremendous resource for information on the many fields covering public works, and a stellar list of links to related professional and trade associations.

Contractor Net

http://www.contractornet.com

This is a website for contractors in the building and construction industry. The Contractor Network holds a current certificate of insurance on all contractors that are listed on its website, giving you some assurance that the employers you see here are good.

The Electronic Blue Book

http://www.thebluebook.com

This site provides online access to continually updated construction industry information. *The Blue Book of Building and Construction* publishes regional construction directories in most of the major geographic regions of the United States.

Engineering News Record

http://www.enr.com

This is the weekly of the construction industry. It posts the jobs online and allows access to terrific information. You can search the jobs by job title, keyword, location, or view the ads from specific issues. Jobs out for bid are also listed at this site.

Right of Way

http://www.rightofway.com/

This site has good information for the industries and occupations related to public works. Job listings too. Not sure what they mean by "right of way"? An explanation is provided.

Hardhats Online

http://www.hardhatsonline.com

This website was designed to give construction industry employees a place to display their resumes and search for employment opportunities. Currently categories include engineering, construction management, crafts, craft supervision, and technical positions, but others are always being considered for addition.

Contract Labor Pool

http://www.clp.com

This West Coast contractor is always looking for construction laborers and skilled tradespeople.

Electrical Engineering

IEEE Job Bank

http://www.ieee.org/jobs.html

Jobs posted with the Institute of Electrical and Electronic Engineers (IEEE).

IEEE Computer Society

http://computer.org/computer/career/career.htm

The classified ads posted in the monthly journal published by this division of the IEEE.

EE Times Jobs Online

http://jobs.hodes.com/j2/owa/j2.dyna.page?iid=1001

EE Times is a leading industry journal for electrical engineers, and now it's placing its classified ads online with CareerMosaic. The journal itself includes career articles by Nick Corcodilos, host of "Ask the Headhunter," part of the Motley Fools on America Online.

Electronic News Classifieds On_Line

http://www.sumnet.com/enews/class/class_ol.html

Classified ads for electrical engineers and related industries.

Electric and Other Utilities

Electric Power NewsLink

http://www.powermag.com/employ.html

This site includes jobs and industry information from *Power* magazine.

American Gas Association

http://www.aga.com

A trade association composed of about 300 natural gas distribution, transmission, gathering, and marketing companies in North America. This site includes the current issue of *American Gas,* the association's magazine, a list of member websites, a searchable handbook covering the publicly traded member companies, and jobs.

PMA Job Site

http://www.intr.net/pma/pmajobs.htm

These are employment opportunities for people experienced in managing and marketing power. The Power Marketing Association (PMA) hosts this site.

Electrical World

http://www.electricalworld.com/employ.html

This includes jobs and industry information from *Electrical World* magazine.

Utility Newslink

http://www.itforutilities.com/employ.html

The editors of *Information Technologies* prepare Utility NewsLink for *Utilities/IT,* a leading magazine covering IT and business issues for electric, gas, and water utilities and communications companies.

Environmental Engineering

See the "Environment/Geographic Information Systems/Earth Sciences" section in Chapter 8.

Facilities Maintenance

Association for Facilities Engineers CareerNet

http://www.afe.org/jobs.shtml

This includes employment opportunities for persons working in facility and plant maintenance.

FacilitiesNet Forums

http://www.facilitiesnet.com/forums/cgi/get/jobs.html

Facility engineers and others involved in plant maintenance can register as users of these forums for free access to networking opportunities and job listings.

Food Processing

At-Sea Processors Association

http://www.atsea.org/employ.html

This site lists work opportunities for processors on fishing trawlers at sea. It also includes information describing the realities of working on the oceangoing processing plants, which anyone considering this work should read.

FishJobs

http://www.fishjobs.com

These are listings of employment opportunities in various aspects of the seafood/fishing industry. Opportunities are listed by geographic region, and postings are retained for only one month.

Manufacturing

Edmonds Personnel Inc.

http://www.edmondspersonnel.com

Edmonds specializes in the placement of individuals in all areas of engineering, technical, data processing, and management with manufacturing companies located throughout the United States.

Food Processing Machinery and Supplies Association

http://www.fpmsa.org/

The Food Processing Machinery and Supplies Association (FPM&SA) represents nearly 500 member companies which provide processing and packaging equipment, supplies, and services to the food and beverage industries domestically and internationally. Their agent and distributor profiles cover the entire world, and each listing includes a contact name, address, phone number, and the list of United States and international companies they represent. You are thinking "potential employers," aren't you?

Manufacturing Marketplace

http://www.manufacturing.net/resources/jobs/default.htm

You can search for a job or post your resume here. The site also includes good information for the manufacturing industry.

Kolak Enterprises

http://www.mindspring.com/~jkolok

This recruiter specializes in engineering, technical, manufacturing management, and managing of information systems/data processing. A list of current openings is available on the site.

Rothrock Associates, Inc. (RAI)

http://www.raijobs.com

These are recruiters for materials, purchasing, engineers in design and manufacturing, and all human resources disciplines for plant, division, and corporate locations.

Mathematics

American Mathematical Society

http://www.ams.org/employment

This association is a great resource for all mathematicians. Jobs in academic and nonacademic areas, and terrific professional and career resources.

Rollins Search Group

http://www.rollinssearch.com

A recruiter looking for actuaries to work in the insurance industry.

Mechanical Engineering

ASMENET, the American Society of Mechanical Engineers

http://www.asme.org/index.html

This website for mechanical engineers includes information for professional development, industry news, and jobs (*http://asme.org/jobs/index.html*).

Mechanical Engineering Magazine

http://www.memagazine.org/contents/current/jobs/jobs.html

These are the monthly classified ads from the journal of the ASME.

Mining/Drilling/Offshore

Info-Mine

http://www.info-mine.com/

This is probably the most informative mining site on the Internet. Some job listings are public, while others require you to have a paid subscription, but it is incredible.

Offshore Guides

http://OffshoreGuides.com/

Need information on the offshore oil and gas industry or on looking for a job? Offshore Guides gives you free access to job openings arranged by category and ranging from engineers to divers to catering to clerical staff. While you are here, look over the free handbook on employment in this industry, including rig types, employment trends, and work conditions. Note the capital letters in the address. They might be important.

e-Mine

http://www.rci.co.uk

This is the mining industry site for Europe, including the Mining World employment listings, and Mining Europe, with links to more resources and opportunities for employment.

MineNet Job Mart

http://www.microserve.net/~ldoug/jobmart.html

This site posts jobs listings as well as position wanted ads. The main page has information on the U.S. mining industry. It's not as well done as Mining USA, but is a nice complement.

Mining USA

http://www.miningusa.com/

Here you will find mining industry jobs in the United States and around the world. All of the ads are dated as to when they were posted. Other great information on the industry is also available at this site.

Optical Engineering

Optics.org

http://optics.org/employment

Optics.org is sponsored by *The SPIE: Society for Optical Engineering*. It includes job resources and a resume bank, but these services are not limited to members.

Semiconductor Industry

Semi/Sematech

https://www.sematech.org/semi-sematech/

Semi/Sematech is a nonprofit organization representing the U.S. semiconductor infrastructure: the equipment, materials, software, and service suppliers to the semiconductor manufacturing industry. Its member list includes links to their web pages, which always means you have a list of potential employers at your beck and call.

Discover a New World of Opportunity . . .

http://www.4chipjobs.com/index.html

In the semiconductor industry! This is an introduction to all kinds of career opportunities in the semiconductor industry and includes information on educational paths, training needs, an explanation of semiconductors and their importance, and other great information for considering any of the many employment opportunities available in this industry. Although there are some opportunities for those with high school diplomas, an associate degree or certification from a technical school will take you farther.

Telecommunications

Telecom Publishing Group

http://www.telecommunications.com

Telecom Publishing Group (TPG) has been covering the telecommunications industry for over 10 years. It provides the Telecom Information Clearinghouse, a resource with links to companies, regulations, and other extensive industry information. You should also check out the Telecom Lingo Guide before going into any interviews.

10

Opportunities
in Government,
Public Policy,
and Public Service

This chapter covers opportunities for employment in public service, as well as with the various federal, state, and local government agencies and departments and the institutions that work closely with them. Any international governments listing employment opportunities on the Internet have been included under the appropriate heading in Chapter 13.

Federal Government

The federal government is one of the largest employers in the United States and probably the most diversified. You can find listings for employment opportunities in several locations online and can examine all of them at no charge. Be sure to check the dates on the listings and to note all job code numbers. You may need specific forms in order to apply or you might be asked to include information with your application that is not on your resume, so check for "Information on Applying" at any of the sites. The Library of Congress (*http://www.loc.gov*) is a great place to start searching for information on the many federal departments and agencies, and the White House Web page (*http://www.whitehouse.gov/*) also provides a link to all of them.

Federal Computer Week

http://fcw.com/

This magazine for information systems professionals in the United States government also includes links to job opportunities and career resources in computer, government, and related sites on the Web.

Federal Government Job Hotlines

http://www.unl.edu/careers/jobs/fedhotl.htm

University of Nebraska at Lincoln Career Services has gathered the job "hot lines" for a number of federal agencies into one handy list.

Federal Jobs Digest

http://www.jobsfed.com/

The Federal Jobs Digest (FJD), a private resource for listings of federal jobs, is nicely arranged by job group (science, administration, and law enforcement) and easy to use. Current vacancies include some blue-collar positions. For a fee, you can subscribe to the Hotline Service and have job postings that fit your profile e-mailed to you as they become available.

FEDIX/MOLIS

http://www.rams-fie.com/

Now part of Research Administration Management Systems/Federal Information Exchange (RAMS-FIE), Federal Information Exchange, Inc. (FEDIX) is the largest database of educational and research funding opportunities available. It also provides access to some employment opportunities. Minority On-Line Information Service (MOLIS), the minority database, is an equally good resource for minority research funding and employment opportunities. Register your profile and FEDIX will send you an "Opportunity Alert" via e-mail featuring funding and employment information of interest to you.

FedWorld Jobs, Labor, and Management Web Page

http://www.fedworld.gov/jobs.htm

FedWorld: The United States Government Bulletin Board

http://www.fedworld.gov/jobs/jobsearch.html

The first entry links to the Bureau of Labor Statistics, Department of the Interior Vacancy System and Office of Personnel Management. The second is FedWorld's searchable job database, in operation since its introduction in 1992. FedWorld downloads files created by the Office of Personnel Management (OPM). For a complex search, the USAJobs website is recommended (see page 112), because it is the official server of the OPM. FedWorld provides simple access. Browse the job announcements or search them by region or state and by keywords. Choose the relevance of search terms and the number of hits to be displayed. FedWorld also makes shareware available that can be used in applying for federal jobs. Keep in mind that several agencies list their own job openings, so look for these at their separate websites.

Local Government Institute/Local Government Job Net

http://www.lgi.org

Established in Seattle in 1988, the Local Government Institute (LGI) is a federally recognized independent nonprofit organization dedicated to improving the quality of local government throughout the English-speaking world. One of the services LGI provides online is the Local Government Job Net, where local governments can post job openings for chief executives, human resources personnel, recreation and administrative staff, public works and public safety professionals, and any other employee they might need. The service allows people to post "position wanted" announcements as they search for new work with local government organizations and agencies.

Government JOBS Central

http://members.aol.com/govjobs/index.htm

Dennis Damp, author of a book about federal jobs, has made much of the material from the book accessible online. He includes a Job Hunters Checklist and helpful links to government resources.

Jobs Database from NACE

http://www.jobweb.org/search/jobs/

Although this database by the National Association of Colleges and Employers (NACE) does not feature federal jobs exclusively, it does offer a large number of federal postings. Search by job title or keyword and choose a region of the country, or look at all the possibilities. Information on applying for federal jobs is available, along with an optional application for federal employment.

Planning Your Future: A Federal Employee's Survival Guide

http://safetynet.doleta.gov/

Planning Your Future was created to assist all the individuals who are in transition because of federal government downsizing. You'll find information for the federal employee looking at retirement, buyouts, and reductions in force (RIFS). It also includes links to many job and career resources featuring transitional tools, information on going back to school and starting a business, and other helps for recareering. Contact *brunnerp@doleta.gov* with your comments or questions.

Private Sector Federal Job Information Sites

http://www.govexec.com/careers/privinfo.htm

Developed by a private business, this web page links to several nongovernment sites of interest to federal government job seekers. Its links include a guidebook for resume writing, the NACE site, Government Jobs Central, and a fee-based database of federal job opportunities.

USAJobs

http://www.usajobs.opm.gov/

USAJobs is the official site for employment information and jobs listed with the Office of Personnel Management. Search the current job listings, then fill in the online application (note: you must have a copy of the Supplemental Qualifications Statement and the vacancy announcement to apply online), or contact the agency that posted the position for more information. There's an additional link to career transition assistance at the Department of Labor website.

The X-118 Qualification Standards for Federal Jobs

http://safetynet.doleta.gov/text/require.htm

This document explains how the series numbering works and the basic requirements for all jobs with the United States government. Suppose, for example, you are interested in a job as an accountant, and you find a few listings on the USAJobs website. Look at the "series" at the top identifying this as a Series 0510 GS 12. The X-118 tells you the basic requirements for an 0510 job and the added requirements to get to the GS 12 rating. This provides very useful information for people in government wanting to change jobs or for others wondering how to evaluate a job listing against private sector skills.

The Military

dod.jobs

The newsgroup for posting job announcements from the United States Department of Defense.

Career Opportunities and Information from DefenseLink

http://www.defenselink.mil/other_info/careers.html

DefenseLink, the official World Wide Web information service of the Department of Defense, was developed with the objective of providing up-to-date, easily accessible, and accurate information to American citizens, wherever they may be.

Today's military service provides all kinds of incentives for enlistment, including technical training and education, monetary and social benefits from living on base, other special opportunities, and an enlistment bonus. Link to information about the Defense Department and its many parts, check out the job possibilities in the four branches through the DefenseLink gateway, or use the URLs that follow to get to the specific sites.

United States Army Recruiting Home Page

http://www.goarmy.com/

"Be all you can be!" Contact *kelleyk@emh2.usarec.army.mil* or send in your address to receive more information via the postal service.

Navy Opportunities

http://www.navyjobs.com/

Call (800) USA-NAVY or check out the Navy's website (*www.navy.mil*) for more information.

Welcome to the Air Force

http://www.airforce.com/

For more information, fill in the online form or call (800) 423-USAF.

The Few. The Proud. The Marines.

http://www.usmc.mil/wwwmcrc/mcrc.htm

Check out the MarineLink website (*www.usmc.mil/*), contact a Marine Corps recruiter, or call (800) MARINES for more information.

Other Federal Departments and Agencies

This section is a sampling of some federal agencies and departments maintaining job listings on their own public Internet sites. You can check other departments and agencies yourself by using the Library of Congress or the White House websites to link to them. USAJobs (described earlier) also will carry almost all of the job announcements found on the individual sites.

Library of Congress

http://lcweb.loc.gov/homepage/about.html#working

gopher://marvel.loc.gov/11/employee/employ/

The Library of Congress (LC) provides many employment and volunteer opportunities, and sponsors several internships and prestigious fellowships, including the new Mellon Foreign Area Fellowships. The website links directly to a gopher menu of LC job postings, with information for applying and additional pointers to other job listings. Be aware that not every job posted here is for librarians!

Department of Justice

http://www.usdoj.gov/careers/careers.html

Check out the career opportunities for lawyers, paralegals, and correctional facility officers. The Department of Justice (DOJ) recruits for its offices, boards, and divisions, including Immigration and Naturalization, Office of the Inspector General, and the Drug Enforcement Administration.

National Science Foundation

http://www.nsf.gov/home/chart/work.htm

The National Science Foundation (NSF) maintains a workforce of over a thousand individuals performing many functions, including clerical, administrative, engineering, and scientific. The foundation also employs scientists, engineers, and educators on a rotating basis from academe, private industry, and other eligible organizations. It is recommended that you read the NSF Factsheet (linked from the site) to get an overview of the foundation. You can check out the current vacancy announcements online or call the Jobline at (703) 306-0080 or (800) 628-1487.

Department of the Interior Automated Vacancy Announcement System (AVADS)

http://info.er.usgs.gov/doi/avads/index.html

Interior Department postings are updated on Thursdays. Because applications are not accepted online, job seekers need to read the application guidelines for each bureau or service (Indian Affairs, National Park Service, etc.), then search, view, or download the weekly vacancy announcements and follow the guidelines for applying.

State and Local Governments

The Internet Job Source at statejobs.com

http://www.statejobs.com/

The Job Source links to government jobs in most of the states, dozens of agencies within the federal government, and many of the Fortune 500 companies. Search for a job by major industry or state, or click to check out the major newspapers, magazines, and other news and government resources available through this site. Some state listings are pages maintained by Job Source.

Jobs In Government

http://www.JobsInGovernment.com/

This site provides access to all kinds of jobs in government and the public sector, including positions with many county and municipal agencies. Search by keyword and other criteria or by employer and location, or submit your resume. Also included is a helpful list of related associations.

What follows is a list of sites we have found that provide access to jobs in state government. Some of them are recruitment or human resources pages for the state, others are commercial sites, and many have a variety of career resources and job links. You will find other career resources for states, counties, and municipalities in Chapter 12. Don't overlook America's Job Bank, with the combined job banks of the state employment services.

Alabama

http://204.29.92.2/alapers/index.htm

Alaska

http://www.state.ak.us/local/jobs.htm

Arizona

http://www.adc.state.az.us:81/ADCweb/hrd2.htm

California

http://www.spb.ca.gov/

http://www.statejobs.com/ca.html

Colorado

http://www.statejobs.com/co.html

http://www.state.co.us/gov_dir/interns/ (internships)

Connecticut

http://www.statejobs.com/ct.html

District of Columbia, Metro-Washington Council of Governments

http://www.mwcog.org/geninfo/jobs.html

http://www.statejobs.com/va.html (Virginia and the District of Columbia)

Delaware

http://www.state.de.us/spo/empsvc.htm

Florida

http://fcn.state.fl.us/fcn/centers/job_center/

http://www.statejobs.com/fl.html

Georgia

http://www.state.ga.us/GMS/

http://www.statejobs.com/ga.html

Hawaii

http://www.state.hi.us/hrd

Idaho

http://www.ipc.state.id.us/

Illinois

http://www.statejobs.com/il.html

Indiana

http://www.state.in.us/acin/personnel/index.html

Iowa

http://www.state.ia.us/jobs/index.htm

Kansas

http://www.ink.org/public/perssvcs/

Kentucky

http://www.state.ky.us/agencies/personnel/jobspage.htm

Louisiana

http://www.dscs.state.la.us/csjobopp.htm

Maine

http://www.state.me.us/bhr/career/career.htm

Maryland

http://www.statejobs.com/md.html

Massachusetts

http://www.magnet.state.ma.us/refshelf.htm#jobs

http://www.statejobs.com/ma.html

Michigan

http://www.mdcs.state.mi.us/Employ/Emp_info.htm

http://www.statejobs.com/mi.html

Minnesota

http://www.doer.state.mn.us/

http://www.statejobs.com/mn.html

Mississippi

http://www.spb.state.ms.us/

Missouri

http://www.state.mo.us/oa/stjobs.htm

Montana

http://161.7.163.2/state/state.htm

Nebraska

http://www.das.state.ne.us/das_dop/index.html

Nevada

http://www.state.nv.us/nvjobs.htm

New Hampshire

http://www.statejobs.com/nh.html

New Jersey

http://www.state.nj.us/personnel/vacancy/vacancy.htm

http://www.statejobs.com/nj.html

New Mexico

http://www.state.nm.us/spo/

New York

http://www.cs.state.ny.us/

http://www.statejobs.com/ny.html

North Carolina

http://www.osp.state.nc.us/OSP/

North Dakota

http://www.state.nd.us/www/jobs.html

Ohio

http://www.state.oh.us/das/dhr/emprec.html

gopher://gizmo.freenet.columbus.oh.us/11/governmentcenter/stateofohio/
State%20Government%20Job%20Opportunities (via the Greater Columbus Freenet,
Columbus, Ohio)

http://www.statejobs.com/oh.html

Oklahoma

http://www.state.ok.us/_opm/

Oregon

http://www.dashr.state.or.us/

Pennsylvania

http://www.state.pa.us/jobpost.html

http://www.statejobs.com/pa.html

South Carolina

http://www.state.sc.us/jobs/

http://www.state.sc.us/jobs/esc/ (State Employment Security)

South Dakota

http://www.state.sd.us/state/executive/bop/listings/openings.htm

Tennessee

http://www.state.tn.us/personnel/

Texas

http://www.twc.state.tx.us/joblists/gvjb.html

http://www.statejobs.com/tx.html

Utah

http://www.dhrm.state.ut.us/

Vermont

http://www.state.vt.us/pers/employ.htm

Virginia

http://www.state.va.us/~dpt/menu

http://www.statejobs.com/va.html

Washington

http://www.wa.gov/dop/employ.html

http://www.statejobs.com/wa.html

West Virginia

http://www.state.wv.us/admin/personel

Wisconsin

http://badger.state.wi.us/agencies/der/empopp.htm

gopher://badger.state.wi.us:70/11/agencies/der

Wyoming

http://personnel.state.wy.us/stjobs/

Public Policy Institutions

Brookings Institute

http://www.brook.edu/

The Brookings Institute is America's oldest policy think tank. This site contains information about the institution and its work. The internship information and employment opportunities are accessible through a link from the home page. Brookings also operates a 24-hour-a-day job line at (202) 797-6096, which is updated weekly.

The Heritage Foundation

http://www.heritage.org/

You'll find information about this organization, along with internship and employment possibilities, at this site. The foundation also sponsors a free job bank for conservative individuals and prospective employers, with a convenient online application form.

International Monetary Fund

http://www.imf.org/

The Fund is continually recruiting for economists, although it never formally advertises the positions. Instead, find out when and how to apply, download an application form, and learn about what kind of employment opportunities are usually available.

RAND

http://www.rand.org/

The RAND Corporation has been around since the end of World War II, created as a research and development organization and initially sponsored by the Air Force. Today, it continues to get funding from the government, as well as from private sector and charitable organizations. You can find the employment opportunities, updated monthly, in the "Reaching RAND" section.

Law Enforcement and Protective Services

United States Department of Justice

http://www.usdoj.gov/careers/careers.html

The DOJ is not only recruiting for lawyers and paralegals but also for many correctional facilities that fall under its area of responsibility.

The Police Officer's Internet Directory

http://www.officer.com/

This site features links to law enforcement agencies around the world, criminal justice resources, and jobs.

National Fire Protection Association

http://www.nfpa.org/

This website puts you in contact with the fire departments, building code regulators, emergency services, fire and safety associations, and anyone else you can think of who would have a part in fire protection and safety regulation in the United States and abroad. Many of these organizations and fire protection departments have information on job openings or job lines for you to call.

Public Administration

Florida State Career Center Job Openings and Placement Administration Help

http://www.fsu.edu/spap/job_intern/jobs/job_listings.html

The Askew School of Public Administration and Policy at Florida State University maintains this server, which stresses job openings and related services for government employees and students in Florida State's Masters of Public Administration Program. Several lists of job links lead to entry-level jobs.

11

Entry-Level and Summer Employment, Internships, and Co-ops

If you are a college student, your first stop for cooperative and internship information should be your department head or college career center. However, if they don't have anything of interest to you, we have gathered some leads that might help you find a position. In addition to these resources, use the virtual libraries to identify other organizations in your major field and contact them about possible work. Use Internet indexers and search engines to search the keywords "intern," "internship," "co-op," "cooperative education," and "summer" or "temporary" for some other possibilities. Another tip—check college and university webservers in the region where you would like to work to see if they have any possible leads from local organizations. You can use Yahoo!, the Master List of Servers, and the Peterson's Guides to target these sites (see Chapter 3). Freenets and other resources in Chapter 12 may also provide some contacts. The major job listing sites included in Chapter 4 can also be good sources for this type of employment, so search their databases as well.

Entry-Level Positions and Internet Resources for New Graduates

CollegeConnection

http://www.careermosaic.com/cm/cc/

CareerMosaic brings you another great resource, with the emphasis on college students and new graduates. Look over the list of employers and submit your resume free if you like what you see, or link to one of the internship sites. Get help with your resume, learn about the hidden market, or use the other career resources.

College Grad Job Hunter

http://www.collegegrad.com/

Search the entry-level job or internship databases by keyword, or review the entire list of openings. You can also limit your search (by zip code) and look for selected opportunities only, or ask the career specialist a question.

The Entry Level Job Seeker Assistant

http://andromeda.einet.net/galaxy/Community/Workplace/joseph-schmalhofer/jobs.html

The Assistant continues to be an excellent source of information for finding an entry-level position through the Internet. This site includes links to companies, online recruiters, and organizations with positions available for entry-level employees. Many of these organizations will also accept cooperatives and internships. Search related Usenet newsgroups or leave a copy of your HTML resume to be linked by major field or specialty.

1st Steps in the Hunt

http://www.interbiznet.com/hunt/

Another good CareerMosaic effort, 1st Steps is a web letter targeting new job hunters and career changers. The Archives is available online, along with other career resources and links to over 1,000 companies and their job listings.

Princeton Review

http://www.review.com/careers/

Fill out the Birkman Career Style Summary to help you figure out what career is right for you, or learn about dozens of careers. Join the career discussion group, search Jobtrak for a job, or check out Dilbert and his "Daily Mental Workout"!

StudentCenter.com

http://www.studentcenter.com/

More help for the recent graduate. You'll find career advice and planning tools, and help in creating the right resume and acing the job interview. Research the companies you're interested in working for and sign up for the site's free newsletter.

Youth Resource Network of Canada

http://www.youth.gc.ca/

Created to help prepare youth for the workplace and the job hunt, the Network is a partnership between several agencies of the Canadian government and the private sector. The Network provides self-assessment tools and career resources, along with job opportunities and resources for starting your own business.

Internships, Co-ops, and Summer Opportunities

California Polytechnic State University

http://www.careerservices.calpoly.edu/

California Polytechnic's Career Services page has information about part-time, summer, and cooperative education positions along with some good career resources. Students who have registered can use the Web Walkup (wwu) login page to sign up for hundreds of job opportunities.

Career Center Internship Index

http://www.carleton.edu/cgi-bin/intern/internwais.pl

Carleton College has pulled together this collection of internships. Choose one of 12 categories, and then search for a position that interests you. Contact the business or organization directly.

Case Western Reserve University

http://www.cwru.edu/CWRU/Admin/cpp/summer.html

Find a *hot* summer job or part-time work at this site. Lots of jobs and they are updated regularly.

Intern-NET

http://www.vicon.net/~internnet/

Intern-NET provides helpful information and links to other resources for potential interns. Search for an internship by geographic location or by category, or check out the resources in the Intern-NET Library.

International Agribusiness Internship Center

http://www.usu.edu/~iaic/

Utah State University administers the International Agribusiness Internship Center (IAIC), a clearinghouse for agribusiness interns and internships. Submit a student profile and the IAIC will try to match you with an appropriate organization. Internship openings are sorted by fields, then position titles.

Internship and Fieldwork Listings Nationwide

http://www.virginia.edu/~career/intern.html

This is an excellent resource with internship listings for all majors throughout the country. The University of Virginia (UV) Office of Career Planning supports this service with additional resources for UV students only.

JobTrak

http://www.jobtrak.com

Your college or university must be a member of JobTrak for you to gain access to the job listings! So, see if your institution is listed; if so, call your career center and ask for the password. This site has some tremendous resources. Those who cannot access the job listings might be able to target the companies listed to ask about opportunities.

Jobnet Internships

http://www.westga.edu/~coop/internships.html

Here you'll find links to internships in the Carter Center and several major companies, plus opportunities in many different disciplines.

The Mighty Internship Review

http://www.daily.umn.edu/~mckinney/

Look here for an internship in journalism. The Review links to opportunities in daily and weekly newspapers and other media as well. A handy resource is the review section, where interns are encouraged to leave information about their experiences.

New England Board of Higher Education Opportunities for Minority Students

http://www.nebhe.org/minority_intro.html

This website has a nice collection of resources for high school students, college students, and beyond. Search the links of interest to you.

Office for Special Learning Opportunities (OSLO)

http://oslo.umn.edu/

Through this site, OSLO provides experiential learning opportunities for students at the University of Minnesota through its internship, career services, and field learning and community service program. It also links to other great internship sites for students nationwide.

Peterson's Guides

http://www.petersons.com/career/

Peterson's Guides, Inc., has organized this listing of study-abroad programs, learning adventures, and summer camp opportunities for teenagers.

Russian and Eastern European Internship Opportunities

http://www.indiana.edu/~reeiweb/indemp.html

The REEIweb lists internships available in Eastern European countries along with non-academic and academic positions. Check this site for information on funding of related studies and additional links.

University of California, Berkeley's Work Study Home Page

http://workstudy.berkeley.edu/

The Berkeley site is divided into an employer area and a student section with job search instructions. This is a great matching service that enables Berkeley students to locate part-time and summer jobs, internships, and so on in their areas of study.

Government-Sponsored and Political Internships and Volunteer Resources

AmeriCorps

http://www.cns.gov/americorps.htm

AmeriCorps members work for a year to meet the needs of individual communities while earning money for college. If you're interested in the National Civilian Community Corps (NCCC) or Volunteers in Service to America (VISTA) programs, call (800) 942-2677 to request an application. If you're interested in one of the hundreds of local community projects, check out the online AmeriCorps Program Directory, print off the application form, fill it out, and send it in.

AmeriCorps*VISTA

http://www.libertynet.org/~zelson/vweb.html

VISTA Link

http://bcn.boulder.co.us/community/vistalink/

AmeriCorps presents this resource detailing volunteer opportunities in Volunteers in Service to America (VISTA). Since 1964, thousands of Americans have been placed with community-based agencies through the VISTA program. Search the database for current openings or look through the links to other AmeriCorps programs. You can link directly to the VISTA Link's Assignment Database through the Boulder recruiting site.

VISTA-L, VISTA On-Line

To subscribe: listserv@american.edu

Message: subscribe vista-l yourfirstname yourlastname

This biweekly electronic bulletin features information about VISTA, including immediate openings, program updates, and national service news of interest to career centers, volunteer offices, libraries, professional groups, and potential volunteers. For more information, send e-mail to the list owners at VISTA-L-*request@american.edu*.

Peace Corps

http://www.peacecorps.gov/

You'll find background information on the organization and access to a transition service for returning Peace Corps volunteers (RPCVs) at this site provided by the Peace Corps. Check out the database for current positions, and then send in your application using the guidelines outlined on the web page.

Project Vote Smart

http://www.vote-smart.org/

This national nonpartisan, nonprofit organization researches federal and state candidates and elected officials to provide factual information to the public regarding their voting records and stands on issues. Ninety percent of the Project Vote Smart (PVS) workforce consists of volunteers or college students, many selected through its National Internship Program. Generous scholarships are available. Print the application for an internship off the PVS website, or contact the organization for more information via e-mail at *intern@vote-smart.org* or by phone at (800) 622-SMART.

UCLA YES

http://www.yes.ucla.edu/voices/intern.html

The University of California—Los Angeles (UCLA) has a Youth Enhancement Service (YES) that sponsors this resource for individuals thinking about applying for the Congressional Internship Program. The internship page includes some FAQS and a sample letter to use in contacting your congressional representative about a position. Search the Congressional Directory by state or name for contact information.

Washington Intern Foundation

http://interns.org/

This foundation is a nonprofit organization that assists individuals in locating and successfully completing internships in the Washington, D.C., area and on Capitol Hill. View the dozens of currently available internships listed on the website, both on "the Hill" and off, or post your resume free.

The White House Fellowships

http://www.whitehouse.gov/WH_Fellows/

The White House fellowship program spans multiple fields and provides gifted young Americans first-hand experience in the process of government, either in the Office of the President or in one of the Cabinet-level agencies. You'll find information about applying here.

Places to Check for Miscellaneous Opportunities and Seasonal Work

CollegePro Painters

http://wanda.phl.pond.com/mall/collegepro/

You've seen the signs—these people are painting houses all over the country! Job and internship descriptions, plus information about the availability of local franchises, is online. You can apply online or contact them via e-mail at *collegepro@pond.com*. Include the name of your hometown in the message so it can be forwarded to the office nearest you.

Cool Works

http://www.coolworks.com/

Check out the loads of seasonal jobs at this website. Ranch jobs, ski resort jobs, and cruise jobs are a click away! Search by state or use the menu of job categories. Cool Works links you to information about the job and the organization's web page, if available, along with contact information so you can follow up on the lead.

Project America Home Page

http://project.org/

Project America is a nonprofit organization designed to promote community involvement. Read the "Guide to Community Service" to get ideas for local projects and how to organize them, or link to specific community project sites.

studyabroad.com

http://www.studyabroad.com/

Studyabroad provides links and contact information for thousands of opportunities in dozens of countries. Search by country or use the menu for language programs, internships, or summer jobs only. Consult the "Study Abroad Handbook" for tips on living abroad or check off the "Pre-departure Checklist." Contact the specific sites for more information about their programs.

Summer Jobs

http://www.summerjobs.com/

Search these summer jobs by keyword or geographic location, or link to *The Wall Street Journal*'s top 10 job sites and other career and training resources.

Teach for America

http://www.teachforamerica.org/

The national teacher corps is looking for new graduates who will commit two years to teach in rural and urban public schools in need. Teacher certification is not required in order for you to participate.

More Possibilities

The following two sites are unique in their attention to colleges, careers, and the entry-level employment scene. Take a look around. Check out the "Real Life Tales from the World of Work" or send a question to a career professional. Ask your career counselor if you need help in using the resources these sites have linked together.

The Catapult, Career Service Professionals Homepage

http://www.jobweb.org/catapult/catapult.htm

JobWeb, The National Association of Colleges and Employers

http://www.jobweb.org

You can also search America's Job Bank (*http://www.ajb.dni.us*) plus the individual state job banks linked from the sites for local opportunities.

12

State and Local Resources for the United States

Each of the resources in this chapter is specific to a city, state, region, or territory of the United States. They include local community networks (Freenets), regional services, state-sponsored job service sites, and several Usenet newsgroups. We did not include the hundreds of U.S. colleges and universities in this list, but you can easily find them through Yahoo! by accessing Christina DeMello's listing of institutions (*http://www.mit.edu:8001/people/cdemello/univ-full.html*) or by using a Web search engine. These institutions usually collect information pertinent to their local communities and list their own employment opportunities on their public servers.

Community networks frequently carry local job listings and provide all kinds of information for a region, including available housing and lists of local businesses. Although each community net is organized differently, you can generally find helpful career information in the listings of government resources and services, community centers, and libraries. Business or commercial resources may give the names of companies or people to contact about potential work opportunities. The downside is that many of these networks restrict access to good information to registered members only. If this is so, see if you can register as a user.

The growth in Internet resources for local and regional employment opportunities and information has been phenomenal since the first edition of this guide was published. State and local governments, regional sites organized by grassroots initiatives or with help from local institutions, and grant-funded community networks are coming online. Newspapers are publishing their help wanted ads online, and many are adding value by including career advice or articles, or company profiles. Many others are linking to career resources such as JobSmart (*http://jobsmart.org*), which already has a great reputation as a career information provider. To access dozens of the nation's top newspapers on the Web, go to CareerPath (*http://www.careerpath.com*). You'll find many other newspaper sites in this chapter on local resources.

Because the number of state governments putting their employment opportunities online has grown so rapidly, we've provided a list of them in Chapter 10. We have included some of the larger county or municipal job sites here, as well as other state job resources, including the offerings of the Job Service partnership with America's Job Bank.

Although we have a lot of information here, it's possible that we still don't have exactly what you need. In this case, use the resources and strategies in Chapter 3 to help you find more local sources for employment. The general resources at the beginning of this chapter will also serve you well.

General Resources

America's Job Bank

http://www.ajb.dni.us/

A joint effort of the 2,000 offices of the state employment services, America's Job Bank (AJB) brings you the job listings of the state employment service agencies and Guam. The site offers a variety of ways for you to search, including military specialty codes so those leaving the military might be able to match their skills to jobs in the private sector. You'll also find a link to the state employment services with Internet job databases available. Keep watching this site, as many improvements are in the works. Check the first entry in each of the states in this chapter, or use America's Job Bank to jump directly to an alphabetical list of these agencies.

Library of Congress Information on State and Local Governments

http://lcweb.loc.gov/global/state/stategov.html

NASIRE (National Association of State Information Resource Executives)

http://www.nasire.org/

The Library of Congress has linked together several similar lists and other resources that can lead you to good information about a region. Representing information resource managers, NASIRE has a unique StateSearch which organizes state government information by subject. The Statejobs site is loaded with links to government and private sector employers sorted by state.

Statejobs.com

http://www.statejobs.com/

State and Local Government on the Net

http://www.piperinfo.com/state/states.html

Our listing of state government resources was originally researched through Dana Noonan's list at Piper Resources. She updates this list as the states and local governments announce new services, so check with this site for the latest information. State and local government servers can be fantastic sources of information! Beyond providing information about themselves, they often list businesses within the state, educational institutions, and other leads to help you out. The state employment services have incredible lists of opportunities waiting for you to walk in the door and view, or surf into their site and browse. You support them with your tax dollars, so use them!

States are presented in alphabetical order with state job services listed first. All other resources within the state are listed alphabetically by name after that.

Alabama

Alabama State Employment Service Job Search

http://al.jobsearch.org/

The easiest way to find jobs in Alabama's Job Bank is to browse using the Menu Search. You can also search job titles by keyword or search by Dictionary of Occupational Titles (DOT), military code, or job number.

AlaWeb

http://www.state.al.us

Alabama's official website provides access to all kinds of information, including links to state newspapers and their classified ads, a directory of businesses, and state employment resources.

hsv.jobs

This is a newsgroup for jobs in Huntsville.

Jefferson County Personnel Board (Birmingham)

http://www.bham.net/pbjc/index.html

This site features announcements for county government jobs available through the Personnel Board in Birmingham. Click on a job title to view more detailed information about that job.

Times Daily Classified

http://www.timesdaily.com/classified/classif2.htm

The Times Daily serves Muscle Shoals and several other small communities in Alabama. There's a link from the home page to job-related terms such as sales, jobs wanted, or help wanted. Click on the term that's most appropriate to your situation to view the current postings.

Alaska

State of Alaska Jobs and Job Services

http://www.state.ak.us/local/jobs.htm

Alaska's Job Bank

http://labor-aix.state.ak.us/cgi-bin/jobs

The state Job Services page links to a number of helpful resources for job seekers and career changers, including jobs in government and education, the State Trooper Recruitment page, and the Job Bank. Alaska's Job Bank opens with a colorful map of the state. Scroll down until you see the word "Search." Use the pulldown menus to select the area of the state and the job category you're interested in, then click on the Search button to view the available jobs.

Alaska Job Resources

http://www.state.ak.us/local/akpages/LABOR/esd_alaska_jobs/ak_resor.htm

Alaska Job Seeker Page

http://www.state.ak.us/local/akpages/LABOR/jobseek/jobseek.htm

The Alaska Department of Labor (DOL) maintains both these pages, which provide access to state resources, job opportunities, newspapers, and more!

Alaska Jobs Center

http://www.juneau.com/alaskajobs/

The center assists Alaskans who are looking for work by linking to helpful sites, including economic indicators, relocation information, and a site exclusively developed for women in the job market. Check out the classifieds in a number of newspapers or the job postings from some of the largest employers. Information about education, government, and seasonal job opportunities is just a click away. Questions? Send e-mail to *info@juneau.com*.

Anchorage Daily News

http://www.adn.com/

Click on the classified ads to get to the employment section and hundreds of jobs. You can choose the current day's ads or those from the previous Sunday. Browse through the job categories or search by keywords.

Finding Work in Alaska

http://www.state.ak.us/local/akpages/LABOR/esd_alaska_jobs/ak_over.htm

Created for the individual in the lower 48 who dreams of starting all over in Alaska, this site contains a lot of helpful information about the state and its resources. If you're thinking of starting a new life in Alaska, check out this site!

Juneau Empire Classifieds

http://juneauempire.com/Classified/classc.htm

Select your job category using the pulldown menu, and choose Browse to view all the current postings in your field. Or select "search category," click on the Submit button, and use keywords to refine your search. Click on the Search button to view the results.

SLED: Alaska's Statewide Library Electronic Doorway

http://sled.alaska.edu/

Developed by the State Library and the University of Alaska, SLED provides free, easy, and equitable access to electronic information. Choose the "Alaska" link to reach job sites, community information, and business and educational resources throughout the state.

Arizona

Arizona's Job Bank

http://az.jobsearch.org/

The easiest way to find jobs in Arizona's Job Bank is to browse using the Menu Search. You can also search job titles by keyword or search by Dictionary of Occupational Titles (DOT), military code, or job number.

Arizona Careers Online

http://www.diversecity.com/jobs.html

Search the Help Wanted USA database. Type in as many as 10 keywords that describe the job you're looking for. Select the method of searching (all the words, any of the words, etc.), click on the Search button, and look over the results. You can also post your resume to ResumeXpress or access a listing of Arizona Job Hotlines.

Arizona Central

http://www.azcentral.com/class/employsearch.html

The *Arizona Republic*'s answer to electronic access! Choose to look through this Sunday's or the previous Sunday's classified ads. Select the job category, and add some keywords to the mix (optional). Click on Search and view the results.

az.jobs

This is a popular newsgroup for jobs in Arizona.

StarNet Electrifieds

http://www.azstarnet.com/public/electrifieds/

Brought to you by Arizona's *Daily Star* newspaper, the Electrifieds feature categories generally associated with classified ads. View the last seven days' newspapers one day at a time, or click on Employment to see all the jobs at the same time.

Arkansas

Arkansas Job Bank

http://ar.jobsearch.org/

The easiest way to find jobs in Arkansas's Job Bank is to browse using the Menu Search. You can also search job titles by keyword or search by Dictionary of Occupational Titles (DOT), military code, or job number.

Arkansas Employment Register

http://www.arjobs.com/

The *Arkansas Employment Register,* a biweekly publication, is distributed on alternate Mondays. Search for a job or click on a link to other Arkansas resources on the Web.

Arkansas Employment Security Department

http://www.state.ar.us/esd/ark_esd.html

Arkansas's all-purpose job and career resources page! Information about the labor market, the state's Job Bank, and other career resources are a click away from the departmental home page.

Arkansas Online

http://www.ardemgaz.com/class/cl05.htm

The online version of the *Arkansas Democrat-Gazette*'s classified ads is updated daily. Browse through the employment categories or search for a job. Arkansas's Voice on the Internet is a great source for news and links of interest to Arkansans everywhere.

WE CAN Job Search

http://www.onestop.org/jbsearch.htm

The WE CAN initiative, developed by the Eastern Arkansas Private Industry Council, provides this one-stop center. There are links to all kinds of human services here, along with a Cartoon of the Day. The Career Page has links to the Job Bank and other helpful job and career resources. Coming soon: a resume posting service.

California

California's Job Bank

http://ca.jobsearch.org/

The easiest way to find jobs in California's Job Bank is to browse using the Menu Search. You can also search job titles by keyword or search by Dictionary of Occupational Titles (DOT), military code, or job number.

ba.jobs

ba.jobs.contract

ba.jobs.misc

ba.jobs.offered

ba.jobs.resumes

These newsgroups discuss jobs around the San Francisco Bay Area.

Bay Area Jobs Home

http://www.sonic.net/cory/ba_jobs.html

Access over 1,000 Bay Area employers! Search by region or resource, find your job, and then check out the local real estate information.

California Career and Employment Center

http://www.webcom.com/-career/

An affiliate of Help Wanted USA, one of the largest online recruiters around, the center provides access to career, business, and educational resources. Post your resume or check out the Career Mall. Join the online forum, where participants can inexpensively advertise their services and products.

California State Government

http://www.ca.gov/

California has been a leader in bringing state information online, and it shows. Excellent representation of the state with legislative information, agencies, and other resources are all linked together. The Working page provides access to a wealth of career information and job leads. Check out the Living & Learning link for helpful consumer, education, and state agency information. Use this site to access it all!

Employment Development Department

http://wwwedd.cahwnet.gov/

The Employment Development Department (EDD) is the agency that links people with jobs in California. At this site you'll find labor market information, links to training opportunities, and links to jobs and Experience Unlimited Job Clubs. Check here for the address of the regional Job Service office closest to you.

The Gate: The Bay Area's Home Page

http://www.sfgate.com/

The *San Francisco Chronicle* and *Examiner* newspapers online include links to their help wanted ads. Look through other sections of these newspapers for housing information or to find out more about the Bay Area. The Career Search section gets you to the employment ads and articles that could be helpful in your job search. You can also research a company in the newspaper archives, or sit back and receive an e-mail alert when job postings of interest to you are received at the papers.

Jobs Jobs Jobs

http://www.jobsjobsjobs.com/

Updated daily, Coolware's Bay Area job site has positions submitted locally as well as copied from other sources. You won't get career advice here—just lots of great job listings! Search by keyword or browse by broad topics. With the Bay Locator, you can click on a section of a map and pull up all of the job listings within that area.

JobSmart: California Job Search Guide

http://www.jobsmart.org

One of the best sites going in online career resources, JobSmart is the creation of librarian Mary-Ellen Mort. Salary surveys, resume writing tips, and guides to the hidden job market—this site has it all! Job resources are scored according to their relative helpfulness to California job seekers. There's a similar rating for blue-collar job opportunities. Ask Electra for career advice or browse through the wealth of information available. Job seekers can choose to search the Bay Area, Sacramento, or Los Angeles exclusively.

la.jobs

This popular newsgroup is for jobs in or around Los Angeles.

Los Angeles Times

http://www.latimes.com/HOME/CLASS/EMPLOY/

The *L.A. Times* JobSource is a classified section with added value. To search the classifieds, click on the category that interests you and type in additional keywords to refine your search. Press Search Jobs and view the results. The JobSource also features plenty of career advice and job search tips!

Palo Alto Online

http://www.PaloAltoOnline.com/

Palo Alto's community network has loads of information about the area. Check out things to do in Palo Alto, use the guide for getting around the area, or click on the link to the classified ads.

Palo Alto Weekly Online Edition

http://www.service.com/PAW/home.html

This is the local newspaper from Palo Alto. Check the classifieds for employment opportunities, and, if you miss a day, you can also check the back issues. The searchable, full-text "morgue" covers several years. It includes lots of great listings, and apartment information should you need it. Contact *marc@service.com* with your questions.

The *Sacramento Bee*

http://www.sacbee.com/classads/ads/today/employment_index.html

This link connects to the job ads in the *Sacramento Bee*. Type in a keyword and press enter to view the results. Or browse through all the ads at one time.

San Bernardino County Employment Opportunities

http://www.co.san-bernardino.ca.us/ht/jobs/mainjobs.htm

You'll find all the information you need to apply for a job in San Bernardino County. The jobs are broken down into two categories, those with deadlines and those for which employers recruit regularly. For more information, call (909) 387-8304.

San Diego Jobs

http://www.sandiegojobs.com/

This free service provides access to job leads and major local employers on the Web. You'll soon be able to post your resume online. The site posts jobs for all levels, both temporary and permanent. Job listings are obtained from agencies or directly from the employer. They are up to date, automatically expiring after 30 days.

San Francisco Cityspan Information Center

http://www.ci.sf.ca.us/infoemp.htm

Check here for employment opportunities with the municipal and county government. The Department of Human Resources posts some of the available jobs, but not all of them. For information on other job opportunities, call the Jobs Hotline: (415) 557-4888.

San Francisco Bay Area Volunteer Information Center

http://www.meer.net/users/taylor/

You'll find information about volunteer opportunities in the Bay Area and the over 100 organizations that participate in the center. Don't overlook this site if you're interested in working in the nonprofit sector. Where there are volunteer positions, there might be job opportunities as well! The center has additional links to national nonprofit groups.

San Jose Mercury

http://spyglass.sjmercury.com/class/help/index.htm

This link takes you directly to the San Jose newspaper's Talent Scout job search page. You can search the current day's ads or those from the last Sunday edition, or browse by broad categories. Post your resume, read career-related articles, or look over the company profiles. Tell them what you think via e-mail: *class.feedback@sjmercury.com.*

San Mateo Times, and . . .

http://www.newschoice.com/default.asp

Check out the classified ads of the *Alameda Times-Star, Fremont Argus, Hayward Daily Review, Oakland Tribune, Pleasonton Tri-Valley Herald,* or *San Mateo Times.* Go directly to the classifieds, click on the map for the region you're interested in, then choose appropriate categories and keywords. Voilà! Jobs!

sdnet.jobs

This newsgroup is for jobs around San Diego County.

The SofTech Jobs Board

http://www.northbay.com/softech/index.html

The North Bay Software and Information Technology Association in Marin County is a nonprofit organization dedicated to the advancement of software and information technology. Click on the category you're interested in, select the companies listed to view their available job openings, or link to other job boards.

su.jobs

This newsgroup lists jobs at Stanford University.

ucb.jobs

This newsgroup presents jobs at or around the University of California, Berkeley.

ucd.jobs

This is a newsgroup listing general jobs at or around the University of California, Davis.

ucd.cs.jobs

This newsgroup is for computer science jobs at or around the University of California, Davis.

Job Hunt (formerly Webdog's Job Hunt)

http://csueb.sfsu.edu/jobs.html

The California State University Employment Board sponsors this site, which includes links to the Best Job sites, hand picked by the Webdog himself! You'll find up-to-date job postings specific to the Bay Area, career guides, and more. This continues to be a great site for both general and San Francisco Bay Area resources.

WorkBase

http://www.workbase.com/

Looking for a job in the Palo Alto area? Fill out a form online, and all the businesses will know you're available! Select the type of business you're interested in and then click on "Get me a job." Complete the form and you'll be part of the local job database.

Yahoo! Los Angeles

http://la.yahoo.com

Yahoo! San Francisco Bay Area

http://sfbay.yahoo.com

These local Yahoos are great information resources for the areas they cover. You'll find links to employers, employment, housing, and anything else you need to make your relocation and job search a success.

Job Search Tip: Planning a Move? If you are relocating, monitor the Usenet newsgroups for the area you are moving to for job listings and other good information about the area.

Colorado

Colorado's Job Bank

http://co.jobsearch.org/

The easiest way to find jobs in Colorado's Job Bank is to browse using the Menu Search. You can also search job titles by keyword or search by Dictionary of Occupational Titles (DOT), military code, or job number.

ACLIN (Access Colorado Library & Information Network)

http://www.aclin.org/

A statewide network of libraries and information resources, ACLIN provides access to over 200 library catalogs plus a wealth of community, government, business, and consumer information. The Employment and Career section has links to the Job Bank, State Department of Labor, and other helpful information for job seekers and career changers.

Boulder Community Network

http://bcn.boulder.co.us/

The Boulder Community Network connects you to city and county information, job listings, and several other Colorado-specific job resources. The One-Stop Career Network just keeps getting better! It is a wonderful collection of information and links to employment opportunities in the Boulder area and throughout the state.

Boulder County Government

http://www.boco.co.gov/jobs.html

Search here for employment opportunities with Boulder County Government. You can also call the 24-hour Job Line: (303) 441-4555.

Colorado Jobs Information

http://www.state.co.us/jobinfo.html

Colorado Jobs links to the Governor's Job Training Office and the Department of Labor and Employment. You'll find employment statistics and other resources, in addition to the traditional job services provided for both employers and job seekers.

The *Denver Post* Online

http://www.denverpost.com/jobs/jobs.htm

The *Denver Post* employment ads are available on CareerPath (www.careerpath.com).

You can use the *Denver Post* URL as a gateway to the ads, or go to CareerPath directly. The newest Sunday ads are available late on Saturday afternoon and stay online until the next update.

Inside Denver : Colorado Jobs

http://InsideDenver.com/jobs/

The *Rocky Mountain News* brings you job ads along with some employer profiles and a Networking Calendar. Click on the Jobs link and choose the category you're interested in. Select the current day's or the previous Sunday's ads. Add some keywords or browse through all the leads in your chosen category. A nice feature is the AdRover, who will "fetch" the ads and send them to your e-mail address.

Connecticut

Connecticut's Job Bank

http://ct.jobsearch.org/

The Job Bank is a joint Department of Labor (DOL) and Connecticut Works initiative. The easiest way to find jobs in Connecticut's Job Bank is to browse using the Menu Search. You can also search job titles by keyword or search by Dictionary of Occupational Titles (DOT), military code, or job number.

Connecticut Works

http://www.ctdol.state.ct.us/

The Connecticut Department of Labor provides these tips for job hunting, programs, and services for job seekers and career changers, and information about the labor market. You can also link to the School-to-Career System, other government resources, and the Job Bank.

Hartford Courant Newspaper

http://news.courant.com/class.stm

The *Hartford Courant* posts its employment ads on CareerPath (*http://www.careerpath.com*). Use this URL as your entrée to that site, or go directly to CareerPath.

Jobfind.com

http://www.jobfind.com/

Jobfind.com is a great resource for jobs in New England. Research the corporate profiles or post your resume online. To look for a job, click on "job search," and then choose the state you're interested in. Select the job category, add keywords, and search.

ne.jobs
ne.jobs.contract

Both of these newsgroups are for jobs in New England.

Delaware

Delaware's Job Bank

http://de.jobsearch.org/

The easiest way to find jobs in Delaware's Job Bank is to browse using the Menu Search. You can also search job titles by keyword or search by DOT, military code, or job number.

Search here for work or link to helpful education, business, and career resources.
Call (302) 761-8102 for more information.

Del-AWARE

http://www.lib.de.us/business/jobs_and_careers.html

A joint project of the state's libraries and Delaware Technical & Community College, the
Digital Library of the First State provides access to libraries, government information,
and DelaWeb, a collection of helpful Internet resources. Check the Business section for
company information or to link to the Jobs and Careers page. From there, you can access
the Job Bank along with other major career resources.

District of Columbia

District of Columbia's Job Bank

http://dc.jobsearch.org/

The easiest way to find jobs in the District of Columbia's Job Bank is to browse using
the Menu Search. You can also search job titles by keyword or search by Dictionary of
Occupational Titles (DOT), military code, or job number.

balt.jobs

This is a very active newsgroup for jobs in the Baltimore/Washington, D.C., area.

dc.jobs

This popular newsgroup lists jobs in Washington, D.C., and surrounding areas.

The Washington Post

http://204.146.47.74/search.html

The CareerPost has a new look, with more jobs, a better search tool, and a career page
hosted by the dean of career counselors, Richard Bolles. If you're not quite ready for
the job search yet and need a little guidance, go directly to What Color Is Your
Parachute: The Net Guide (*www.washingtonpost.com/parachute*). Dick offers reviews
of the resources available for job seekers and career changers along with his always
helpful advice.

Yahoo! Washington D.C.

http://dc.yahoo.com

These local Yahoos are great information resources for the areas they cover. You'll find links
to employers, employment, housing, and anything else you need to make your relocation
and job search a success.

Florida

Florida Communities Network (FCN)

http://www.state.fl.us/

The FCN is the major link to Florida's government, business, and community information. Lots of good resources here! Search for specific information or browse by category. The Florida Jobs One-Stop Service Center is a great site, with links to all the major job sites in the state, including academic, government, and private sector jobs.

Locating Government Job Opportunities in Florida

http://www.state.fl.us/fcn/centers/job_center/vacancy/

This is a fantastic service! Updated weekly, this link to the FCN includes job listings for government agencies all over the state. Search by county or the entire state at once, then narrow your search by occupation. The resulting list gives you a job title and full description, a pay grade, a phone number for contact, and the opportunity to apply online.

fl.jobs

This is a newsgroup for jobs in Florida.

Job Board

http://www.fsu.edu/Jobs.html

Job Board, located at Florida State University, includes job postings for all the state universities in Florida. Choose the university you're interested in, or use the site's search capability to find a position of interest. Listings are for faculty, administration, and support personnel. Select the category, add keywords to refine your search, click on Submit, and view the results. You'll find information on salary ranges, links to other internal resources, and additional links to other academic job sites.

Tallahassee Free-net

http://www.freenet.tlh.fl.us/Employ.html

Tallahassee has created a very nice information network. The job resources listed as "Local & Florida" are quite extensive, and other helpful business, government, and community resources are available on the server. And more good news—most of the information seems to be open to all, visitors and registered users alike!

Workforce Florida

http://www.floridajobs.org/

Another good job resource brought to you by the Florida Department of Labor. Search private sector jobs by county or region, keyword, or job order number. If you register, you will have access to contact information for the small and growing number of employers who provide that information. Otherwise, contact a local office with the job order information. You can also link to the One-Stop Center and other helpful career resources from this site.

Yahoo! Miami

http://miami.yahoo.com

These local Yahoos are great information resources for the areas they cover. You'll find links to employers, employment, housing, and anything else you need to make your relocation and job search a success.

Georgia

Georgia's Job Bank

http://www.dol.state.ga.us/eshtml/eshtml02.htm

Accessible through the state's Department of Labor (DOL) home page (*http://www.dol.state.ga.us*), the Job Bank is searchable by location and job category. The DOL also provides labor market information, links to jobs in state government, and other assistance for job seekers.

Atlanta Classifieds

http://www.atlantaclassifieds.com/

The *Atlanta Journal-Constitution* has partnered with Cox Interactive Media to develop this site. From this opening page, click on the employment choices. Then browse through all the jobs or select a job category. Add some keywords to refine your search, click the button, and view the results. Like other classified sections, this one has a range of offerings so you can find an apartment or buy a vehicle while you're at it!

Atlanta Web Guide

http://www.webguide.com/

The Atlanta Web Guide is the closest you can come to visiting a city without paying the airfare! Sunbelt Advertising maintains this site featuring local companies' products, restaurants, and interesting sites for tourists to visit. The links to universities in the area provide an entrée to job sites, if you're willing to work through half a dozen layers.

Atlanta's Computer Job Store

http://www.atlanta.computerjobs.com/

You'll find industry and career information for computer professionals in the Atlanta area here, plus links to the other Computer Jobs sites in Chicago, Texas, and the Carolinas. This is a great-looking site with information about the Atlanta job market and company profiles for the Atlanta area (not just for those that advertise here). Check out the hundreds of job listings and add your name to the skill registry.

atl.jobs

This newsgroup covers positions available in Atlanta.

City of Atlanta Jobs

http://www.atlanta.org/employ/employ.htm

The City of Atlanta home page (*www.atlanta.org*) provides all kinds of information about the community. Links to local events, government information, news, and interesting Internet sites are all accessible here. Click on the job page for instructions on applying for a position and for a list of current employment opportunities. You can also call the Job Line at (404) 330-6456 for employment information.

Fulton County Employment & Job Opportunities

http://www.co.fulton.ga.us/employ.htm

Fulton County needs thousands of employees on its payroll to maintain the services and man the departments of county government! New job opportunities are posted to this site as they become available.

git.ohr.jobs.digest

This is a newsgroup for listings provided by the Georgia Institute of Technology.

Yahoo! Atlanta

http://atlanta.yahoo.com

These local Yahoos are great information resources for the areas they cover. You'll find links to employers, employment, housing, and anything else you need to make your relocation and job search a success.

Guam

Guam's Job Bank

http://gu.jobsearch.org/

Search this database of thousands of jobs! Select a job category, refine it if necessary, and view the job listings. As with the nation's other job banks, salary, experience requirements, location of the position, and a job number are all part of the posting. Information about the application procedure is also available here.

Guam Chamber of Commerce Directory of Members

http://www.guamchamber.com/directory/

The chamber of commerce for any region is guaranteed to be an excellent source of information about the community it serves, and this one is no different. The directory is divided into industry categories, so select those that interest you to find information on the organizations included. Many have web pages linked from this list. Potential employers are always easy to find, don't you think?

Hawaii

Hawaii's Job Bank

http://hi.jobsearch.org/

Search this database of thousands of jobs! Select a job category, refine it if necessary, and view the job listings. As with the nation's other job banks, salary, experience requirements, location of the position, and a job number are all part of the posting. Information about the application procedure is also available here.

Hawaii Department of Labor and Industrial Relations

http://www.aloha.net/~edpso/

The Department of Labor and Industrial Relations (DOLIR) page links to information about unemployment benefits, labor laws, and labor statistics. Check Job Information for a link to Hawaii's Job Bank, financial aid, and other career resources on the Web. Coming soon: a link to the One-Stop Career Center from this page!

Hawaii Home Page

http://www.hawaii.net/

Started in 1994 by a group at the University of Hawaii, this home page seeks to provide an access point for all aspects of information about the islands. It does just that! You'll find links to businesses, educational resources, government information, and more. Search for specific information or browse the broad categories. A search for employment brings up links to career services resources at the University of Hawaii, a temp agency, and the state DOL.

Hawaii JobPage

http://www.lava.net/hijobs/

Surf through the Hawaii JobPage! Updated weekly, the JobPage presents opportunities in many fields. Click on the job category you're interested in to see what's available, or call the Jobline at (808) 592-9675.

Maui Web Directory

http://www.mauimapp.com/

Everything you want to know when you visit Maui! Places to see, entertainment and activities, and restaurant and lodging information. You'll also find links to government information and a directory of numbers to call for employment assistance.

Idaho

Idaho Works Job Bank

http://www.doe.state.id.us/pubjs/jsmain.asp

Idaho's Job Bank is set up a bit differently from the usual menu of options. Select an area of the state to search in, an occupational grouping, and a specific occupation. Press the Search key and view the results. With the results, you get application information. Do *not* call the Job Service office. Rather, Idaho residents should go to the nearest office. Out-of-state applicants can fax, e-mail, or "snail mail" (regular mail) a cover letter along with a resume.

Idaho Works

http://www.doe.state.id.us/

Idaho Works is maintained by the state Department of Labor. Come to this site for labor market information, job training programs, and other information to assist both the employer and the job seeker. You can also link to the Job Bank from here.

Internet Tip: Reading News on the Web. You can set up your web browser to allow you to read Usenet newsgroups you see on web pages. However, two things must be set up at your site to let this work. First, your web browser must have the newsreader software added and configured to read news; second, your local provider must carry the newsgroups you want to read. If a problem occurs, talk to your own help desk before you send messages to web page maintainers.

Illinois

Illinois Job Bank

http://il.jobsearch.org/

The easiest way to find jobs in the Illinois Job Bank is to browse using the Menu Search. You can also search job titles by keyword or search by DOT, military code, or job number. You'll find additional links to labor market information, state training centers, and the Department of Commerce and Community Affairs.

Champaign-Urbana *News Gazette*

http://www.news-gazette.com/

Access the classifieds from the *News Gazette* Online home page. Choose "employment" to see the full range of job opportunities in the Sunday newspaper. You can submit your resume, but keep in mind that the service is not confidential, and anyone with access to the Internet can view it.

chi.jobs

This is a popular newsgroup for jobs in Chicago.

ChicagoJobs.org: the Definitive Chicago Area Job and Career Guide

http://www.chicagojobs.org/

ChicagoJobs is one of the newest Internet job search resources and should prove to be a helpful one. Regional newspapers and smaller subject-oriented sites are featured along with the major national sites, making this a comprehensive resource for Chicago-area job seekers.

Chicago Newspaper Network

http://www.chicago-news.com/classified/Employment.html

Chicago Sun-Times

http://www.suntimes.com/classified/Employment.html

Access the employment ads from 70 Chicago area newspapers! The *Sun-Times* and Pioneer Press newspapers are among the participants. Choose the job category, add keywords if you wish, and click on Search to view the results, 15 at a time. Or go directly to the *Sun-Times* site and do the same search in that newspaper only.

Chicago Tribune

http://www.chicago.tribune.com/

Here's another site that just keeps getting better! Find news about Chicago's high-tech industry in the Silicon Prairie, and then link to the high-tech job postings. Check out the profiles of hot companies to work for, or link to CareerPath's Resume Connection, where you can assemble a professional and confidential resume to post for potential employers. The *Tribune* posts the help wanted sections from the past three Sundays online. Select a category and choose to download the ads, or refine your search and view the results. Very nicely done.

Chicago WorksMart: Directory of City Services

http://www.ci.chi.il.us/WorksMart/

From the WorksMart page, you can link to all the city's agencies and services. Click on Personnel to learn more about working for the city and current employment opportunities. If you find a job you're interested in, apply at the Application Service Center at City Hall.

You can also learn about job possibilities through the 24-hour Job Hotline: (312) 744-1369. The city also sponsors a regular program on its cable channels. *Looking for Work* features job searching tips, job leads, and live interviews with Chicago-area job seekers. If you're unemployed and would like to appear on the program, send a copy of your resume to City Hall, Room 1100. For more information, call (312) 744-5394.

Digital City Chicago

http://chicago.digitalcity.com

This site, sponsored by the *Chicago Tribune,* has information on business, entertainment, and anything else you might want to know about Chicago and its surrounding communities.

Heartland Regional Network, the Community Network for Central Illinois

http://hrn.bradley.edu/heart.htm

Heartland includes a link to the Illinois Job Bank. You can also link to the extensive Internet resources of some of the communities of central Illinois, along with business, education, and government information.

Illinois Department of Commerce and Community Affairs

http://www.commerce.state.il.us/dcca/menus/wfjt.htm

The Department of Commerce and Community Affairs (DCCA) provides a lot of good information for starting a new business, getting the training you need to compete in today's job market, and searching for a job. You'll also find government, tourism, and other information about the state.

il.jobs.misc
il.jobs.offered
il.jobs.resumes

These popular newsgroups are for discussions about work in Illinois.

Peoria Journal Star

http://www.adquest.com/local/pjstar/employ.asp

Choose a category and a geographic location. Add up to three keywords to search the database. You can also use the new ReQuest Employment service and have the classified ads sent to you via e-mail. And, if you call (800) 373-3547, you can have the results of your search faxed or sent to you by regular mail! Talk back to the *Journal Star* by e-mail at *chawley@pjstar.com.*

uiuc.cs.jobs

This newsgroup lists computer science jobs at the University of Illinois.

uiuc.misc.jobs

This is a newsgroup for general job announcements at the University of Illinois, Urbana-Champaign.

Yahoo! Chicago

http://chi.yahoo.com

These local Yahoos are great information resources for the areas they cover. You'll find links to employers, employment, housing, and anything else you need to make your relocation and job search a success.

Indiana

Indiana's Job Bank

http://in.jobsearch.org/

The easiest way to find jobs in Indiana's Job Bank is to browse using the Menu Search. You can also search job titles by keyword or search by Dictionary of Occupational Titles (DOT), military code, or job number.

Access Indiana

http://www.ai.org/index.html
http://www.state.in.us/

Indiana's official website provides access to loads of good information—even a link to grants, loans, and scholarships! State government resources, links to community networks, and business information are all just a click away.

HoosierNet

http://www.bloomington.in.us/

HoosierNet pulls together a wealth of community information for the Bloomington area, including educational resources, libraries, and social services and business and job information.

in.jobs

This newsgroup lists jobs in Indiana.

Indiana Workforce Development

http://www.bloomington.in.us/employment/

This is another helpful site for job seekers in Bloomington. You'll find links to local discussion groups and career resources, in addition to the traditional job services.

Indianapolis Online

http://www.indianapolis.in.us/

Browse using the Quick Topic Links or search the site for helpful job and career information. Billing itself as the "Community Network for Indianapolis," this site provides access to lots of good resources—housing, government, education, business, and other informative Internet sites, plus great local and state jobs links!

Star/News Online

http://www.starnews.com/

The *Indianapolis Star* and *Indianapolis News* have teamed up to provide access to the newspapers online. From the opening page, click on the classified icon to get to the employment opportunities, or you can go directly to the job page (*classified.starnews.com/classifieds/employ.qry*). Choose the job category of interest to you, select the current day's paper or the previous Sunday's classified section, add keywords, and search. After you've done your job search, kick back and read the news digest, or check to see what's happening in the realm of local sports!

Iowa

Iowa Jobs

http://www.state.ia.us/jobs/

Iowa's Job Bank includes full- and part-time job listings, jobs available with the state, and information on finding federal job listings. Job openings are sorted by the city in which they are located, so use the Find feature in your web browser to locate keywords. If your browser doesn't support frames or you have a slow connection to the Internet, you can choose the text or no-frames options.

Iowa Jobs Hotline

http://www.unl.edu/careers/jobs/iowahotl.htm

The University of Nebraska has compiled this list of job hot lines for major employers in the state of Iowa.

Iowa Workforce Development

http://www.state.ia.us/iwd

Iowa Workforce Development (IWD), the Job Services agency in Iowa, encourages lifelong learning and skill development through its services and programs for both employers and job seekers. From here you can link to the Job Bank, get labor market statistics, or find the local Workforce office near you.

IowAccess

http://www.state.ia.us/government/iitt/iowaccess/index.htm

At press time, not much was available for job seekers and career changers, but we think this is a site with a future. The IowAccess mission is to "provide citizens with a single electronic gateway to a wide variety of government services and information."

Kansas

Kansas Job Bank

http://www.ink.org/public/kdhr/jobbank.html

The easiest way to find jobs in Kansas's Job Bank is to browse using the Menu Search. You can also search job titles by keyword or search by Dictionary of Occupational Titles (DOT), military code, or job number. This Job Bank has additional links to a resume service, public message board, and other workforce development materials.

Kansas City Star

http://www.kcstar.com/

Browse the newspaper online or go directly to the KCcareers page (*http://www.kccareers.com/*). Check out the employer profiles; submit your resume; or look over some of the career articles, tips, and advice. To search the employment ads, select the category and date of the newspaper (the current day or last Sunday). Add keywords unless you want to see all the jobs available in your field. Click on the Search button to view the results.

Kansas Department of Human Resources

http://www.hr.state.ks.us/

This site links to the Job Bank, the One-Stop Centers, and training and career resources. You can also reach this and all of the other Kansas state agencies through the Information Network of Kansas (*http://www.ink.org*).

Topeka Capital-Journal Classifieds

http://voyager.stauffergold.com/clbrowse/clbrowse.dll

Go directly to this page to search by job classification. Add keywords or look at all the jobs available. Updated daily, the classifieds are also accessible through the *C-J* Online's home page (*http://www.cjonline.com/*).

Wichita Area Chamber of Commerce

http://www.wacc.org/index.html

The local chamber of commerce has pulled together a nice page of Wichita community information. You'll find business and government information and a link to job postings at the Wichita NationJob Network. Updated weekly, the system is underwritten by local employers. Search by job specialty or link to the home pages of the employers. Contact the Chamber for more details at *webmaster@wacc.org.*

Kentucky

Kentucky's Job Bank

http://ky.jobsearch.org/

The easiest way to find jobs in Kentucky's Job Bank is to browse using the Menu Search. You can also search job titles by keyword or search by DOT, military code, or job number.

Commonwealth of Kentucky Workforce Development Cabinet

http://www.state.ky.us/agencies/wforce/des/des.htm

Here you'll find links to the job services and Job Bank, along with labor market information and services for veterans. Kentucky also is working on a School-to-Work initiative that will lead to a better-trained workforce. Learn more about it at *http://www.stw.ed.gov/states/ky3.htm.*

Louisville *Courier-Journal*

http://www.courier-journal.com/
http://classifieds.courier-journal.com/cv3/lville

You'll find material of interest throughout the newspaper, so after you've looked it over, click on "classified" to get to the employment opportunities. You can also use the second URL to go directly to the classified section. Choose the category "help wanted," select Sunday or the current day and the number of results you want displayed (maximum of 50). You have the option of choosing a subcategory or adding keywords to the search. Click on Go, tag the interim results, and then view the detailed job ads.

Louisiana

Louisiana's Job Bank

http://www.ldol.state.la.us/JIS/JISMAINC.HTML

The Job Information Service (JIS) allows you to search the state by geographic location and then job family (professional, clerical, and so on). Note: Education jobs are in a different database.

The *Baton Rouge Advocate*

http://www.theadvocate.com/classifieds/employ.htm

To find jobs in the *Advocate,* choose a job category, and browse through the resulting job opportunities.

Department of Labor (DOL)

http://www.ldol.state.la.us/homepage.htm

One of the finest Web services available for users, the DOL server includes a set of Frequently Asked Questions (FAQS) for employers, job seekers, and others who need its services, as well as links to exceptional job and career information (including the database of teaching jobs). The career resources provide some particularly helpful articles and links for entry-level job seekers and new high school and college graduates.

lou.lft.jobs

This newsgroup covers jobs in Lafayette.

Maine

Maine's Job Bank

http://me.jobsearch.org/

The easiest way to find jobs in Maine's Job Bank is to browse using the Menu Search. You can also search job titles by keyword or search by Dictionary of Occupational Titles (DOT), military code, or job number.

Jobfind.com

http://www.jobfind.com/

Jobfind is a great resource for New England jobs. Research the corporate profiles or post your resume online. To look for a job, click on "job search," and then choose the state you're interested in. Select the job category, add keywords, and search.

Maine State Government

http://www.state.me.us/

Maine has built a very nice webserver for the state government, including a link to current state job openings. You can also link to communities statewide and get help starting your new business. Access the Department of Labor (or go directly to *http://www.state.me.us/dolbes/labor.htm*), its services, and links to other helpful career resources.

ne.jobs
ne.jobs.contract

These popular newsgroups are for jobs in New England.

Portland *Press Herald* / Maine *Sunday Telegram*

http://www.portland.com/
http://www.maineclassified.com/

Scope out the newspaper in its entirety, or go directly to Maine's Biggest Classified Marketplace. Choose which of the seven days to search, select at least one of the job categories, and look through the results.

Maryland

Maryland's Job Bank

http://md.jobsearch.org/search.html

The easiest way to find jobs in Maryland's Job Bank is to browse using the Menu Search. You can also search job titles by keyword or search by DOT, military code, or job number.

balt.jobs

This newsgroup lists jobs in the Baltimore/Washington, D.C., area.

The *Capitol* Online

http://192.41.44.21

Serving the Annapolis area, the *Capitol* makes it easy to get to the employment ads. Select "classified" on the pulldown menu and click Go. Choose "help wanted" and refine with keywords, or press the Search button to bring up all the available jobs.

Maryland's CareerNet

http://www.careernet.state.md.us/

A nicely organized page of links for Maryland job seekers and employers, CareerNet provides access to career planning and job training information. You can post your resume, search for a job, or link to other helpful resources.

Sailor: Maryland's Online Public Information Network

http://sailor.lib.md.us/sailor/

Developed by the libraries of Maryland, Sailor has as its primary focus the connecting of its communities with state and local information and library databases. It also links to selected Internet sites. Click on "topics" to get to the career resources and job information. You'll find a wealth of career information, with additional links to the City of Annapolis, the Black Collegian, CC-Link (southern Maryland jobs), libraries, universities, and other sites with job listings.

The *Washington Post*

http://204.146.47.74/search.html

The CareerPost carries numerous jobs and terrific business information for the area surrounding Washington, D.C.

Massachusetts

Massachusetts Job Bank

http://ma.jobsearch.org

Employment opportunities in or near Massachusetts with contacts for all local Division of Employment and Training (DET) offices are provided here. If you are not in Massachusetts, you may fax or mail your resume to a DET office. You must cite the job order number for which you are applying and your Social Security number. If employer information is given in a listing, you may contact the employer directly. You can also search in the database for area job training programs by topic. This site can also be accessed through the server for the Massachusetts government (*http://www.magnet.state.ma.us/*). Click on "services" and you'll find it on the listing of employment resources.

Boston Online

http://ftp.std.com/www/NE/boseconomy.html

Boston Online sponsors this collection of links to business and economic information for Boston and Massachusetts, including links to the NYNEX yellow pages, Securities and Exchange Commission filings, and a list of Boston-area businesses. Only a few of the resources are duplicated in the Cambridge list.

Boston.Com, the *Boston Globe* Online

http://www.boston.com/
http://careers.boston.com/

Click on "careers" to start the job search, or go directly to the career page. Choose the current week, or the prior three weeks, then select from the many job categories. Boston.Com claims to have the largest database of Boston-area jobs. Currently, it lists over 12,000 employment opportunities, and new listings are added every day.

City of Cambridge Employment Opportunities

http://www.ci.cambridge.ma.us/employment.html

Look here for job opportunities with the city and more! Cambridge, just across the river from Boston and home to MIT and Harvard, has job listings and employment information for the local youth services program, and provides a resource called "High-Tech in Cambridge" (*http://www.ci.cambridge.ma.us/hightech.html*), a link to the high-tech companies in the Cambridge area. Many of these organizations post job opportunities on their servers. There are also additional links to local and state job sites, along with some national resources that could be helpful.

Jobfind.com

http://www.jobfind.com/

Jobfind is a great resource for New England jobs. Research the corporate profiles or post your resume online. To look for a job, click on "job search," and then choose the state you're interested in. Select the job category, add keywords, and search.

ne.jobs
ne.jobs.contract

These popular newsgroups are for jobs in New England.

Tango! Telegram and Gazette

http://www.telegram.com/

Search Worcester's *Tango!* classified section for jobs or peruse the entire newspaper. Choose the Employment category and decide which day's newspaper you want to search, or leave it blank to see the entire week. You can narrow your search by choosing a subcategory or typing in some keywords. Click "search!" and view the results.

Town Online

http://www.townonline.com/
http://www.townonline.com/working/

Search for news and information in any of the dozen towns represented on this site. Community calendars, current events, and information of local interest are all available here. Use the second URL to go directly, or click on "working" to delve into the employment opportunities in eastern Massachusetts. Ask an expert a question about work, or join a bulletin board discussion or real-time chat! Register your resume to take advantage of the job-matching service. Search for jobs by company or category, or look for helpful articles in the Career Resources. Nicely done.

Yahoo! Boston

http://boston.yahoo.com

These local Yahoos are great information resources for the areas they cover. You'll find links to employers, employment, housing, and anything else you need to make your relocation and job search a success.

Michigan

Michigan Jobs Commission

http://www.mjc.state.mi.us/mjc/index.htm

Check out the Holiday Helpers Program for temporary work during the holidays or register for Michigan's Talent Bank. The Employment Security Agency has included links to helpful career information, labor market statistics, and the School-to-Work initiative. Choose to search the entire state or click on the area of the state you'd like to work in. Type in a keyword and begin the job search.

MEL: Michigan Electronic Library

http://mel.lib.mi.us

This is a joint project of the Library of Michigan, the University of Michigan's MLink project, the Merit Network, and Michigan's libraries. It is an excellent one-stop site for your Michigan information needs, including businesses (potential employers) and job resources for the Great Lakes State.

Michigan Government Internet Sites

http://www.state.mi.us/

From here, you can link to any of the state's other government websites, including the Employment Security Agency.

mi.jobs

This newsgroup covers jobs in Michigan.

umich.jobs

This newsgroup lists jobs at the University of Michigan.

Minnesota

Minnesota's Job Bank & SkillsNet

http://www.des.state.mn.us/

The residents of this state have two powerful job resources at their disposal; the Minnesota Job Bank and the Minnesota SkillsNet. The Job Bank provides online access to its jobs database, labor market information, and unemployment information. The Minnesota SkillsNet will scan your resume into its electronic database, let you e-mail a copy, or even let you compose a resume online. Your education, experience, and up to 80 skills are identified and screened continuously against job openings listed with the job service. If your resume is matched to an opening, you will be called before your resume is sent to an employer. What a service!

Employment Hotlines for Minnesota

http://www.disserv.stu.umn.edu/TC/Grants/COL/hotline.html

Here are the hot lines and detailed information for contacting a few of the area's larger employers.

METRONET

http://www.metronet.lib.mn.us/

METRONET is a multitype library organization serving academic, public, and special libraries in the Twin Cities (Minneapolis–St. Paul). This is an especially good site for librarians, with links that include a Minnesota Job Pathfinder and web page creation tips. Click on Minnesota to link to a list of other helpful resources, compiled by the METRONET librarians.

North Star: Minnesota Government Information and Services

http://www.state.mn.us/

The One Start link takes you to the Minnesota Government Hotlist. Jobs are the first choice on the list, and other state agencies and services are only a click away.

Twin Cities Free-Net

http://freenet.msp.mn.us/

Set up to serve the Minneapolis–St. Paul region, Twin Cities has a very nice selection of links to information and resources for the area. Select Resources by Subject to find the business and employment section with its links to the Twin Cities jobs page and other great local resources, including the Minnesota Department of Employment Security Job

Bank and several local businesses. Not limited to the Twin Cities, but excellent resources for that area.

umn.cs.jobs

This newsgroup is for jobs at the University of Minnesota, Computer Science Department.

umn.general.jobs

This newsgroup is for general job postings from the University of Minnesota.

umn.itlab.jobs

Newsgroup for jobs for the information technology (IT) lab at the University of Minnesota.

WorkAvenue.com

http://www.startribune.com/mcu/workave/stonline/content/workave/work_main1.shtml

Brought to you by the *Minneapolis Star Tribune,* this is a searchable index of jobs as well as a place to post resumes and match them to employer needs. Get help creating your job-winning resume! Check out the company profiles or scan the classified ads for leads.

Yahoo! Twin Cities

http://minn.yahoo.com

These local Yahoos are great information resources for the areas they cover. You'll find links to employers, employment, housing, and anything else you need to make your relocation and job search a success.

Mississippi

Mississippi's Job Bank

http://ms.jobsearch.org/

The easiest way to find jobs in Mississippi's Job Bank is to browse using the Menu Search. You can also search job titles by keyword or search by DOT, military code, or job number. You'll find additional links to labor market information and other resources on this server.

Mississippi Employment Security Commission

http://www.mesc.state.ms.us/

In addition to linking to the Job Bank, the Mississippi Employment Security Commission (MESC) also makes the Labor Market Information Guide and information on job fairs in Mississippi and surrounding areas available here.

State of Mississippi

http://www.state.ms.us/

This page is a gateway to all kinds of information about the state! You can reach agencies and departments within the state by linking through the list of websites or using the contact information. You'll find dozens of other Mississippi websites further down the page, and can link to more information about the state at Ole Miss (arranged alphabetically) and Mississippi State (arranged topically). While you're at it, you can check out the job opportunities at either of the schools!

Missouri

Missouri Works! Job Bank

http://www.works.state.mo.us/search/index.htm

Use the map of Missouri to choose which area of the state you want to work in, or search the whole state for employment opportunities. If you're conducting a statewide search, use the pulldown menu to choose job-related categories and add keywords to customize your search. If you're interested in a teaching position or a job in law enforcement, search the separate databases that have been set up for those professions. Click on Show Me to see your results!

Department of Labor and Industrial Relations

http://www.dolir.state.mo.us/

The DOLIR site links to the Job Search page, America's Talent Bank, and other agencies and services that could be helpful to Missouri's job seekers and career changers.

Kansas City, Missouri

http//www.kcmo.org/

Check here for all kinds of information about the city, its services, and a calendar of upcoming events. Work for the "City of Fountains"—the job listings are just a click away!

Missouri State Government Web

http://www.state.mo.us/

The state website links to the usual government agencies and services. You can also click on State Job Opportunities to get to a nice assortment of job links—the universities, state personnel site, individual agency postings, and a link to jobs in St. Louis.

POSTnet

http://www.stlnet.com/

Use your mouse to click on "classifieds." You can browse the *St. Louis Post-Dispatch* job leads by clicking on the button to the left of the word "employment," or search for a particular job by typing in a keyword and pressing the Go! button.

St. Louis Employment Links

http://members.tripod.com/~Jablon/assess.html

Moira Jablon-Bernstein has created this helpful listing of job links for St. Louis job seekers. She includes companies, positions in St. Louis, and organization websites.

stl.jobs

This active newsgroup is for jobs in or near St. Louis.

Montana

Montana's Job Bank

http://jsd.dli.mt.gov/

This server is full of information to help you find work in Montana, with links to additional Internet resources. You can do a self-directed search by occupational category and location. Updated daily, each listing includes the job title and a brief description, pay rate, and location. To apply for a job, visit the Job Service office within the region where the job is located. There are links to the education positions database and to state government job listings, neatly categorized by the recruiting agency. You can also link to the statewide online Resource Directory of community services, and search it by category, services, keyword, or provider.

Montana Vacancies in Education

http://jsd.dli.mt.gov/state/edu.htm

Check here for job opportunities in the state's schools, from K–12 through university! The Teacher Placement Office provides the listings and a standard application procedure, but applicants need to apply to the person or office listed in the job posting. Call (406) 444-7362 for more information.

Nebraska

Nebraska's Job Bank

http://ne.jobsearch.org/

Use the Internet self-service Job Search System, link to the services at the state's Department of Labor, or look up the Job Service office nearest you.

Employment Hotlines for Omaha, NE

http://www.unl.edu/careers/jobs/omaha.htm

The University of Nebraska at Lincoln maintains this listing of Omaha-area job hot lines.

Frequently asked questions about Nebraska

http://www.state.ne.us/faq/faq.html

Find a Job in Nebraska links to the Job Service and Personnel pages, and provides access to the state's newspaper classified sections as well. You'll also find information on relocating to Nebraska and answers to your other frequently asked questions about the state and its resources.

Nebraska Department of Labor

http://www.dol.state.ne.us/

Link to the state's Job Service website or learn more about the local labor market. You can also access the Job Training Division resources and other services provided by the DOL.

Nebraska State Government

http://www.state.ne.us

Nebraska's official website does a great job of linking you to information about the state. Beyond its links to the Department of Personnel, the Job Service resources, and the other state agencies on the Internet, the state website links to two sites that provide comprehensive information about the state, the Nebraska World Wide Web Registry and NebraskaLink.

Nebraska Web

http://www.nebweb.com/

Brought to you by the *Lincoln Journal Star* newspaper, Nebraska Web features an update on the news plus a Campus Guide to survival in academe and the city's annual progress report, FutureLinc. You'll also link to the classified job listings, or go directly (*lincoln.lee.net/*). Click on Employment to view all the job categories, or search for job leads using a specific job title.

Nebraska World Wide Web Registry

http://www.novia.net/~rfulk/web/

This registry is an extensive collection of links to the state's schools, city information, nonprofit organizations, and commercial enterprises. Search the site by selecting the category of information you're interested in (e.g., business, college). You have the option of choosing a subcategory. Click GO! to see the results. You can also go directly to Internet resources for a specific city.

NebraskaLink

http://www.neblink.com/

This comprehensive community index is an attempt to provide access to *all* of the Internet sites in the state. Check out the community you're interested in to see all the information that's been made available on the Web. Choose any of the items on the easy access menu to get to schools, government information, and more! The Career Page is also just a click away. It features links to many of the major job sites for the state, with additional links to Dilbert and a Relocation Salary Calculator.

Omaha CareerLink

http://www.omaha.org/careerlink.html
http://www.careerlink.org/index.htm

Maintained by the Applied Information Management (AIM) Institute on behalf of Nebraska's technology industry, Omaha CareerLink matches professionals and college interns with available Nebraska job openings, especially in the information technology, telecommunications, and engineering sectors. You can also look over the local business community, or link to community information and the Omaha Freenet.

Nevada

Nevada's Job Bank

http://nv.jobsearch.org/index.html

Search for work in Nevada, and link to other Job Service offerings including the helpful Working in Nevada page.

Las Vegas Review-Journal

http://www.lvrj.com/

Scope out the local news and headlines, or link to other Las Vegas area sites. The *Review-Journal* makes its classified ads available online. Link from the front page or go directly (*http://www.lasvegas.com/classifieds/*). Search last Sunday's ads or the newspaper archives. You can narrow your search by choosing salary requirements and full- or part-time work. Select Employment Opportunities to look at all of the ads, or choose a letter of the alphabet to view only those job titles that begin with that letter.

NevadaNet

http://www.nevadanet.com/

Developed and maintained by *Reno's Gazette-Journal,* NevadaNet is a guide to the Reno and Lake Tahoe area. Separate links on the home page take you to the newspaper or to the daily classifieds. You can also go directly to the classifieds (*http://www.renoclassifieds.com/*). Click on the Employment category and GO! to see all of the job leads, or refine your search by choosing a subcategory or adding keywords.

Working in Nevada

http://www.state.nv.us/detr/index.html

The Department of Employment, Training, and Rehabilitation page provides all kinds of helpful information for job seekers and employers alike. Link to the Job Bank or look over the employment opportunities at the dozens of other Nevada sites accessible from here. You'll discover links to additional government, business, and education resources, or learn more about the labor market or reemployment services.

New Hampshire

New Hampshire's Job Bank

http://www.nhworks.state.nh.us/

Updated daily, the Employment Security Department site features more than a link to the Job Bank. Career resources, other employment sites, and economic and labor market information are all available from this page. You can also link to WEBSTER and other New Hampshire resources.

Jobfind.com

http://www.jobfind.com/

Jobfind is a great resource for New England jobs. Research the corporate profiles or post your resume online. To look for a job, click on "job search," and then choose the state you're interested in. Select the job category, add keywords, and search.

ne.jobs
ne.jobs.contract

Both of these newsgroups are for jobs in New England.

The *Telegraph* on the Web

http://www.nashuatelegraph.com/

The *Nashua Telegraph* maintains this newspaper plus! Take a virtual tour of downtown Nashua or read the News Digest. Check out the community information or the Sausage Factory (hint: "You never saw such links!"). If you want to focus on the employment opportunities, click on Classified Ads to reach the job leads, select Employment and hit the Search button to view the results. You can also refine your search by job title, skills set, area code, or experience.

WEBSTER: the New Hampshire State Government Online Information Center

http://www.state.nh.us/

Maintained by the New Hampshire State Library, WEBSTER is the official website for the state. From here you can link to state agencies, a fact-filled New Hampshire Almanac, and information about the cities and towns of the state. WEBSTER also hosts a directory with links to many of the state's businesses and organizations. Click on Employment to get to job resources within the state or to access the employment resources compiled by the state's librarians.

New Jersey

New Jersey's Job Bank

http://nj.jobsearch.org/

Search for a job or link to New Jersey's premier Workforce site!

IN Jersey

http://www.injersey.com/

The *Asbury Park Press* and *Home News Tribune* bring New Jersey's Internet Network to you. Read the online newspaper and link to the classified ads, or go directly to the job leads (*http://www.appclassifieds.com/doc/employment.shtml*). Click on a job category to browse through all of the ads of that type. You also have the option of limiting the job selections by adding a keyword or defining a range of salaries. Hit the Search button to view the results.

New Jersey Home Page

http://www.state.nj.us/

"What a Difference a State Makes!" New Jersey's official website provides access to resources statewide. Information for consumers, for and about businesses and about the counties and municipalities of New Jersey, is at your fingertips. You'll also find information about the Prosperity New Jersey initiative and links to education, government, and the state library. Click on Employment Info to reach links to job search tools, Workforce New Jersey, and other job leads.

New Jersey News.com: Your One-Stop for Garden State News

http://www.newjerseynews.com/

News.com has linked to all of the major newspapers in the Garden State, making it easy for New Jersey job seekers to check out the classifieds for job opportunities. Truly a one-stop news service!

New Jersey Online

http://www.nj.com/

Brought to you by the *Star-Ledger,* New Jersey Online lets you search the news archives or check your stocks and portfolio online. Scope out the South Jersey link or find what you need in the Yellow Pages. Read the helpful articles in the Career Center. Then use the Career Search to find a job lead in the *Trenton Times,* the *Star Ledger,* or both newspapers simultaneously! Choose a job category and click on the Search button to view the employment opportunities.

NJ Jobs

http://www.njjobs.com/

Updated weekly, NJ Jobs is maintained by Advanced Interactive Communications and features postings from New Jersey businesses and employment agencies. Jobs are posted according to the week they are received, and are listed alphabetically by job title. View this week's jobs (from A to M or N to Z), or look through the previous week's offerings. Use the Find feature of your web browser to look for keywords. Contact an employer or agency directly to apply for a listed position.

Philadelphia Online/Philly Jobs

http://www.phillynews.com/programs/ads/SUNHLP

Online home of the *Inquirer* and the *Daily News,* Philadelphia Online also serves the people of South Jersey in separate print and online editions. All of the classified ads are available to both communities.

Workforce New Jersey Public Information Network

http://www.wnjpin.state.nj.us/

Workforce New Jersey has developed this comprehensive website of career resources, public services, and employer information. It features excellent information on the job search in general, and career resources for you to explore. You can also link to the other state agencies from here. You'll find additional information about the local communities, the One-Stop Career Sites, and starting your own business.

New Mexico

New Mexico's Job Bank

http://nm.jobsearch.org/

Use the menu for a self-directed search for work in New Mexico.

ABQjournal: *Albuquerque Journal* Online

http://www.abqjournal.com/

Check out the News You Can Use for a guidebook to information about the state and news on other issues that affect individuals and businesses in New Mexico. Information about farming in New Mexico, "globe-rattling" news, and the classified ads are all just a click away! To search the classifieds, select Employment and hit the Search button. Browse all of the ads or limit your search by choosing a job title, skill set, level of experience, and area code. Type in keywords to further refine your search. View the results, 15 at a time, or revise your search strategy and try again.

La Plaza Telecommunity

http://www.laplaza.org/

The community network for Taos, La Plaza features links to government and education accessible from the front page. You'll also find a nice selection of business and employment links.

New Mexico Department of Labor

http://www.state.nm.us/dol/

The DOL seeks to "enhance the quality of life for all" by "providing employment opportunities, income maintenance assistance, and protection of employee rights and benefits." Link to the Job Bank or learn more about the services available to the state's job seekers, career changers, and employers. You can also link to other state agencies by subject or agency name, and to other websites that could be helpful.

nm.jobs

This newsgroup covers jobs in New Mexico.

New York

New York's Job Bank

http://www.labor.state.ny.us/dolemp.htm

Job Search, plus all kinds of other helpful information! You'll find direct links to career resources, tips on starting your own business, and facts about teens in the workforce. There's also a direct link to the *Employment in NYS Newsletter*, featuring articles about the state's job market. A welcome addition to the Internet, this site is similar in structure to other state banks with easy forms to guide you to job descriptions. To apply for a job found on this database, fill out the online form, print it, and fax or mail it to the office indicated on the form.

Brooklyn Public Library Education, Job and Computer Center

http://www.brooklynpubliclibrary.org/central/ejcc.htm

The EJCC is another great resource for New York residents looking for work. Library staff members have developed these links to many helpful sites with career, employment, and job-search information. They also provide education directories, test-preparation materials, and company information online.

New York State Department of Labor

http://www.labor.state.ny.us/

Link directly to the Job Bank or to other agencies and initiatives in New York State. Statistical information, resources for youth, and information about doing business in New York are a click away. Check the Contact Us link for a list of local Department of Labor (DOL) offices and contact information for employers and job seekers.

li.jobs

This newsgroup is for jobs on Long Island.

New York City Reference

http://www.panix.com/clay/nyc/

Clay Irving maintains this reference page of NYC resources. Click on Employment to get to the regularly updated career links. The Employment page is annotated with a brief description for each listing. Use the Reference Page to find a job. Then use it to learn about the community and its resources!

New York Times on the Web

http://www.nytimes.com/

Although access to the *Times* is free, the publisher of "all the news that's fit to print" asks that you register before you use the paper. Check out the regular features and current events, plus thousands of job listings! Click on Job Market to see the latest Dilbert cartoon, read career-related articles, and link to the help wanted classified ads. You can browse through all of the ads (whew!) by using the alphabetical index of job titles, or search using specific job titles and/or keywords.

Newsday.com

http://www.newsday.com/

This is the online home of *Newsday*, the newspaper for Long Island and Queens. Click on Jobs & Careers to link to helpful career resources. From there you can check out the local calendar of events or go to the classified ads to search for job leads. Choose a broad job category (health opportunities, sales, etc.) to see all of the positions currently available in that line of work.

NYC Employment, Career & Job Resources

http://www.allny.com/jobs.html

This site is slow to load, but full of information! You'll find listings of NYC employment agencies sorted alphabetically by type or agency name. Resume services and listings of job resources on the Web, along with all the other New York City links make this a "must-see" site for job seekers in the Big Apple. Also provided is access to job-related newsgroups, job counseling services, and helpful career resources beyond NYC.

NYC LINK: the Official New York City World Wide Web Site

http://www.ci.nyc.ny.us/

Honored for the second consecutive year as a "Best of the Web" state and local government website, NYC LINK provides quick and easy access to information about New York City's services, agencies, and programs. Among the offerings are information for starting and growing a business in the city, including many forms and permit applications available for downloading. To reach the Job Training and Placement Services at the Department of Employment, click on Services and use the alphabetical listing of agencies to link to the department. To see if there are any positions available in city government, use that same listing of agencies to link to the Department of Citywide Administrative Services. You'll find information here about summer employment and internships, along with general information about working for the city of New York.

nyc.jobs
nyc.jobs.contract
nyc.jobs.misc
nyc.jobs.offered
nyc.jobs.wanted

These are all Usenet newsgroups that post opportunities for or discuss working in New York City.

The Red Guide to Temp Agencies

http://www.panix.com/~grvsmth/redguide/

Not just a guide to temporary agencies in New York, the Red Guide offers advice on how best to work the temp agencies. Agencies are evaluated for types of jobs staffed, pay rate, general length of employment, and other qualifiers. The reviews are done by temps who have worked with the various agencies, and they want to pass on to you the good word or the timely warning. Editor Angus Grieve-Smith has posted the review form on this site, making it easier for temps to submit information. Agencies can use a different form (also available online) to have information about their services included in a separate database.

Syracuse Online

http://www.syracuse.com/

Brought to you by the *Herald American, Herald-Journal,* and *Post Standard* newspapers, Syracuse Online includes all the features you'd expect from an online paper, with added value. Take virtual field trips, look over the high school reunion forum, or check out the current mortgage rates at a glance! Learn the Fact Du Jour or read the personal ad of the week before you click on the "Help wanted" link to search for a job. These classified ads from the most current Sunday are arranged by broad job categories. Choose the category that interests you (professional, clerical, etc.) and use the Find feature in your web browser to locate the listings you are interested in.

Western New York Jobs

http://www.wnyjobs.com/

Here are jobs and career links for employers in the Buffalo, Jamestown, Niagara Falls, and Rochester areas. Post your resume for a small fee, or check out the employer and school links. Updated twice a week, the job leads are organized in broad categories. Choose the category you're interested in and look through all of the positions that are currently available. The site maintainers suggest that you may need to click on your web browser's Reload or Refresh button to see the latest listing.

Yahoo! New York

http://ny.yahoo.com/

The local Yahoos are great resources for information about the areas they cover. You'll find links to employers, employment, housing, and anything else you need to make your relocation and job search a success.

North Carolina

North Carolina's Job Bank

http://www.esc.state.nc.us/jis/

Developed by the North Carolina Employment Security Commission (NCESC), North Carolina's Job Bank (NCJB) is one of the best. Use the self-directed search or the NCJB form, entering your request and clicking "ok" to receive a list of the job leads that meet your requirements. Employment opportunities are updated daily, between 4:00 A.M. and 5:00 A.M. EST. The maintainers have included a file of FAQS to answer your questions, and information about applying for jobs in state government.

Carolina Career Center

http://www.webcom.com/nccareer/

Maintained by Webcom, the Career Center features a Welcome page of information for newcomers and travelers to the state. You can post your resume online or have it distributed to dozens of organizations in the Carolinas. The Job Seeker Resource Center has a listing of Carolina job hot lines and links to major local employers.

Carolina ComputerJobs Store

http://www.carolina.computerjobs.com/

Here you'll find industry and career information for computer professionals in the Carolinas, plus links to the other Computer Jobs sites in Chicago, Texas, and Atlanta. This is a great-looking site with information about the local job market and company profiles for the area (not just for those who advertise here). Check out the hundreds of job listings and add your name to the skill registry.

Charlotte.com: The *Charlotte Observer* Online

http://charlotte.com/

Although this page is graphics intensive, Charlotte's online newspaper provides a great deal of helpful information. After you've updated your portfolio, checked out the news, and read the article about living in Charlotte, you can search for work with Job Hunter. Choose a broad category from the pulldown menu, add optional keywords, and decide how many results you want to view at a time. You can display as few as five or all of them simultaneously. You also have access to the yellow pages of local employment agencies and helpful career-related articles. Job seekers are encouraged to post their skill inventory to the Resume Connection, a confidential database that employers can search for potential employees.

Charlotte's Web

http://www.charweb.org/

The community network for Charlotte provides access to a wealth of information. You'll find schedules for local buses, trains, and airlines, along with links to government in Mecklenberg County (*http://www.charmeck.nc.us/*), to local schools and libraries, and to area businesses and business organizations. Any of these links could provide job leads as well, or go directly to the Job Page and its "Gobs and Gobs (and Gobs) of Jobs!!"

Employment Security Commission of North Carolina (*NCESC*)

http://www.esc.state.nc.us/

ESC Online links directly to the Job Bank, or you can use the other services provided at this site. Submit your skill inventory to Skillnet, the resource for employers who want to find qualified employees quickly, or market your qualifications in the Talent Bank, the nation-wide electronic resume system. Access labor statistics or link to the career resources at the North Carolina Navigator. ESC is also accessible through the State of North Carolina main page (*http://www.state.nc.us/*).

The *News and Observer* Classifieds

http://www.news-observer.com/classads/employment/
http://www.nando.net/classads/employment/

One of the first online newspapers, the *News and Observer* remains one of the best! You can also check out Nando.net, a cousin to the *News and Observer* (*http://www.nando.net/*) and a presence on the Web since July of 1994. To get to the job leads, click on the Classified Online icon, and then choose Employment. You can search the entire database, which includes the ads from Durham, Raleigh, and Chapel Hill, otherwise known as the Research Triangle. You can check ads for the current day, the next day, or the last Sunday. Then type in a keyword from the job title or description you're looking for. Decide how many postings you want displayed. You can view as few as 10 or as many as 100. Click on the Search button to see the results. Don't forget to check out the *News and Observer*'s employment opportunities while you're there!

North Carolina Information Server

http://www.state.nc.us/

The official "World Wide Web server for the state of North Carolina" provides access to all of the agencies of government, information for small and large North Carolina businesses, and links to education and other government resources. You can get to the ESC site from here, and other state information is just a click away!

North Carolina's Job & Career Navigator

http://www.esc.state.nc.us/NCJC/

Another great career resource developed by the state's Employment Security Commission! Use the buttons at the top of the page to navigate the site. You'll find interviewing tips and advice on presenting yourself to a potential employer, assistance in creating your resume, and information about different careers. Self-assessment tools, financial aid and training information, a directory of all the secondary schools in North Carolina, and links to job listings are all easily accessible here.

Philanthropy Journal of North Carolina

http://www.philanthropy-journal.org/
http://www.pj.org/

The journal grew out of a column about the nonprofit sector that appeared in the *Raleigh News & Observer*. More than a newspaper, the journal funds its activities through grants and subscriptions, and seeks to bring people together to exchange ideas and learn from one another. The Nonprofit Jobnet is accessible from the front page. Choose the section of the United States you'd like to work in to view a list of job leads. You could also link to another nonprofit job site to see its current employment opportunities or check out several national career resources.

Raleigh Online

http://www.webs4you.com/raleigh/ral2.htm#jobs

You'll find links from golf to hardware stores here. To save yourself time, be sure you type in the full URL (include the #jobs) and you'll get to the half dozen or so links to major employers. If you have more time, you might enjoy perusing the Raleigh-area businesses and organizations represented here.

triangle.jobs

A newsgroup discussing work in the Research Triangle of North Carolina (Raleigh, Durham, Chapel Hill).

North Dakota

North Dakota's Job Bank

http://nd.jobsearch.org/

Use the Self-Directed Search to find a job in North Dakota.

Job Opportunities in North Dakota

http://www.tradecorridor.com/jobs.htm

Maintained by the Central North American Trade Corridor Association, these jobs are posted free, but at the discretion of the webmaster. All jobs are located in North Dakota, and the focus is on professional positions. As we go to press, the site lists opportunities for mechanical engineers, line welders, and drafting personnel.

Job Service North Dakota

http://www.state.nd.us/jsnd/

Link to the job search information, or use the other helpful links for job seekers and employers. Check out current labor market and economic information or access the job training site. The Job Service also links to career-related sites. Click on Jobs & Job Search Info to get to the Job Bank, state government employment opportunities, and education vacancies in the state. Look at the education jobs by grade level (elementary, vocational, etc.) or browse through all of them.

Information for applying is included with each listing.

North Dakota State Government

http://www.state.nd.us/

North Dakota's official website provides access to agency information, road reports, education information, and economic development resources. Choose the executive link to go to the Department of Labor and the Job Service sites. The Department of Labor has additional links to labor laws, employment agencies, the Central North American Trade Corridor Association, and its business directory.

Northscape

http://www.gfherald.com/

A service of the *Grand Forks Herald,* Northscape presents the usual sports, news, and weather for its customers. You can also browse the *Herald*'s archives (along with the other Knight-Ridder newspapers) or peruse the business section. The classified ads should be available for job seekers by the time this book is published.

Ohio

OBES: Ohio's Job Bank

http://www.state.oh.us/obes/

The Ohio Bureau of Employment Services (OBES) links you to the Job Bank to state government jobs, OBES openings, and other helpful job and career resources. For your job search, the state of Ohio provides a handy map. Click on the region you're interested in, then choose the county (or consult the alphabetical listing of counties) to look at the employment opportunities. You're also encouraged to register for Ohio Job Net, where your application is electronically evaluated and matched to job leads. An OBES staff member will call you or write to begin the referral process. If you do take advantage of this service, you'll need to update your application every 120 days. Let your OBES contact know if you get a job using the service.

Cincinnati Enquirer

http://enquirer.com/

Cincinnati Post

http://www.cincypost.com/

The *Enquirer* sports a dynamic home page with the usual weather, sports, and current events. You'll also find links to the day's business news, along with your favorite Cincinnati journalists' columns and the featured cartoon. A quieter local voice, the *Post* also provides the latest in local and international news, plus a link to the *Kentucky Post* for its cousins across the Ohio River. Job seekers will find a link to the GoCinci.Net Careerfinder from both newspapers.

Go Cincinnati!

http://gocinci.net/
http://www.gocinci.com/

Cincinnati's home page, sponsored by the *Enquirer* and *Post* newspapers, includes links to both newspapers, an interactive atlas, and a community guide to more than 100 Cincinnati suburbs. You can also link to the Careerfinder from here.

GoCinci.Net Careerfinder

http://careerfinder.gocinci.net/

Go directly to the Careerfinder for job leads and more! You'll find job search tips, hints on preparing your resume, and strategies for cover letters and interviews. You can even get help in evaluating your job skills and a list of helpful career books to read. To start your job search in the *Enquirer* and *Post* classifieds, select a category from the pulldown menu (accounting, retail, etc.), then select which of the seven days to search (or choose all of them). Next, determine the number of results you want displayed and add keywords if you wish. Click on the "Find it here" button to view the results. A nice feature of the Careerfinder is that you can mark the job leads that you'd like to print, and print only those that are in the "print basket."

Columbus Dispatch

http://www.dispatch.com/

"Ohio's Greatest Home Newspaper" features up-to-the-minute news and more. You'll find an index to the newspaper's past investigative reports, a link to the *Ohio* magazine, and the

Dynamic Dinosaur Site, a "fun place to learn about dinosaurs and Ohio geology"! Click on the Employment button or go directly to the employment page (*http://ads.dispatch.com/ employ.htm*) to get to the job hunting tips, Resume Builder, the Dispatch's own employment opportunities, and the CL@SSIFIEDS, which are updated daily. On the Search page, choose one or more of the job categories (hold the Control key to select more than one). You can then specify full- or part-time work, educational requirements, and benefits. Type in keywords to refine your search, and click on Search to view the results. Note: The job categories here are very specific. You might want to try the search without using additional keywords first.

State of Ohio Government Information and Services

http://www.ohio.gov/ohio/index.htm

The state's front page links to information about its three branches of government and provides a handy listing of Ohio information "by topic." There's a FAQ and a listing of the most popular state sites. You'll also find resources for doing business in the state and a link to both state government jobs and the Job Bank.

cinci.jobs

This newsgroup covers jobs in Cincinnati.

cle.jobs

This newsgroup covers jobs in Cleveland.

cmh.jobs

This newsgroup covers jobs in Columbus.

osu.jobs

This newsgroup has jobs at or near Ohio State University.

Work-Web

http://www.work-web.com/

Sponsored by the Private Industry Council of Franklin and Columbus Counties, Work-Web is developing links for all of the states. Choose Ohio and click on GO! to link to the job resources it's partnered with.

Oklahoma

Oklahoma's Job Bank

http://www.oesc.state.ok.us/jobnet/

Search the Job Net by occupation or use keywords. You can also link to other job search sites from here.

City of Oklahoma City Hall

http://www.okc-cityhall.org/

From the city's server, you have access to information about the community and its neighborhoods, plus links to services and departments of the city. Workforce Development administers the Job Training Partnership Act programs (JTPA) and offers skills assessment and counseling services. Personnel handles the human resources needs of over 4,000 employees. A list of current job openings is available with a click, or you can call the Job Information Line at (405) 297-2419.

Connect Oklahoma

http://www.connectok.com/

Link to classified ads in the *Daily Oklahoman* or connect to all kinds of Oklahoma sites. News, community, and business information is just a click away. Link to Volunteer Oklahoma and check out the opportunities there, or look over Vo-Tech Net for job openings or training possibilities.

Oklahoma City and Related Links

http://okccvb.org/okclinks.html

The Convention and Visitor's Bureau maintains this page of links to "all things OKCish." You'll access regional and statewide resources, including educational and governmental institutions, media sites, chambers of commerce, and newspapers. If you want to experience Oklahoma City electronically, check out this site!

Oklahoma Employment Security Commission

http://www.oesc.state.ok.us/

You can link to the Job Bank from here or explore the other resources available for job seekers and employers. Among its other services, the state has developed the Oklahoma Universal Computerized Assistance Network (UCAN) initiative, which provides access to a range of programs, services, and products for the public. From the UCAN page (*http://www.oesc.state.ok.us/okucan*), select the type of service you need and the area of the state in which you reside. You'll be directed to the assistance you need. Included in the UCAN choices is "job search." To look for work, select that item from the menu along with the geographic location. Click on the Search button to view the job leads.

The *Oklahoman* Online

http://www.oklahoman.net/opub/

Oklahoma City's online newspaper provides the usual current news, weather, and sports, along with community and state news. Forums for discussion of many topics, including the Oklahoma City Bombing, are accessible with your web browser's newsreader. You can reach the classifieds from the front page or go directly to them (*http://www.oklahoman.com/ classifieds.html*). Click on "employment" to bring up the list of available jobs, sorted by broad categories. You can refine your search by choosing a keyword. Press the Submit button to retrieve the job leads.

State of Oklahoma Government Information Server

http://www.state.ok.us/

The front door leading to information about the state of Oklahoma! Agriculture, education, and commerce are all accessible from here. Click on the employment link to view the hyper-linked listing of job-related sites, including the state Department of Labor, the ESC, and the Office of Personnel Management.

Oregon

Oregon's Job Bank

http://www.emp.state.or.us/empmtsvcs/

Use the self-directed search to find a job in Oregon, or link to the Employment Department home page for other services.

CascadeLink

http://www.region.portland.or.us/

CascadeLink, created for the global community of Portland, encourages citizen involvement and provides community information online. From the opening page you can link to transportation, education, election, and government information. Nonprofit organizations and businesses also have a large presence here. Regional government websites are linked so their job leads are immediately accessible via CascadeLink.

Mail Tribune

http://www.mailtribune.com/main.htm

Southern Oregon's online news source gives you the usual news, weather, and sports. You can also search its archives or follow the links to other Oregon resources. For your job search, choose the current day's or last Sunday's classifieds. You'll have to scroll past the links to other ads to get down to the employment section. Then click on one of the broad categories (part-time, self-employment, etc.) to view the alphabetical listing of current job leads.

Oregon OnLine

http://www.state.or.us/

The official website for the state, Oregon OnLine is very simple to navigate. Choose a button in your area of interest or click on the menu items at the bottom to get to education, business, and community resources. Choose the government link to access the state's agencies, including the Employment Department. On the Employment page you'll find information about child-care service, a directory of office locations, and labor market statistics. You'll also find links to the job listings, which are updated every two hours. Among the resources are federal jobs and military career information, jobs in state government, and a link to the Job Bank.

Oregon Live

http://www.oregonian.com/

A service of the *Oregonian,* Oregon Live brings you the week in review, bank rates, and stock quotes. You'll find entertainment news, plus a link to Ticketmaster! Click on the Career Search menu item to reach the classified ads. New to the *Oregonian,* Career Search can access thousands of job listings. The newspaper wants to have the ultimate online guide for finding a job, but it needs your help in testing it. So, go ahead; choose a job category (or categories) from the menu. (Hold the Control key to select more than one.) Click the Search key to view the results.

Oregon's Essential Links

http://www.el.com/To/Oregon

This is a great collection of Oregon links! The Essential site itself (*http://www.el.com/*) is a well-organized, highly acclaimed ready reference resource, with good links for dozens of subject areas. Welcome to Oregon is just part of what's available here. There are no job listings, but the links to chambers of commerce, business, government, and education resources, and other attractions number in the hundreds. The business directory (*http://www.oregondirectory.com/*) is searchable by city or industry and links to the state's Employment Department and the PDXJOBS site. Parts of the site are under construction, so keep watching for updates.

PDXJOBS Home Page

http://www.pdxjobs.com/

PDXJOBS is a job placement service. You can search for a job or post your resume free. Employers using the service have to pay a fee to establish an account for job posting and to search the resume database. To search the job listings, choose a category from the menu (medical, high tech, etc.) and specify full- or part-time work. You can select which company you want to search or search all of them. Add keywords to narrow your search and view the results with the best match listed first. If you search without using keywords, the results will be displayed with the newest job postings first.

All of the following are newsgroups for jobs in Portland:

pdaxs.jobs.construction (*construction*)
pdaxs.jobs.engineering (*engineering positions*)
pdaxs.jobs.management (*management positions or trainees*)

pdaxs.jobs.misc (*Can you think of something we didn't list?*)

pdaxs.jobs.resumes (*resumes of persons seeking work*)

pdaxs.jobs.sale (*sales positions*)

pdaxs.jobs.temporary (*short-term employment*)

pdaxs.jobs.wanted (*job seekers*)

Pennsylvania

Pennsylvania's Job Bank

http://pa.jobsearch.org/

Use the self-directed job search to look for work in Pennsylvania.

Carnegie Library of Pittsburgh

http://www.clpgh.org/

The library, whose credo is "Free to the People," has developed and linked to some especially helpful sites for its users. One of its best efforts is the Job and Career Education Center page (*http://www.clpgh.org/clp/JCEC/*). For those of you in the Pittsburgh area, a physical visit to the center could be just what you need to get your job search on target. For those of you linking to the site through the Internet, you'll find interview assistance, resume hints, links to financial aid information, and other career resources. And yes, there are links to job postings as well!

IR Online

http://www.intelligencer-record.com/

The online equivalent of the Harrisburg-based newspapers, the *Intelligencer Record* Online features the news from either local paper, plus the usual weather, entertainment, and business news. You're encouraged to speak out with the Electric Vent and check out THELINES: BuyLines, HomeLines, and PeopleLines. Use the JobLines to search for work. Simply select the job category from the pulldown menu, fill in the zip code or city and state, and decide how far you're willing to commute! Add up to three keywords (optional), click the Search button, and voilà! You have job leads.

JobNET

http://www.jobnet.com/

From here, you can post your resume to a local database free, or have it exported to over 1,000 other sites for a fee. Check out the companies who subscribe to the service, or search the database for hundreds of job leads. To start your search for work, type in keywords from a job title or description. Click the Search button and view as many as

50 job postings at one time. A handy feature at this site is the ability to download all of the current jobs as text in a Zip file. Simply click on "PROJOBS.ZIP" to start the process.

LibertyNet: Linking People and Information in the Philadelphia Region

http://www.libertynet.org/

Founded in 1993 by a group of civic and business leaders, LibertyNet is the largest provider of online regional information in the Philadelphia area. The handy menu bar at the left makes it easy to navigate the site. You'll find information about community services, government and education links, and developing businesses. Under the Business Development section, you won't find actual files of job listings. Instead, you'll find job training and literacy sites, professional associations, and economic development resources. LibertyNet also links to Philadelphia-area businesses, government agencies, and organizations that could have jobs available.

PA-Today: the Best of Pennsylvania's Newspapers Online

http://www.pa-today.com/

PA-Today links to the home pages of over a dozen Pennsylvania newspapers. From here, you can reach the classified sections for Erie, Pittsburgh, Altoona, Johnston, the Susquehanna Valley, Wilkes-Barre, Scranton, Harrisburg, and Philadelphia. Also included is a link to the *Dominion Post,* a West Virginia newspaper. To search for work, click on the individual newspaper's icon and follow the links. Read the directions to search the help wanted ads and get to the job leads.

pgh.jobs.offered

This is a newsgroup for jobs offered in Pittsburgh.

pgh.jobs.wanted

This is a newsgroup for jobs wanted in Pittsburgh.

PHILA.GOV

http://www.phila.gov/

The official website of the City of Brotherly Love! Choose one of the four icons to get to the business, government, community, or attractions links on this site. Philadelphia Marketplace links to area business information, which includes a directory of over 250,000 businesses. You'll find a great assortment of community resources, including neighborhood links, nonprofit and health care organizations, human services, and more. The city of Philadelphia doesn't post its jobs online (yet), but you can find information about applying for a position. Follow the City Services link to the Internal Services listing, and from there you'll reach the Personnel Department.

Philadelphia Online/Philly Jobs

http://www.phillynews.com/programs/ads/SUNHLP

Online home of the *Inquirer* and the *Daily News,* Philadelphia Online also serves the people of South Jersey in separate print and online editions. All of the classified ads are available to both communities. From either edition, click on "classified," and then "employment." You can browse all of the ads, or select categories to view specific job offerings. You can also save your results and look at a list of ads you've chosen over time. You'll also find career planning, resume writing tips, and other career resources.

PhillyWorks

http://www.slipps.com/phillyworks/

Since 1995, PhillyWorks has been providing information for Philadelphia-area job seekers and career changers. You'll find lots of helpful links here, including career counseling and training sites, chambers of commerce, and resources for minorities. There are also links to major businesses and newspapers in the area. The maintainers continue to add resources as they are developed or discovered.

phl.jobs.offered

This newsgroup covers jobs available in Philadelphia.

phl.jobs.wanted

This newsgroup covers jobs wanted in Philadelphia.

Three Rivers Free-Net

http://trfn.clpgh.org/

Three Rivers is a Pittsburgh-area, community-based computer network. Its purpose is to provide free access to local information and the world of the Internet. Click on the Subject Guide to get to an alphabetical listing of topics available through the Freenet. Business, education, government, and social services are all good choices for information about the community. To get to the job and career information, visit the Employment link. Three Rivers has made a concerted effort to link to all the local job sites. Placement services, summer opportunities, and job training are all accessible here. Click on the Job Postings to search for work in the area.

Rhode Island

Rhode Island's Job Bank

http://ri.jobsearch.org/

Use the self-directed search to look for work in Rhode Island.

Jobfind.com

http://www.jobfind.com/

Jobfind is a great resource for New England jobs. Research the corporate profiles or post your resume online. To look for a job, click on "job search", and then choose the state you're interested in. Select the job category, add keywords, and search.

ne.jobs
ne.jobs.contract

Both of these newsgroups are for jobs in the New England area.

Ocean State Free-Net (OSFN)

http://osfn.rhilinet.gov/
telnet://osfn.org

As we go to press, there are job resources available via Telnet for registered users only. The website is currently in a state of development. We hope that by the time you read this, there will be links to job and career information through the Web.

Projo.com

http://www.projo.com/

The website of the *Providence Journal-Bulletin* features a handy pulldown contents menu. Without it, navigating through the busy graphics can be confusing. Select "careers" and click on GO! to link directly to the employment page. The newspaper staff has developed a large number of resources for job hunters. You'll find articles; a database of occupation options; and helpful hints for resume writing, interviewing, and the job search. To search for work in the current week's editions of the paper, type in a keyword(s). Decide whether you want the results ranked according to relevance, alphabetical order, or date, then click on GO! to display the job leads. Once you find that job, consult the site for information on the local communities.

Providence RI Home Page

http://www.providenceri.com/

This URL will take you to the Mayor's Home Page. From marinara sauce to beautiful photographs, this site has an interesting combination of links. There are no links labeled "employment," but there is information that could be helpful to you. City government, schools and universities, local businesses, and organizations all have information available online. You'll find many of them linked from this site. To find out if there are jobs available with city government, call the City Department of Personnel at (401) 421-7740, ext. 237.

RIDLT: Rhode Island Department of Labor and Training

http://www.det.state.ri.us/

This service is similar to other state employment offices online, with its easy directions and simple forms. Link to the state's Job Bank or to others in the New England states. A directory of local employment offices is available online along with links to government resources, career information, classified job ads, and additional Internet resources. Very well done.

State of Rhode Island Home Page

http://www.state.ri.us/

Developed and maintained by the Secretary of State's office, this public information kiosk links to many helpful resources. The First Stop Business Information Center provides business assistance, economic development resources, and a listing of corporations by name. The state links include state agencies, community information, cities and towns, and schools and universities.

South Carolina

South Carolina's Job Bank

http://sc.jobsearch.org/

Use the self-directed search to look for work in South Carolina.

Charleston.Net Home Page

http://www.charleston.net/

Sponsored by the *Post and Courier* newspaper, Charleston.Net provides an easily searchable page. There are links to local government information and an archive of stories going back to 1994, with a librarian ready to assist you with your other requests for *Post and Courier* information! The Net Gateway links you to other educational, informational, and recreational sites on the Internet. To search for work, click on the classified button and choose the employment link. Type in a keyword and decide how many job leads you want displayed. The default is 20 and is easily changed. Choose a category and click on "begin search" to view the results.

SCIway . . . Gateway to Online South Carolina

http://www.sciway.net/jobs/index.html

No glitz or glamor here, just access to loads of information for the people of South Carolina! The simple menu structure makes it easy to find exactly what you need.

Directories links to a wonderful collection of yellow pages for the state. Many of the entries are also accessible by county or city. The home page leads to libraries, newspapers, government, and education sites. You'll also find a directory of medical facilities, links to state and local organizations, and more! To get to the employment links, click on "jobs." Private employment services, the state Job Service, listings by type of organization, and links to other helpful career-related sites are all here. Click on the Newspaper employment ads to reach the state's online newspapers, linked from each of their job search pages. You can power search the classifieds here, without having to go through the other sections of the newspapers!

South Carolina Employment Security Commission

http://scjob.sces.org/

Established in 1936, the ESC plays a vital role in the state's economic development. Visit its site to check out the services that are available. Link to the Job Bank or check out the job training site. Information on the School-to-Work and One-Stop initiatives is also at your fingertips.

State of South Carolina Public Information Home Page

http://www.state.sc.us/

South Carolina's window on the Internet provides access to the many departments of state government. You can check out the state jobs, link to the Clemson University Cooperative Extension Service, the Departments of Commerce and Education, or the Employment Security Commission from here. Consumer information, libraries, and the Higher Education Tuition Grants Commission are all accessible.

Job Opportunities in South Carolina

http://www.state.sc.us/jobopps.html

This page links to the Job Bank and to opportunities in state government.

South Dakota

South Dakota's Job Bank

http://sd.jobsearch.org/

South Dakota's Job Bank features simple choices of occupational area, field, and geographic location to get you to the jobs you'd like to see. To apply for a job you see online, fill in the online form, print the screen, and fax or mail it to the office indicated.

Madison Daily Leader

http://www.madisondailyleader.com/

The *Leader* serves the Interlakes area of the state. The classified ads are easily accessible from the front page. On the ad page, hit "click here" to view the classifieds and choose "employment" to get to the job search page. Note: AdQuest supplies the job leads and includes thousands of ads from other regions of the United States. Be sure you specify South Dakota in your search. When we visited the paper, there were a dozen job leads for *Daily Leader* readers.

Pierre Home Page

http://www.pierre.org/

Maintained by the local chamber of commerce, the Pierre page includes links to local businesses, current legislative information, and business resources. You'll find information about the state's capital city here, too!

Sioux Falls

http://www.siouxfalls.org/

The "Gateway to the Plains" also serves as a doorway to local information. When we looked, some of the features were still under construction, but much was already accessible. You'll find a listing of major employers in the area, although the contact information isn't readily available. Information about city and county government, state resources, and the local chamber of commerce is at your fingertips. One of the most helpful features is the Sioux Falls Directory, searchable by category or business name. You can also browse the listings by subject. The word "employment" brought up listings for employment agencies, the state job service, and a couple of other employment service agencies.

South Dakota Department of Labor

http://www.state.sd.us/state/executive/dol/

The Department of Labor manages the Job Bank, the Job Service program, and all other aspects of employment and training for the people of South Dakota. You'll find links to those services, along with labor market information and the School-to-Work initiative, on this site. From here, you can also link to job openings with the state, or take a quiz to see how much you know about welfare in South Dakota.

South Dakota Popular Internet Places

http://sodapop.dsu.edu/

This site's designers and maintainers, many of whom are students at Dakota State University, would like to make this a one-stop source for local information and more. When we visited the site, they were well on their way! At South Dakota Popular Internet Places (SoDa PoP), "where actual human beings organize sites into categories," you can search for specific information or use the handy contents menu to browse by topic. Among the offerings are links to colleges and universities, vocational education and community colleges, federal and state resources, information about individual communities, and business resources. Sign up to receive the mailing list of new sites. You can also send in your feedback via the handy online form.

Tennessee

Tennessee's Job Bank

http://tn.jobsearch.org/

Use the self-directed search to look for work in Tennessee.

Knoxville News-Sentinel Online

http://www.knoxnews.com/

The *News-Sentinel* features the usual news, weather, and sports. Choose "classified" and click on GO! to get to the job opportunities. A nice feature is AdRover, the electronic equivalent of man's best friend. AdRover will look over the classified ads every day and send you the results of the search by e-mail. Or you can look for yourself. Simply click on the Employment link to browse through the listings. To search for specific job titles, choose a broad category, select the current day's or the previous Sunday's paper, and add or exclude keywords (optional). Click on the Search button to view the results.

memphis.employment

This newsgroup covers jobs in Memphis.

Metropolitan Government of Nashville and Davidson County

http://janis.nashville.org/

Local government in Nashville has provided access to some helpful resources here. You'll find listings of the departments and a telephone directory of "who to call" in local government. There are links to agencies, information about starting a business in the metropolitan area, and links to several Nashville websites. If you're interested in working for county government, click on the Employment Opportunities link. When we last checked, there were more than a dozen jobs advertised here.

Memphis *Commercial Appeal*

http://www.gomemphis.com/

For fans of the King of Rock and Roll, the *Commercial Appeal* provides an "Elvis Archive," accessible from the opening page. The site maintainers suggest that you click your web browser's Reload or Refresh button to see the latest updates. Check out the business news and keep up with local and national news. To look for employment, choose the Searchable Classifieds link from the easy-access menu. This takes you to the main classified page. Note: You can search the Knoxville paper and some out-of-state papers here also. Click on the employment sign, and choose either the current day's or the previous Sunday's listings. Select a specific area of interest (health care, clerical, etc.) or select all of them. Type in one or two keywords, and narrow your search further by excluding terms. For instance, if you are a nurse and don't want to work nights, the word "nights" would be a good one to exclude. Click on the Search/Browse button to see the job leads.

Tennessee Department of Employment Security

http://www.state.tn.us/employsecurity/

From here, you can link to the Job Bank or check out the other services offered by the department. Among the other offerings are labor statistics, industry trends, and other labor market resources. You can also reach this site from the State of Tennessee Home Page (*http://www.state.tn.us/*).

Texas

Texas Job Bank

http://www.tec.state.tx.us/
http://www.twc.state.tx.us/twc.html
telnet://hi-tec.tec.state.tx.us/
telnet://twcdirect.twc.state.tx.us/
Login: jobs

Texas has *two* job banks! One is known as the Governor's Job Bank, with Texas state agency job listings, and the other is the Texas Workforce Commission Job Express, where you'll find the private industry job leads. Both of them are accessible from this page. Information about job training, employment laws, labor market information, and child-care service recommendations are at your fingertips. You can also Telnet to the job databases.

Austin360: The City Site for Austin

http://www.austin360.com/

Brought to you by the *American-Statesman,* Austin360 is among the online Texas newspapers asking users to register. You can access the job opportunities without registering by choosing Classifieds from the menu. To search for job leads, type in a keyword or phrase from the job title, description, or category you're looking for. Choose the day or days (you're limited to the current day and the previous six days) you want to search. Click on Employment and the Fetch! button to view the results of your search.

Austin City Links

http://www.austinlinks.com/

Voted a "1997 Best of Austin" award winner for the best website, City Links has a lot to offer job seekers and career changers! The Austin government link leads to the city's home page and its job postings. There are also education and organization links, and a listing of Austin businesses on the World Wide Web. Other links will tell you more about the community and its resources. If you click on Employment, you'll find links to the job leads or the human resources pages of all the major employers in the area. You can power search through the employment opportunities! There are additional links to newsgroups and career resources, including online resume assistance.

austin.jobs

This is a newsgroup for jobs in Austin.

Dallas Examiner

http://www.dallasexaminer.com/

As we go to press, the _Examiner_ classified ads are under construction. We hope they'll be available by the time you read this.

dfw.jobs

This newsgroup covers jobs in Dallas–Fort Worth.

Express-News Online

http://www.express-news.net/

San Antonio's contribution to online news services! Note: Resources with a an asterisk can be accessed by registered users only. The employment ads are available without registering. Choose "classified" from the handy menu and click GO! to reach the ad page. Select Employment & Education, specify the broad category from the menu, add a keyword, and click on the Submit button to view the results.

Galveston County Daily News

http://www.galvnews.com/

Sound off on the news forum or join in a live chat group. Texas's "oldest daily newspaper" joins the legion of newspapers that are featuring additional services in the new online environment. Note: You must register to use the forums, chat groups, or archives. You can also subscribe to a mailing list to receive highlights of the day's events through e-mail. To look for work, click on "classified" on the Services menu. Choose Employment to browse or search the ads. Select a job category (management, domestic, etc.) to view only those leads in your area of interest, or EMPLOYMENT to see all of the ads.

Houston Chronicle Interactive

http://www.chron.com/

The *Chronicle* asks that you register, although we were able to browse through the career resources and look for job leads without doing so. Choose Job Source from the handy content menu to access resume and interviewing tips, relocation information, and advice for career changers. If you're only interested in doing a quick job search, choose the HCI Quick Classified Search. Click on the employment link and choose a job category to view the job leads.

houston.jobs

houston.jobs.offered

These newsgroups are for jobs available in Houston.

houston.jobs.wanted

This newsgroup is for jobs wanted in Houston.

State of Texas Government Information

http://www.state.tx.us/

http://www.texas.gov/

From the front page, this server links you to state and local agencies, the state library, institutions of higher education, information about doing business in Texas, and current highway conditions. The State Electronic Library (*http://link.tsl.state.tx.us/*) has loads of information about the state, the workings of the government, and its services. You'll also find links to the state's Job Banks here. Easy to navigate, with lots of good information!

Texas ComputerJobs Store

http://www.texas.computerjobs.com/

Here, you'll find industry and career information for computer professionals in Texas, plus links to the other Computer Jobs sites in Chicago, the Carolinas, and Atlanta. This is a great-looking site with information about the local job market and company profiles (not just for those who advertise here). Check out the hundreds of job listings and add your name to the skill registry.

Texas One

http://www.texas-one.org

Although it provides no job postings, Texas One does have a search feature that connects to business listings. To search the directory, type in keywords, or browse by Standard Industrial Classifications (SIC) code or geographic location. Dozens of other states and countries are included here also.

tx.jobs

This newsgroup is for jobs in Texas.

ut.jobs

This newsgroup has jobs from the University of Texas, Austin.

utcs.jobs

This newsgroup covers jobs from the University of Texas, Austin, Computer Science Department.

Yahoo! Austin

http://austin.yahoo.com/

Yahoo! Dallas/Fort Worth

http://dfw.yahoo.com/

These local Yahoos are great information resources for the areas they cover. You'll find links to employers, employment, housing, and anything else you need to make your relocation and job search a success.

Utah

Utah's Job Bank

http://ut.jobsearch.org/

Use the self-directed search to look for work in Utah.

Deseret News

http://www.desnews.com/

Salt Lake City's *Deseret News* has thoroughly incorporated the world of the Internet with the newspaper business. Among its online offerings is an archive dating back to 1988. Access to stories from the previous six months is free, and older stories are available to subscribers. Explore Cyberworld, a great resource for students, their families, and teachers. Of interest to job hunters are the Utah links available in the ETC section. Links to educational, business, and government resources, including the Department of Employment Security, are available here. The classified ads, available from the menu on the front page, are updated daily by 6 A.M. Choose employment from the list on your left and select the category of interest from the pulldown menu. "Help wanted" is generally the most useful category, but look them over first. Decide whether you want to search the current day's or the previous Sunday's listings. Then enter up to three keywords. Without keywords, the search will bring up a list of all job opportunities. Click the Search button to see the results.

Herald Extra

http://www.daily-herald.com/

Provo's *Daily-Herald* maintains this 24-hour information service. You'll find up-to-date news, weather, and sports, as well as local and regional news and access to a growing archive. A handy feature is the classified ad search at the bottom of the opening page. Simply type in a keyword describing the position you're interested in (accounting, sales, etc.). Click on GO! to view the results. Another way to search for work is to choose the classified ads from the menu on your left. The Find feature on your web browser is helpful here. Use it to find Help Wanted on the classified page, and use it again after you click on the link to go directly to jobs that interest you.

SmartUtah

http://www.smartutah.org/

Its goal is to "facilitate the development of community networks across the state." Business, educational, and government services will be made available to the citizens electronically. Keep your eyes on this site as it develops!

State of Utah: Employment

http://www.state.ut.us/html/employment.htm

The state of Utah has pulled together some great resources here. From this page, you can link to the Job Bank and the other services provided by Workforce Services, get answers to your Utah employment FAQS, and link to the state's major universities. But that's not all! The state newspapers and many of the major employers also have a presence on this site. Lots of Utah job leads and potential employers accessible from one website!

Utah Department of Workforce Services

http://dwsa.state.ut.us/

The Department of Workforce Services is the lead agency for job- and career-related services in the state. From here, you can link to the Job Bank or America's Talent Bank, the nationwide database of skill inventories. Or learn more about the other services provided by the agency, JTPA, labor market statistics, employment centers, and more!

utah.jobs

This is a newsgroup for jobs in Utah.

Vermont

Department of Employment and Training

http://www.det.state.vt.us/

Vermont's employment page is frames free, easy to navigate, and full of helpful information! Link to the Job Bank, get job referrals, or submit your resume to the Talent Bank. Need help putting your resume together? No problem, the DET is there to help. Want your skill inventory displayed on the World Wide Web? Say yes and it's done, free. Check out the labor market statistics (Statistics R Us) and trends in the U.S. job market, or get help deciding what you want to be when you grow up. There are additional links to training and education information, internship and job opportunities with state government, and other employment resources and agencies. A must-see for Vermont job hunters!

Addison County Independent

http://www.addisonindependent.com/

The Middlebury, Vermont, newspaper maintains a handy Business and Service Directory. Simply click on the subject that interests you to get to that section of the list. You could also browse or use the Find feature of your web browser. Link to other community sites or scope out the classified ads. They're accessible from the opening page. Click on "help wanted" to view all of the current job leads. Using Find would be helpful here also.

Central Vermont Home Page

http://www.central-vt.com/

Maintained by the Central Vermont Chamber of Commerce, these pages feature several helpful resources. Individuals thinking of starting a new business or those needing help in growing a business can find tips for financing, site planning, and registration information. You can look over the towns in the area, or find housing or education information. Check to see which towns have jobs, or use the main employment page to see all of the possibilities. Labor statistics, major employers, and industry trends are all accessible from this page, as are the job leads.

Jobfind.com

http://www.jobfind.com/

Jobfind is a great resource for New England jobs. Research the corporate profiles or post your resume online. To look for a job, click on "job search," and then choose the state you're interested in. Select the job category, add keywords, and search.

ne.jobs

ne.jobs.contract

Both of these newsgroups are for jobs in New England.

State of Vermont Home Page

http://www.state.vt.us/

Your entrée to the Green Mountain State, this page features the most up-to-date informa-tion about local ski conditions! You'll also find a link to state maps here, along with the usual links to agencies, legislators, and the business of state government. From the opening page, you can link to the great career resources at the Department of Employment and Training or check out the job possibilities with state government. There are also links to the state's public libraries and educational resources, and a link to other Vermont and New England sites on the Internet.

Virginia

Virginia's Job Bank

http://va.jobsearch.org/

Use the self-directed search to find work in Virginia.

Blacksburg Electronic Village

http://www.bev.net/mall/index.html#employ

A pioneer in the online community, the Village has a wide assortment of helpful links. You'll find government and education links, business resources, and information about the offline community as well. Use this URL to get directly to the employment page and its links to newspapers, career resources, and local job opportunities.

Department of Personnel and Training

http://www.state.va.us/~dpt/

In addition to the part the DPT plays in recruiting and maintaining the state government's workforce, it provides links to other job sites and state agencies here.

Gateway Virginia

http://www.gateway-va.com/

Graphics intensive, but worth the effort for Virginia job seekers. The Gateway pulls together a wealth of resources for the area, including the newspapers for Charlottesville, Danville,

Lynchburg, and Richmond. Check out any of the papers for additional links. The Charlottesville paper alone has links to local government, regional networks, and major universities—all good targets for job hunters. You can keep in touch with business and government by following the links to DC Dateline and Virginia Business Online, or search for information in the Richmond Internet Yellow Pages. To reach employment opportunities advertised in the *Richmond Times-Dispatch,* click on "classified ads" or "local listings." Press the employment button and browse through any of this week's job leads. Choose the category you're interested in to view a list of job offerings.

Pilot Online

http://www.pilotonline.com/

The *Virginian-Pilot* is based in Hampton Roads. From the opening page, you can use the pulldown menu (and press GO!), or use the menu and icons on the right side to navigate. A nice feature is the Biz Search Yellow Pages. With the default set on the Hampton Roads area, it's easy to find businesses by type or name. The "new and improved classifieds" section is also at your fingertips. To go directly to the employment resources, choose "jobs" from the pulldown menu. You can check out jobs at the *Pilot;* look over the classified ads; or link to CareerWeb, a D.C.–area jobs site, for a job search or to post your resume. To search the classifieds, choose a category (medical, help wanted, etc.) or select all. Narrow your search through the use of a keyword, and click on Search to view the results. Once you get the job leads, you can use another helpful feature, the ADD box. Simply click in the ADD box of any of the job leads that interest you. It "collects" them at the end of your session and allows you to print out only the jobs you've selected.

Virginia Employment Commission

http://www.state.va.us/vec/

Link to the Job Bank or check out the other services available through this site. Labor market statistics, links to Private Industry Council sites in the state, a collaborative Reemployment Project for displaced federal workers, and other job seeker services are available here.

The Washington Post

http://204.146.47.74/search.html

The CareerPost has a new look, with more jobs, a better search tool, and a career page hosted by the dean of career counselors, Richard Bolles. If you're not quite ready for the job search yet, and need a little guidance, go directly to What Color Is Your Parachute: The Net Guide (*www.washingtonpost.com/parachute*). Bolles offers reviews of the resources available for job seekers and career changers, along with helpful advice.

Washington

Washington's Job Bank

http://wa.jobsearch.org/

Use the self-directed search to find work in Washington.

Home Page Washington

http://www.state.wa.us/

The home page sports a different image every time you visit. George Washington's likeness from Mount Rushmore, a piece of petrified wood, and the state bird are among the images you might see at different times. Beyond the look of the site, you'll also find considerable content. There are links to state, local, and federal resources, business and educational sites, and consumer resources. The Jobs page links to the state's employment services, government job leads, career information, and other Internet employment resources.

Job Hotlines for Washington

http://www.gspa.washington.edu/Career/hotlines.html

These lists of telephone numbers are collected by the Graduate School of Public Affairs at the University of Washington and made available on its server. Use these telephone numbers to get information on available jobs in the Seattle/Kings County area. You will either be connected to a recorded list or to a live person, depending on the hot line.

Seattle Community Network

http://www.scn.org/

This is one of Seattle's great public networks! You'll find good information about the neighborhoods, local businesses, and organizations here.

Seattle Online

http://www.pan.ci.seattle.wa.us/

The Public Access Network (PAN) is the other great public network for Seattle. This also serves as the official website of the city of Seattle. Select Business from the front page to access information on local businesses, links to city job openings, regional job lines, and other job leads.

Northwest Source: The Seattle Times Company

http://www.seatimes.com/

The Pulitzer Prize–winning *Seattle Times* has developed a wonderful online resource for Washington residents. You'll find easy access to Washington's largest daily newspaper, along with the *Seattle Post-Intelligencer,* the *Issaquah Press,* mirror *Drive-Thru* newspaper for teens, and the *Community News Group.* A nice feature is the seattletimes.com yellow pages, searchable by business type or name. You can also browse by topics such as "community" or "shops & services." The *Times*'s and *Post-Intelligencer*'s classified ads are updated each night at 8:30 P.M. Pacific time. You can browse them by category, although we don't recommend it because there are dozens of help wanted files to go through. To search the database for career assistance such as counselors or resume writers, choose the career directory category. To search for work, select Employment, then enter keywords to describe the job title or description, and specify whether you want all ads since Sunday or only the new ads. Click on the Search button to retrieve your results.

seattle.jobs
seattle.jobs.offered

This newsgroup is for jobs available in Seattle.

seattle.jobs.wanted

This newsgroup is for jobs sought in Seattle.

TRIBnet

http://www.tribnet.com/

Brought to you by the *Tacoma News Tribune,* this online news source has all the regular features of a local newspaper plus several other helpful resources. In a hurry? Quickscan allows you to scan five days of headlines. Use the Northwest Index (NI) to find all kinds of interesting Pacific Northwest websites. Explore the NI business, education, and government links for possible job leads, and add your own favorite URL to the index! The Special Projects section includes some helpful facts about the local business community, including a listing of the top employers and industries. Click on Classified Can to reach the ads. To start your job search, choose Employment and a broad category. Select a subcategory and click on GO! Use the Find feature of your web browser to look through the job opportunities.

Washington Online Reemployment Kiosk

http://www.wa.gov/esd/employment.html

The Employment Security Department sponsors this site. Press the Job Seeker button if you're looking for work. Click on the Employer button if you're an employer. Services for job seekers include resume posting and writing tips, a calendar of job-related events, career resources, and job leads. All of it available through the site's kiosks! Washington residents can visit their local Job Service Center in person to learn more about the possibilities for training and career development.

Yahoo! Seattle

http://seattle.yahoo.com/

These local Yahoos are great information resources for the areas they cover. You'll find links to employers, employment, housing, and anything else you need to make your relocation and job search a success.

Washington, D.C.*

See District of Columbia.

West Virginia

West Virginia's Job Bank

http://wv.jobsearch.org/

Use the self-directed search to look for work in West Virginia.

Charleston Gazette Online

http://www.wvgazette.com/

The *Gazette* encourages its readers to take advantage of the Internet and e-mail their news tips, letters to the editor, and questions and comments. It has also developed online forums where readers may post their views. Of course, the site hasn't overlooked the traditional news, weather, and sports! And it is continuing to post job leads in the classified section. To look through these ads, click on the classified menu item on the home page. Choose to look at the whole week or one of seven days, select Employment, and add a keyword from a job title or description. Click on Find It! to view the results.

Dominion Post Online

http://www.dominionpost.com/

The *Dominion Post* dates back to 1864, about the time the state was created. Family owned and operated, it provides a number of interesting features in its online edition. Among them is a section for seniors and information for local college sports aficionados. The InfoLine is a free voice information system that offers a range of news and information by phone. To start your quest for work, click on the Classifieds icon on the front page. To browse the ads, select Help Wanted from the scrolling menu, choose the day(s) you're interested in, and click the Browse button. To search for specific job leads, select Help Wanted, make the choice of the current day's, Sunday's, or both newspapers, and type in keywords from the job title or description. Click on the Search button to view the results.

InfoMine Reference Links

http://www.wvlc.wvnet.edu/commish/ref.html

InfoMine is sponsored by the state Library Commission, the agency charged with maintaining and improving library services. There are links to the West Virginia libraries' collective catalog, information about the services available for the blind and physically handicapped, and a state newspaper index. You'll also find links to all the state's libraries and schools. The Reference Links include the state's online newspapers, businesses and organizations, the regional chambers of commerce, and other resources that could be helpful to job hunters.

State of West Virginia Home Page

http://www.state.wv.us/

One of the delightful aspects of viewing this home page is watching the scenic "postcard" change to another beautiful landscape! In addition to the scenery, you get ease of navigation here. Links to the state's agencies, including the Bureau of Employment Programs, are readily available. An innovative new program allows West Virginians to add their own URLs to the site. As a result, you'll find a growing number of nongovernmental links. These are accessible through the menu on the left, or you can use keywords to search the site.

West Virginia Bureau of Employment Programs

http://www.state.wv.us/bep/

You'll find information about all of the state employment programs here. Link to the Job Bank, find out about job training programs, or look up the customer service office nearest you. Services for employers, labor market statistics, and publication information are all available here. The bureau's online job search makes this one of the most popular of the state's government sites.

West Virginia Online

http://www.wvonline.com/

An interesting collection of West Virginia links! Individuals can submit their own links, so you'll find college home pages, businesses online, and some personal pages here. You can search the site or use the topical headings to browse. Our search for the word "employment" resulted in more than half a dozen websites, including the state's official page, a job accommodation association for the disabled, and the West Virginia Army National Guard.

Wisconsin

Wisconsin JobNet

http://167.218.251.8/jobnet/

This database includes the listings for the Wisconsin Job Service. The organization is similar to that of the other state job services in that you choose a job category, select a job title, and identify a region of the state. You will be asked to register for this server, but you can arrow past, submit the form, and continue from there. Don't skip over the sample documents, because they are great guides to writing resumes and preparing for an interview, and include a list of 20 basic questions to use in interviewing.

City of Madison

http://www.ci.madison.wi.us/

For the past two years, Madison has ranked in the top 10 best places to live in America. If you'd like to work for a top-10 city, click on the employment link to see the job possibilities. New job listings are posted each Monday.

madison.com

http://www.madison.com/

When you stop at this site, you're linking to two newspapers online, *The Capital Times Cyberzone* and *The Wisconsin State Journal*. They've provided a searchable archive of staff-written articles available back to 1989. You'll find features similar to those you find in other papers, plus links to Badgers/Packers information and local resources. To get to the job ads, click on the classified button on the menu bar. Look over all of them by clicking on Employment, or be more selective and choose the employment category from the pull-down menu, type in a keyword from the desired job title or description, and click the Submit button.

Milwaukee Journal Sentinel

http://www.jsonline.com/

If you're a fan, check out the Packer Plus and Badger Plus links while you're here. There's an archive of information about your favorite teams and photographs, too. A catalog of licensed team merchandise is accessible online for your reading or purchasing pleasure. To search for work, click on "classified" on the menu bar and on the advertising link on the next page. (Don't overlook the opportunities at the *Sentinel* posted here.) Choose "employment" and a subcategory (full-time, health care, etc.), or select all. Fill in your geographic location and add up to three keywords. Hit the Search button to view the results.

milw.jobs

This newsgroup covers jobs in Milwaukee.

State of Wisconsin Department of Workforce Development

http://www.dwd.state.wi.us/

This agency oversees the employment services of the state. There are links here to information about its services, and to other information for job seekers and employers.

State of Wisconsin Information Server

http://www.state.wi.us/

You'll find links to all of the parts of state government here, including the employment services. This server also has links to municipal, county, and community websites, along with the University of Wisconsin. More potential employers!

West Bend Community Career Network

http://www.careernet.org/

This is a source of great information for choosing and researching a career, deciding if you need more education, and, finally, looking at local and state employment opportunities and linking to other career resources and job listings. A cooperative effort of business, government, and educational institutions, the site's CareerInfoNet was designed for students and job hunters in the community of Washington County.

Wyoming

Wyoming's Job Bank

http://wyjobs.state.wy.us/region.htm

Use the map to select the area of the state you're interested in, or choose from the list. Enter a keyword from a job title or description. Add the name of a community and/or a date. To save time and avoid misspelling, you can shorten or truncate the keyword or city name. For example, use "account" for "accountant," or "casp" for "Casper." Search, and voilà! Job leads. Updated daily.

trib.com

http://www.trib.com/

Wyoming's Internet newspaper has the usual up-to-the-minute news and weather, plus some added features. Take a tour of Wyoming or visit Dino-Mite, "the dinosaur site for kids"! The site also provides a simple Internet search page so its users can look for information on the World Wide Web. Link to the classified ads through the Marketplace menu item. Click on *Casper Star-Tribune* and scroll through the ads to get to the Help Wanted section.

Wyoming Department of Employment

http://wydoe.state.wy.us/

Resources accessible through this well-organized home page include the state's Job Bank, the state employment offices, jobs in state government, and the University of Wyoming's job openings. For the warm-blooded, there's an additional link to information for getting through a winter in Wyoming! The state has provided some nice programs, services, and links to Internet resources to help its customers meet their "employment, training, income, or information needs."

13

International Opportunities

This chapter features Internet resources for finding employment opportunities in countries other than the United States. We have arranged it by region in order to facilitate searches in neighboring countries. Many international recruiters based in one country place employees in several other countries in that region, so you may want to check neighboring countries for references.

Since the first edition of this guide came out, the growth of websites with a regional focus has been phenomenal. Yahoo! has led the way, with several sites focused on particular countries or regions of the world, and many more designed to cover U.S. metropolitan areas. CareerMosaic and the Online Career Center, both well known to job seekers in the United States, now have several sites designated for specific regions of the world. There also are other, lesser known efforts, and the result is good for job hunters. By bringing the resources of a given locale together in one website, the individual spends his or her time searching materials in the region of interest, not the entire world of Internet resources. We've included sites with the geographic areas they represent.

Many of the larger Internet job sites in Chapter 4 carry international postings, and that includes America's Job Bank. Some international sites listing jobs in a given specialty have been placed with that specialty, such as mining and academe.

Services with Listings for Multiple Countries and Regions

Aupair JobMatch

http://www.aupairs.co.uk/

Aupair on the Internet is an automated job-matching service for families and au pairs. Choose the language of your choice to register free and submit a photograph if you'd like to. Search the family database of several thousand possibilities by location or nationality.

CareerMosaic International Gateway

http://www.careermosaic.com/cm/gateway/gateway1.html

CareerMosaic has expanded to include career resources for several areas of the world. Check out the thousands of postings in the JOBS Database or search the Usenet newsgroups that contain job postings. Post your curriculum vitae or resume, or look over the company profiles. CareerMosaic also provides materials to assist in your job search and other career resources. Highly recommended.

Expat Forum

http://www.expatforum.com/

The Expat Forum does not have job postings, but does have a great deal of information for individuals who are working, living, or doing business overseas. Information on the cost of living, using the telephone, time zones, and cultural differences are accessible on the

Forum. Find weather reports, a language translator, and links to other helpful resources. The site recently started a Jobs and Careers section on the Expat Chat! message board. You will need to register to contribute or ask questions.

ICEN-L International Career and Employment Network (NAFSA)

To subscribe: listserv@IUBVM.UCS.INDIANA.EDU
Message: subscribe icen-l yourfirstname yourlastname

This mailing list, maintained at Indiana University, discusses international employment. If you have any question about the ICEN-L list, write to the list owners at the generic address (*ICEN-L-request@IUBVM.UCS.INDIANA.EDU*).

International Herald Tribune Recruitment Ads

http://www.washingtonpost.com/wp-adv/classifieds/careerpost/iht.htm

The *International Herald Tribune* features up-to-date job listings for administrative and executive positions all over the world.

International Job Search Resources

http://www.overseasjobs.com/resources/jobs_main.html

Part of the Overseas Jobs site, Jeff Allen's guide links to hundreds of other job listings and information resources. Click on Industry type to start your search.

International Organizations with Job Openings on the Internet

http://www.psc-cfp.gc.ca/intpgm/epb6.htm

The Public Service Commission of Canada produces this site as a service to its citizens. Arranged alphabetically by organization name, this is an excellent source for international job openings.

International Rescue Committee

http://www.intrescom.org/toc.html

The International Rescue Committee (IRC) is the leading nonsectarian, voluntary organization providing relief, protection, and resettlement services for refugees and victims of oppression or violent conflict. Employment opportunities are listed for all parts of the world in a wide range of job categories.

Online Career Center International

http://www.occ.com/occ/international.html

Online Career Center (OCC), the granddaddy of Internet job sites, has broadened its service to include jobs worldwide. Go to the international site or directly to the one that covers the geographic region you're interested in. Search for jobs or post your resume.

Overseas Jobs Web

http://www.overseasjobs.com/index.html

Search the jobs database by keyword or browse the categories. Join the Overseas Jobs Express (OJE) discussion list, submit your curriculum vitae or resume, or link to other helpful Internet resources. For more information, send e-mail to jeff@overseasjobs.com.

Les Pages Emploi

http://emploi.hrnet.fr/

This site provides access to a collection of Internet job sites located throughout the world. Search by geographic location, check out the top 100 of the hottest job sites, link to Usenet newsgroups, or find helpful mailing lists. Leave a copy of your curriculum vitae or resume. Main page is primarily in French and English.

Yahoo!

http://www.yahoo.com

What can you find here? Well, under Government is a list of embassies as well as international governments; under Regional is a list of countries; under Higher Education is a list of colleges by country; and under everything is something using the word "international" or a geographic heading to describe itself. Take your time and really search all of the avenues available here. And don't forget the national Yahoos. Information in these "baby Yahoo" sites is customized for each country.

North America

Resources for the United States are included in Chapter 12.

CANADA

These resources have been divided by province and then listed alphabetically by title. Resources with listings for the whole country are at the beginning of the section.

ActiJob

http://www.activemploi.com/tp_menu.html

ActiJob features free resume posting, job search tips, and job listings for the major cities in Canada. You can also view the corporate profiles of a few of the major employers.

can.jobs

This is a popular newsgroup for jobs in Canada.

These resources have been divided by province and then listed alphabetically by title. Resources with listings for the whole country are at the beginning of the section.

Canada WorkInfoNet

http://www.workinfonet.ca

Formerly the CanWorkNet, WorkInfoNet (WIN) is a bilingual Internet directory that connects to resources helpful to job seekers and career changers. It numbers more than 1,300 links, including career resources, financial information, and community services. This is an excellent resource. In addition, several of the provinces have launched local sites for the project.

Alberta	http://www.edsg.com:80/canwin/
British Columbia	http://workinfonet.bc.ca/
New Brunswick	http://www.gov.nb.ca/ael/lmab/cwnhome.htm
Northwest Territory	http://siksik.learnnet.nt.ca/career/
Quebec	http://www.workinfonet.ca/cwn/english/quebec/
Saskatchewan	http://www.sasked.gov.sk.ca/careers/

You can also click on "Contacts in Your Province" to find directory information for your local WorkInfoNet representatives.

CareerMosaic Canada

http://canada.careermosaic.com/

CareerPlace

http://www.careerplace.com/

CareerPlace is an initiative of the Native Women's Association of Canada, a nonprofit organization representing aboriginal women across Canada. A job search support service, CareerPlace targets the same population. The site contains limited information about the organization, as well as information on how to submit a resume.

Electronic Labour Exchange

http://ele.ingenia.com/

This huge database of employment opportunities is run by the Canadian government's Human Resources Development Canada–Dévelopment des ressources hamaines Canada (HRDC-DRHC). Choose your language preference, then search the exchange for a job.

Human Resources Development Canada

http://www.hrdc-drhc.gc.ca/

The Canadian government sponsors this site and other HRDC-DRHC sites in the individual provinces. It features a full range of career and human resources services. You can choose to see the material in English or French. To reach the Job Bank, click on Work, then on Job Opportunities. Search by job title, occupational categories, or National Occupational Classification code number. You can also restrict your search to the newest listings (posted within 48 hours) or listings for students. As with many of today's job sites, you can search using a job profile you create, called a Personalized Service Code. Although many of the regional job banks have been closed since the development of the national site, you can still link to those that remain at http://www.st-thomas.hrdc-drhc.gc.ca/work/jblist.html.

JobSAT

http://www.jobsat.com

The JobSAT database provides free access to thousands of job listings from Canada and some selected U.S. locations. JobSAT also provides career resources such as labor market information, interviewing tips, and links to other job sites. Register for a free membership and post a resume summary to the Resume Database, or develop a search profile for future use. Positions range from entry-level to executive.

National Graduate Register

http://ngr.schoolnet.ca/engine/

Industry Canada provides the National Graduate Register (NGR) for the youth of Canada. Students can register in the NGR database or visit the Career Centre for career and job information. Click on "Worklink" to search for jobs by area of study, location, or job type in the Campus Worklink database.

Online Career Center Canada

http://www.occ.com/occ/Canada.html

Positionwatch Information Technology Employment Network

http://www.positionwatch.com/

Positionwatch is an information technology job site. Search by keyword or check the employer list for vacancies.

Public Service Commission of Canada

http://www.psc-cfp.gc.ca

Search here for jobs with the Canadian federal government.

Strategis

http://strategis.ic.gc.ca/

Strategis is a full-service business information resource. Locate business information by sector, or get information about starting a small business or laws related to investing in

Canada. Find out about individual companies or link to some job sites. You'll also find consumer information and learn the latest business news.

Sympatico

http://www.sympatico.ca/

Choose the closest mirror site in French or English, and then check out this Canadian guide to news and information. You'll find a focus on general business information, links to business-related discussion groups, and some great career articles.

Ward and Associates

http://www.ward-associates.com/

Ward provides a good resource for information technology jobs. You can search for jobs by location, job category, salary, or operating platform; or register to be notified of new openings automatically. Ward also provides some career information, related links, and a listing of upcoming events that might be of interest.

WorkWeb: Canada's On-Line Campus Career Centre

http://www.cacee.com/

Sponsored by the Canadian Association of Career Educators and Employers (CACEE), a partnership between Career Centre personnel and employer recruiters from across Canada, the WorkWeb provides tips for job searching and resume writing along with other career resources. You'll also find a listing of upcoming career fairs and other information helpful to educators, employers, students, and recent graduates.

Yahoo! Canada

http://www.yahoo.ca/

Youth Resource Network of Canada

http://www.youth.gc.ca/

Created to help prepare young people for the workplace and the job hunt, the network is a partnership between several agencies of the Canadian government and the private sector. The network provides self-assessment tools and career resources, along with job opportunities and resources for starting your own business.

Alberta

Calgary Free-Net

http://www.freenet.calgary.ab.ca/home.shtml

Click on the community pages to get down to the business and education directories. The Employment Opportunities section features hundreds of job-related links.

Job Search Tip: Don't Forget the Freenets! Canada has several great Freenets that have been established all over the country. Use Peter Scott's HYTELNET (another great Canadian product at *http://library.usask.ca/hytelnet*) to find them and put them to good use! Look for "business" or similar headings.

Career and Placement Services (CAPS)

http://www.ualberta.ca/~caps/homepage.htm

The University of Alberta maintains this resource that includes an Electronic Job Bank with listings in various fields throughout Canada. It also features career and job search counseling and information on career fairs.

Edmonton FreeNet

http://freenet.edmonton.ab.ca/

Check out the business listings for information about local companies. Look at the government and education sections for more information about helpful services. You'll find the job postings under the Careers and Employment section.

Government of Alberta Home Page

http://www.gov.ab.ca

This site lists government jobs for the province of Alberta. It provides a link to the Labour Department page with information on the laws that govern many Canadian professions. The Jobs Board includes information on how to apply for a position and additional information on the governmental units so that you can research the jobs before applying for them.

British Columbia

BC Ministry of Employment and Investment

http://www.ei.gov.bc.ca/

The ministry is considered the lead agency for economic development and job creation in British Columbia. Click on the Job Postings to link to hundreds of jobs searchable by region or classification.

Bridge Information Technology Inc.

http://www.bridgerecruit.com/index.cfm

Located in and serving the Vancouver area, this company has been working since 1991 to assist organizations in finding software engineers, developers, project managers, business analysts, network administrators, and technical writers for contracting/consulting assignments. Bridge features a skills bank that is matched against opportunities in the information technology field. Search the current job listings for a position. Register your skills profile and receive a periodical newsletter via e-mail featuring emerging trends and career advice.

Greater Victoria Chamber of Commerce

http://www.chamber.victoria.bc.ca/chamber/

Search the business database by keyword or browse through the menu for information about local companies.

The Parksville-Qualicum Career Centre

http://www.island.net/~careers/

The Career Centre provides links to local and national job postings, career planning resources, self-assessment tools, and information on the local labor market. Immigration information and links to government and educational resources are all just a click away.

Prince George Free-Net

telnet://frodo.pgfn.bc.ca
Login: guest

The business and employment section has numerous links to resources for Canadian jobs. The Employment Centre provides a daily update of job listings. Guest login is limited to 30 minutes. The Free-Net web page at *http://www.mag-net.com/freenet/* gives more detailed information for logging on and becoming a member.

Vancouver CommunityNet

http://www.vcn.bc.ca

Check the Community Information pages for education and business resources. Find the job and career information in the Employment and Labour section.

Victoria Telecommunity Network

http://freenet.victoria.bc.ca

The Gateway to Victoria link provides information about many of the area businesses. Also check the education links for helpful information.

Manitoba

Blue Sky Community Networks

http://www.freenet.mb.ca

The Resource Centre has information on local businesses and links to dozens of Internet job sites.

Manitoba Government Home Page

http://www.gov.mb.ca/

Click on the Department of Industry link to find helpful business information, including the Manitoba Companies Database. The Business Database is searchable by sector, by market, and by name of a particular business. You can reach the list of current job listings by clicking on the Employment Opportunities menu item.

Ontario

Halinet (formerly Halton Community Network)

http://www.hhpl.on.ca/

Check out the business, government, and education information available on the community network. The Job Search Resources are nicely annotated and provide links to several good employment sites.

Internet Employment Cafe

http://cafe.sdc.uwo.ca/low/iecmain.html

The Internet Employment Cafe is a division of the University of Western Ontario's Student Development Centre. It features career resources, job postings, and other information of interest to students, alumni, and other job seekers in the area. The listings highlight positions on campus and in numerous towns and cities across Canada, but the majority of jobs are in the province of Ontario.

Internet Job Links

http://www.the-beaches.com/empl.html

This site provides links to Toronto-area, Canadian, and U.S. job and career sites. Other "hot buttons" link to classified ads, professional services, and community information.

kingston.jobs

This newsgroup covers jobs in Kingston.

kw.jobs

This is a newsgroup for jobs in Kitchener-Waterloo.

Niagara's Electronic Village

http://www.npiec.on.ca/
Telnet://freenet.npiec.on.ca
Login: guest

Search this website using keywords or get contact information for the local Job Finders Club. At present, the Telnet menu leads to more helpful information, although the Village appears to be in the process of migrating to the Web. Guests have a 15-minute time limit on the Telnet connection.

ont.jobs

This newsgroup is for jobs in Ontario.

ott.jobs

This newsgroup has jobs in Ottawa.

Sheridan College Career Centre Online!

http://www.sheridan.on.ca/career/home.htm

Sheridan provides a number of career resources for choosing or reevaluating your career, researching a career, or searching for a job. Sheridan also links to resume posting sites and major universities in the area. For access to hundreds of jobs, just click on the job search section.

tor.jobs

This newsgroup covers jobs in Toronto.

Toronto Free-Net, Inc.

http://www.freenet.toronto.on.ca/

Click on the section marked Community and that will lead you to a nice selection of job links. Toronto Free-Net also has a large number of business and economic development resources.

Quebec

qc.jobs

This is the newsgroup for jobs in Quebec.

Latin America and South America

GlobalNet Markets

http://www.bolsadetrabajo.com/main.htm

Latin American employment information is here, most of it in Spanish.

Online Career Center Central America

http://www.occ.com/occ/CentralAmerica.html

Online Career Center Mexico (in English)

http://www.occ.com/occ/Mexico.html

Online Career Center Mexico (in Spanish)

http://www.occ.com/mx/

Online Career Center South America

http://www.occ.com/occ/SouthAmerica.html

Western Europe

REGIONAL RESOURCES

Online Career Center Europe

http://www.occ.com/occ/Europe.html

FRANCE AND BELGIUM

Association Bernard Gregory

http://abg.grenet.fr/abg/

Check here for job listings for scientists in France and other material of interest to the profession. All listings are in French.

CareerMosaic France

http://www.careermosaic.tm.fr/

fr.jobs.off-res

fr.jobs.demandes

fr.jobs.d

These newsgroups discuss job hunting in France.

FROGJOBS—Employment in France

To subscribe: listproc@cren.org
Message: subscribe frogjobs yourname

The French Scientific Mission in Washington sponsors FROGJOBS. This mailing list is intended to help young French scientists pursuing a Ph.D. or postdoctorates abroad prepare for their professional return to France or Europe by providing complete information on scientific employment, job opportunities, and contacts in public and private research centers.

Creyf's

http://www.creyfs.be/

Creyf recruits for technical and engineering personnel in Belgium. Ads are in English, French, and Nederlands, although the English section is still under development. For more information, send e-mail to *creyfs@creyfs.be.*

FDAssociates

http://www.pratique.fr/pro/FDAssociates/

FDAssociates is a recruiter for high-tech positions in France.

Prospective Management Overseas (PMO)

http://www.pmo.be/home.htm

Good news for Belgians—PMO, an overseas construction and technical projects consultant, is urgently in need of employees. Visit the site for the details.

Réseau Européen pour l'Emploi

http://www.reseau.org/emploi/

You'll find many job listings at this site. Submit your resume or curriculum vitae and check out the list of online recruiters for France.

Yahoo! France

http://www.yahoo.fr/

GERMANY AND AUSTRIA

at.jobs

This newsgroup covers jobs in Austria.

bln.jobs

This newsgroup covers jobs in Berlin and the surrounding area.

Breitbach & Partner

http://www.breitbach.com/

Breitboch & Partner provides a brief description of opportunities in Germany (in German).

de.markt.jobs

This newsgroup is for jobs in Germany.

Yahoo! Germany

http://www.yahoo.de/

IRELAND

ie.jobs

This newsgroup has jobs in Ireland.

Irish Jobs Page

http://www.exp.ie/

Search the Jobs Page in either of the databases: one for information technology, the other for the nontechnical positions. Check out the company vacancies or link to the recruiters' page. Register to have the newest job postings sent to you as they come in. You can also link to the Australia Jobs Page, or look at teaching and engineering jobs exclusively. For more information send e-mail to *info@exp.ie.*

NETHERLANDS

Headhunters

http://www.xs4all.nl/~avotek/

Avotek offers several guides to the European job market, including listings of recruiters in various fields (Recruiters Network) and links to international jobs. Try the fast, free IQ test or one of the other personality tests available on the site. Contact Avotek for more information about anything listed in the site via e-mail at *avotek@tip.nl.*

SWITZERLAND

Nexus Job Index

http://www.nexus.ch/

Search for jobs in the Nexus database, look at information on industry, or link to related sites.

SwissWebJobs

http://www.swisswebjobs.ch/

You guessed it, a site for jobs in Switzerland! It includes links to hundreds of job listings, employers, recruiters, and other career resources. This site is mostly in German.

TeleJob

http://www.telejob.ethz.ch

TeleJob is the electronic job exchange board for the Association of Assistants and Doctoral Students of the technological institutes of Zurich (AVETH) and Lausanne (ACIDE). There are plenty of interesting jobs for young academics interested in academe or the business world. The home page is in English, but many job positions are not. For more information, send e-mail to *telejob@aveth.ethz.ch*.

UNITED KINGDOM

The British Council

http://www.britcoun.org/eis/

The British Council's Education Information Service provides a very helpful FAQ page for students working in Britain.

CareerMosaic UK

http://www.careermosaic-uk.co.uk/

EMAP Media Web

http://main.emap.com/media/

Check out the Euroguide Online for service and facility providers or look through the online recruitment service. For more information, send e-mail to *webmaster@media.emap.co.uk*.

Job.net

http://www2.vnu.co.uk/jobnet/

This site is sponsored by VNU Business Publishers. Search by keywords in the assignment listings or by choosing an agency and looking at its listings. Each assignment has very extensive listings and good information. Additional information on contract work and services is also available. Register your profile to make it easier to search or to have the job postings e-mailed to you.

JobServe

http://www.demon.co.uk/jobserve/

JobServe is one of the largest sources of information technology jobs in the United Kingdom. Although the majority of listings are in the United Kingdom and neighboring countries, several other international and U.S. opportunities were listed here at the time of review. In its fourth year, the award-winning job site (1997 Excellence in the Electronic Recruiting Industry) is updated daily, with thousands of new listings each month. The e-mail newsletter can be filtered to your specifications. Listings can be viewed by agency, contract versus permanent positions, and what was added on that day. You can subscribe to the e-mail version of the newsletter at *subscribe@jobserve.com,* and have the option of receiving only the job listings you're interested in.

M & M Recruitment Limited

http://www.mmstaff.co.uk/

Based in the United Kingdom, M & M provides technical recruitment services for the engineering and information technology markets. The jobs posted include many that are international.

NISS, National Information Services and Systems

http://www.niss.ac.uk/noticeboard/index.html

The NISS provides access to employment opportunities at universities in the Commonwealth countries (the United Kingdom, Canada, Australia, etc.). Several disciplines are listed here, with links to more resources.

Price Jamieson Online

http://www.pricejam.com/

This U.K. recruiting agency lists jobs in marketing, media, and communications. The listings include title, a brief description, and salary, and there are entry-level positions here. You can register your resume, or register to have only the job postings that are relevant sent to you.

Reed Personnel Services

http://www.reed.co.uk/

Register your skills at no cost at this site, which features jobs in a variety of fields. Check out the regional salary calculator for the United Kingdom or the Company Factfiles. Note: For those not used to reading international dates, remember that the month and day are reversed, so 2/10/98 is October 2, 1998.

taps.com

http://www.taps.co.uk

Taps features hundreds of jobs, many in the information technology field. Choose either permanent jobs or contract positions, then search by keyword or skill. You can submit your curriculum vitae or resume and apply for advertised positions online. E-mail *suzy@taps.com* for additional information.

THESIS: The Times Higher Education Supplement InterView Service

http://www.thesis.co.uk

The THESIS service is the fastest way to find jobs in higher education. Jobs are updated every Tuesday at 3 P.M., with the ads booked to appear in the following Friday's print edition of *The Times Higher Education Supplement.* THESIS carries lists from all categories of higher-education job vacancies worldwide as advertised in *The Times.* Jobs are sorted into U.K. or international groups and then sorted by their classification type, that is, lecturers and tutors, principal/senior lecturers, professors, and readers and chairs. Listings are retained for about one month or until filled, whichever comes first. This is a great resource for U.K. educational postings. You do not need to be a subscriber to the print version of *The Times Higher Education Supplement* to register to access the new THESIS site.

Work MadeEasy

http://work.madeeasy.com/

Primarily a U.K. site, Work MadeEasy (WME) includes some international listings as well. Postings are taken from uk.jobs.offered as well as from agencies listing with them. Search by skills, roles (job titles), or geographic location, or look through the industry sector menu for jobs in your field. A nice feature is the address list of all agencies in the United Kingdom.

Eastern Europe

REGIONAL RESOURCES

Eastern and Central European Job Bank

http://www.ecejobbank.com

Browse the job listings for many countries in Central and Eastern Europe. Sponsored by ScalaECE, a free resume bank is included, but you must register for a password before being allowed to post your resume.

RUSSIA

relcom.commerce.jobs

This newsgroup has job postings for Russia and other Eastern European countries.

Russian and East European Institute Employment Opportunities

http://www.indiana.edu/~reeiweb/indemp.html

A service of Indiana University, the institute's up-to-date listings cover many fields for people who are seeking employment in Russia or Eastern Europe, or for individuals who have expertise in the languages, history, or cultures of these areas. When postings are removed from the list, they are stored in the archives, accessible through the web page, and filed by company name.

The Russian Word, Inc.

http://www.russianword.com/

The Russian Word, Inc. (RWI) is a Russian-language service provider that specializes in translation, language instruction, and other services. It is looking for translators, interpreters, Russian-language instructors, and other language professionals to add to its database. The site has provided links to other Russian sites that could be helpful. Send e-mail to *rwi@exo.com*.

Scandinavia

REGIONAL RESOURCES

Online Career Center Scandinavia

http://www.occ.com/occ/Scandinavia.html

DENMARK

dk.jobs

This newsgroup lists jobs in Denmark.

SWEDEN

swnet.jobs

This newsgroup covers jobs in Sweden.

Africa and the Middle East

AFRICA

Online Career Center Africa

http://www.occ.com/occ/Africa.html

SOUTH AFRICA

Hampton Consultancy

http://www.hampton.co.za/

Based in South Africa, Hampton Consultancy includes information technology jobs from all over the world. Check the list of international opportunities.

The Personnel Concept

http://www.web.co.za/p-concept/

Look here for engineering, finance, and computing work in South Africa.

za.ads.jobs

This newsgroup lists jobs in South Africa.

ISRAEL AND THE MIDDLE EAST

AACI Israel Jobnet

http://192.116.74.141/images/weleng.htm

The Association of Americans and Canadians in Israel (AACI) brings you this online service with the financial help of the Ministry of Science and The Samis Foundation. Updated daily by the staff and human resource departments all over Israel, the site is searchable by position, company name, or geographic area; or look at only those jobs that have come in within the last 72 hours. Click "help" to get assistance with reading Hebrew online. The "job basket" feature allows you to mark all the positions you're interested in and print or send them to your e-mail address at the end of your session. For more information, contact *info@jobnet.co.il.*

de Marchel von Bakker Inskip, Ltd.

http://www.dmvbi.com/index.html

This firm specializes in headhunting and recruitment in the information technology field. Click on the "jobs" icon to search for a position. Submit your curriculum vitae or resume free of charge.

israel.jobs.misc
israel.jobs.offered
israel.jobs.resumes

Newsgroups for discussions of employment in Israel.

Online Career Center Middle East

http://www.occ.com/occ/MiddleEast.html

SASIS, Inc.

http://www.sasis.com/main.htm

SASIS provides access to hundreds of international jobs, primarily in the Middle East, specializing in the recruitment of Western personnel for contract positions. Search the jobs database or check out related links. Send e-mail to *Sasis@cncnet.com*.

Asia and the Pacific Rim

REGIONAL RESOURCES

Asianet

http://www.asia-net.com

Asianet provides current job postings for professionals who speak English and Chinese, Japanese, or Korean. You can search the job database or register to receive job updates via e-mail. For more information contact *sales@asia-net.com*.

Asia Online!

http://www.asiadragons.com/asia/asiawork/asiawork.htm

The Asia Work Station provides access to job opportunities throughout Asia. Search by geographical location or post your resume free. Employers can search resumes or submit job postings. Asia Online! also has directories for educational, governmental, and cultural resources.

CareerMosaic Asia

http://www.careerasia.com.sg/index.html

Online Career Center Asia

http://www.occ.com/Asia.html

TKO Personnel, Inc

http://www.tkointl.com/

TKO recruits for technical positions and companies in Asia, Japan, and the Pacific Rim region. It has recently expanded to include some U.S. technical jobs. Click on the world map for the job opportunities in the region you're interested in. For more information, call TKO at (408) 453-9000.

Yahoo! Asia

http://www.yahoo.com.sg/

AUSTRALIA

AK Jobnet, Austin Knight Company

http://www.ak.com.au/akjobnet.html

With an excellent listing of job opportunities in Australia arranged by industry sectors, there is also a section of "blind ads" which protects the identity of both the employer and applicant until such time as they are prepared to meet. The Jobnet also links to many job-related Usenet newsgroups.

aus.jobs
aus.ads.jobs

These newsgroups are for jobs available or wanted in Australia.

CareerMosaic Australia (Employment Opportunities Australia)

http://careermosaic.jobs.com.au/cmaust.html
http://employment.com.au/index.html

Careers Online

http://www.careersonline.com.au/

Careers Online is a full-service career site, which provides links to tips on writing resumes, getting ready for the interview process, and other helpful career resources. Get help choosing a career, visit the Small Business Support Network, or search for a job.

Department of Employment, Education, Training and Youth Affairs

http://www.deetya.gov.au/

Check out the Employment Services Bulletin Board or find what's happening on the Australian job front. Search for a job in the Commonwealth database by territory, state, or occupation. Link to other resources and services helpful to the job seeker or career changer.

employment.net.au

http://www.employment.net.au/

This site links to the job listings of several recruiters and major companies. It features many different job categories.

International Academic Job Market

http://www.camrev.com.au/share/jobs.html

This is the Internet version of the job advertisements in *Campus Review,* a respected and widely circulated weekly newspaper on academe. Jobs are mainly in Australia and New Zealand (with the occasional one from Singapore or Hong Kong), and listings are updated daily with plenty of detail. A useful site for those seeking academic careers, though there are few entry-level positions.

Online Career Center Australia

http://www.occ.com/occ/Australia.html

People Bank

http://www.peoplebank.com.au/

A free service for information technology professionals, who can submit their resumes to a database distributed to agencies and employers throughout Australia and the United Kingdom. The site uses agents to protect the confidentiality of the job seekers registered here. You will need a forms-capable browser to register online. You can also check out the current job listings online. Send e-mail to *pb@peoplebank.com.au.*

Professionals On-Line

http://www.webcom.com/wordimg/pro/

Words & Images maintains this service, which is based in Australia and provides technical opportunities and a free Web presence for computer consultants. It also links to other Australian and U.K. sites and placement services. For more information, contact the service via e-mail (*ian@wordsimages.com.*)

Yahoo! Australia & New Zealand

http://www.yahoo.com.au/

CHINA

Alliance-China Online

http://www.alliance-china.com

Alliance is small but has some major corporations as its clients. Search for jobs in its database or submit your resume. For more information, send e-mail to *Mark.Baldwin@Alliance-China.com.*

Career China

http://www.globalvillager.com/villager/CC.html

Career China provides job postings for work with companies in China, Korea, and beyond. There are a few U.S.-based opportunities also.

China Gold

http://www.chinagold.com/

China Gold is in the process of pulling together links to the "best" websites. Currently, there are links to a few business sites and a couple of helpful job-related sites. Send e-mail to *hta@msn.com.*

Job Market China

http://www.jobchina.net/

Choose to view this site in English or Chinese. Jobs are generally posted for 90 days. Browse through the job ads or post your resume free. You must have an e-mail account to register. If you don't have one, you can get one for a year for a fee from *http://www.keysoft.net.* For more information, send e-mail to *keysoft@jobchina.net.*

INDIA

Naukri

http://www.naukri.com/

Maintained by Info Edge in New Delhi, Naukri is a great job and career site for India. Search for a job, submit your resume, learn more about the larger businesses in India, or link to other helpful sites. For more information, send e-mail to *sbikh@best.com.*

JAPAN, HONG KONG, KOREA, AND MALAYSIA

CareerMosaic Hong Kong

http://www.careermosaic.com.hk/

CareerMosaic Japan

http://www.careermosaic.or.jp/

CareerMosaic Korea

http://www.careermosaickorea.com/

The Gaijin Gleaner

http://kyushu.com/kcentral/

The Gleaner serves the English-speaking expatriates of Kyushu, providing information, news, and commentary about Japan and the experience of being a foreigner living and working there. Join the Kyushu Chat or check out the other links.

Gemini Personnel Group

http://www.gemini.com.hk/

With offices in London, Hong Kong, and Malaysia, Gemini is one of Hong Kong's leading recruiters. Check out the job hunting tips or the salary survey. Click on Current Vacancies to find the jobs.

O-Hayo Sensei, The Newsletter of (English) Teaching Jobs in Japan

http://www.ohayosensei.com/

The biweekly newsletter lists positions in Japan teaching conversation and at public schools, colleges, and universities. Check out the classifieds or the current exchange rates.

NEW ZEALAND

InfoTech Weekly Online JobNet NZ

http://www.jobnetnz.co.nz/

This is a good link to technical jobs, primarily in New Zealand. Eight agencies list jobs here, and this page provides direct links to all of those agencies. Search the database by type of position (permanent or contract), location, agency, date, or description (using keywords). Get there by choosing "jobnet" from the home page.

SINGAPORE

BizLINKS Resources

http://sunflower.singnet.com.sg/~g6615000/

BizLINKS offers job and employment opportunities for Singapore citizens or permanent residents. Submit your curriculum vitae or resume, check out the career resources, or search for a job in the hundreds of listings. For more information, contact *g6615000@singnet.com.sg*.

14 Career Resources Online

One of the truly great features of the Internet is the sharing of information and resources between organizations and the ability for anyone with Internet connectivity to access all of this. This chapter provides a list of sites and resources to assist you with preparing for your job search and with conducting research on an organization before you go in for your interview. Many college and university career centers are making their guides and basic information available on the Internet, and you can benefit from this. There are also a number of great sites with information to help you find out more about the places you are about to apply to or interview with, and the better prepared you are the better you will come across.

Career Counseling

National Board of Certified Counselors

http://www.nbcc.org

The National Board of Certified Counselors (NBCC) is a national certification agency for counselors, including career counselors. Certification from this group or from a local licensing or certification board gives you the assurance that this counselor has met certain professional standards. The NBCC will send you a list of board-certified counselors in your area at no charge.

National Career Development Association

http://www.ncda.org

This is the career counseling arm of the American Counseling Association, a group that has been instrumental in setting professional and ethical standards for the counseling profession. Not all members are certified career counselors, but you can contact the association for assistance in finding someone. The National Career Development Association (NCDA) is also working on a career facilitator certification program to establish training and education standards for career professionals who are not certified counselors. Other resources you can find here include articles on counseling and career choices as well as a paper on what to expect from a career counselor.

International Association of Career Management Professionals

http://www.iacmp.org

The association's membership is made up primarily of career management and outplacement professionals around the world. This website provides links to local job networking groups and other valuable career resources.

Career Exploration and Selection

Most of these sites are links to career resource and counseling centers at colleges and universities, but some other organizations are making great information available to help you with your choice of careers.

America's Career InfoNet

http://www.acinet.org

This new service, sponsored by the U.S. Employment and Training Administration, provides information on hundreds of careers that might interest you. Search by industry to find out what occupations are included, or search by occupations to find out what industries employ them. You can also find national and, in some cases, local information on the job market and average wages for any given occupation.

The Catapult, Career Service Professionals Homepage

http://www.jobweb.org/catapult/catapult.html

The Catapult is the springboard to the frequently visited places of Career Service Professionals and other great souls. The National Association of Colleges and Employers (NACE) maintains the Catapult, which contains more than 200 links to career and employment resources. There is great information to begin researching companies and organizations you might want to check for employment opportunities.

JobWeb, The National Association of Colleges and Employers

http://www.jobweb.org

JobWeb is intended to be "the electronic gateway to career planning and employment information, job-search articles and tips, job listings, and company information for college students, recent graduates, and alumni." There are significant resources for college career services and employment professionals, including career and employment information, training, and services sponsored by the National Association of Colleges and Employers, formerly the College Placement Council. A great resource for researching potential employers.

JobSmart

http://www.jobsmart.org

This site is one of the most comprehensive collections of career guides, salary surveys, hidden job market information, and interactive career guidance. It says "California," but most of the information here is applicable everywhere.

Quintessential Career and Job-Hunting Resources Guide

http://stetson.edu/~rhansen/careers.html

Dr. Randall S. Hansen has produced an award-winning guide to job and career resources for the new college grad and experienced workers.

University of California, Berkeley Career Exploration Links

http://www.berkeley.edu/CareerLibrary/links/careerme.htm

The career center library at the University of California at Berkeley provides a very specific and well-organized set of links to career resources in a large number of occupational fields. The creators are quite proud to say what this site includes— no jobs, just information.

The Definitive Guide to Internet Career Resources

http://phoenix.placement.oakland.edu/career/Guide.htm

Oakland University's guide is a favorite site for those who appreciate a huge alphabetical list of job and career resources.

1st Steps in the Hunt

http://interbiznet.com/hunt/assist.html

Job seekers needing daily advice will want to visit this site frequently. Links to recruiters and tools for career advancement make this a valuable place to visit.

About Work

http://www.aboutwork.com

This site has good advice about success at work and how to solve career problems, provided through daily chat and networking with experts. Check out the Birkman Method Career Style Summary questionnaire if you are not sure of your best career fields.

Career Magazine: Career-Related Links

http://www.careermag.com/db/cmag_careerlinks

Career Magazine maintains an interesting assortment of career resource links as well as articles and job information.

Tripod

http://www.tripod.com

Many sources of helpful advice about careers and what jobs are really like can be found here.

What Color Is Your Parachute: Job Hunting Online

http://www.washingtonpost.com/parachute

Richard Bolles has produced a very attractive and informative guide to help job hunters and career changers find the very best career sites on the Internet.

1998–99 Occupational Outlook Handbook

http://stats.bls.gov/ocohome.htm

You can use keyword searching in this valuable handbook to find out where your interests fit in the top 250 occupations in this country. This is a great source for employment projections as well as for descriptions of all the jobs contained within.

Find Your Career: USNews

http://www4.usnews.com/usnews/edu/beyond/bccguide.htm

USNews has produced one of the most outstanding career guides on the Web. Special features of this guide include expert advice on careers in the greatest demand now and in the future, and links to other sources of career information. You can take the Campbell Interest and Skill Survey and receive a printed evaluation for a small fee.

Princeton Review—So You Want to Get a Career . . .

http://www.review.com/career/index.cfm

The Find-O-Rama Career Search Engine brings together very practical career information about daily life, future outlooks, and organizations to contact.

Getting Past Go: A Survival Guide for College Graduates

http://www.mongen.com/getgo

This colorful site is an easy guide to life after college, including such mundane information as insurance, figuring out where the best jobs are, staying connected after college, and job hunting. Very easy to follow and read, it is sponsored by Monumental General Insurance Group.

Getworking

http://www.getworking.msn.com/getworking/toc/default.htm

At last, there is a modern career guide targeted to twentysomethings and written in their language and style.

Graduate Horizons, Career Information

http://www.gold.net/arcadia/horizons/

This site is an excellent resource for the new graduate seeking work in the United Kingdom and for other information on choosing a career. It can be slow at times, but the information is worth the wait.

Self-Assessment Tests

Sometimes a self-assessment test can help you to understand yourself better, but sometimes it can lead to more questions. You can easily get information on career counselors in your area from the National Board of Certified Counselors (*http://www.nbcc.org*) and the National Career Development Association (*http://www.ncda.org*).

Alt.Psychology.Personality Archives

http://sunsite.unc.edu/personality/

You can view the archives of this newsgroup for the discussion of personality typing systems or use links to actual personality tests on the Web.

Career Interests Game

http://www.missouri.edu/~cppcwww/holland.html

This game is designed to help match your interests and skills with similar careers. The University of Missouri—Columbia has created a separate web page for each of the six different Holland groups: realistic, artistic, investigative, social, enterprising, and conventional.

IQ Tests, Personality Tests, and Entrepreneurial Tests on the Www

http://www.2h.com

This is a great collection of self-assessment tests on the Internet, many of which come from Europe.

Keirsey Temperament Web Site

http://www.keirsey.com/

This is the official website for the test developed by Keirsey and based on the Myers-Briggs Temperament Indicator.

E-Span Career Briefcase—AssessmentTools

http://espan2.espan.com/career/p1/dir/care/asse.htm

E-Span has brought together an excellent collection of links to personality tests on the Internet.

Personality and IQ Tests

http://www.davideck.com/

This site has links to many different IQ and personality tests that give back automatic results. Some of them are just for fun.

The Platinum Rule—Personality Style Quiz

http://www.platinumrule.com/

The Platinum Rule will improve your compatibility with others and help you understand yourself. What is the Platinum Rule? Do unto others as they want you to do unto them!

University of Waterloo Career Services—Career Development Manual

http://www.adm.uwaterloo.ca/infocecs/CRC/manual-home.html

Try this six-step process for career- and life-planning success. The first step is self-assessment, but the other five will take you through the job search process and even choosing which job offer to accept.

Assistance for Writing Resumes, Interviewing, and Other Tasks

More resources are available from the various career counseling and placement services at the Catapult and from JobWeb. Many of the major job banks found in Chapter 4 also offer guidance in these areas.

AAA Resume Service

http://www.infi.net/~resume/

A Greensboro, North Carolina, resume writing firm provides this site. In addition to information about its own services, the site provides great information on interviewing and choosing a resume service, and a weekly "hints and tips" page. Substantial links to additional career services and job sites on the Internet are included.

Owl—Online Writing Lab, Purdue University

http://owl.trc.purdue.edu/

This online information resource was set up to help with writing all types of documents. The various guides answer questions on grammar, punctuation, and citations, as well as offer assistance with writing styles and formats for reports, articles, cover letters, and resumes.

Acorn Career Counseling and Resume Writing

http://www.acornresume.com

This site, operated by Fred Nagle, offers great advice on preparing resumes.

Rebecca Smith's eResumes & Resources

http://www.eresumes.com/

Learn about posting online resumes and choosing the best format for you with the help of the author of *Resumes! Resumes! Resumes!*

Resumania On-line

http://www.umn.edu/ohr/ecep/resume

The University of Minnesota has produced this interactive workbook to help you with resume writing.

Resumix

http://www.resumix.com

Resumix is one of the leaders in developing resume management systems. Their site includes excellent advice on creating a resume that scans well for these systems.

Information on Returning to School

Sometimes your best career move is more education.

Comprehensive College Financing Information

http//www.infi.net/collegemoney/

This site has information on getting funding for college. Although it is an advertisement for one bank, the information on figuring interest rates and payment schedules is helpful to anyone.

FinAid, The Financial Aid Information Page

http://www.finaid.org

Sponsored by the National Association of Student Financial Aid Administrators (NASFAA), this is a gold mine of information and resources for sources of aid (traditional and nontraditional), calculators for figuring out your debt load and payback, and scam alerts.

Peterson's Education Center

http://www.petersons.com/

Peterson's is the well-known publisher of guides to colleges. Now the company is taking this information online. This is a great resource for information on undergraduate and graduate programs, as well as summer work, and Peterson's has included sections on professional training and long-distance education programs.

Resources for Researching Potential Employers

The resources in Chapter 3 can also help you locate information in this area. In addition, The Riley Guide has extensive links for researching and targeting employers at *http://www.dbm.com/jobguide/*.

Hoover's Online

http://www.hoovers.com

Hoover's, the well-respected publisher of business almanacs, gives visitors to its website a lot of information on over 10,000 companies. Additional links expand this information even further.

Business Researcher's Interests

http://www.brint.com/interests.html

This is a huge guide to business research resources available on the Internet.

CompanyLink

http://www.companylink.com

CompanyLink has a searchable database of over 65,000 companies. Search by name, industry, location, or ticker symbol. News highlights from many industries are included. The free information includes phone and fax numbers, web page and e-mail address (if available) and a short profile.

Information on Relocating

Every week, the *National Business Employment Weekly* (*http://www.nbew.com*) and *ComputerWorld* (*http://www.computerworld.com*) provide articles on various locations including cost-of-living data. These publications can be found in most public and college libraries, or they offer reprints on their websites. *The Riley Guide* (*http://www.dbm.com/jobguide/*) includes a section on relocation resources, including online telephone directories and maps. The new America's Career InfoNet (*http://www.acinet.org*) is also filled with this information along with links to more services and resources.

CityNet

http://www.city.net

CityNet has listings of information and links to servers in over 113 countries. This is a great way to research locations you are considering moving to or places where you have been offered employment.

State and Local Government on the Net

http://www.piperinfo.com/state/states.html

This extensive guide links to official state and local government resources for the United States and many territories. From here you can find all kinds of helpful information on the various locations you are interested in.

State Occupational Projections, 1994–2005

http://udesc.state.ut.us/almis/stateproj/

This site is filled with labor market information (LMI) from the 50 states. What is LMI? It is the statistics on employment, wages, industries, and other factors affecting the world of work. Although you can view national averages at the Bureau of Labor Statistics (*http://www.bls.gov*), it is best to get the local information for the specific area in which you are interested. This will be a better marker and more valuable to your decision.

Chamber of Commerce International Directory

http://chamber-of-commerce.com

This is the International Chamber of Commerce and City-State-Province Directory. Search the worldwide or the city-state directory.

Employment Directory of American Markets

http://www.careermosaic.com/cm/directory/edl.html

A publication of Bernard Hodes, Inc., CareerMosaic includes this directory of data on "The Top 50 U.S. Markets," "The Top 10 Canadian Markets," and the consumer price index (CPI) in its webserver. This is a great way to check the availability of talent in a given market and to see what major industries are prevalent there.

Working and Living Overseas

http://www.magi.com/~issi

Put together by Jean-Marc Hachey, author of *The Canadian Guide to Working and Living Overseas,* this site says it's a guide for Canadians, but anyone who is considering a move to another country should look it over carefully. It is a clear and concise set of questions and leads for making your move a better one.

Support Groups

Every issue of the *National Business Employment Weekly* has a list of job-search support groups from around the country with contact information for each. Check your local library or career service center for copies.

Career Resource Center

http://www.careers.org/

Career Resource Center claims to be the Internet's most extensive index of career-related websites (over 7,500 links).

Forty Plus of Northern California

http://www.fortyplus.org

Forty Plus of Northern California is a nonprofit self-help group of executives and professionals over 40 who are currently in career transition. There is a fee to use this service.

Resources for Persons with Disabilities from The Catapult

http://www.jobweb.org/catapult/DISABLED.htm

A great collection of links to information resources and employment resources for the disabled, many of these sites include links to legal information, assistive technologies, and support groups, as well as job opportunities.

Careers On-Line at the University of Minnesota

http://disserv3.stu.umn.edu/COL/

Careers On-Line provides local job listings for people with disabilities and valuable links to national disability resources.

President's Committee on Employment of People with Disabilities

http://www.pcebd.gov

This committee has been formed "to facilitate the communication, coordination and promotion of public and private efforts to enhance the employment of people with disabilities." There is terrific information for employers and job seekers.

Women's Wire

http://www.women.com

This site is a great resource for women, including surveys on the best employers.

WWWomen

http://www.wwwomen.com

This is a subject directory similar to the Yahoo! model and is a good place for links to information by and for women and minorities. It includes many career-related sites.

Services for the Experienced Job Seeker

In the work we've done with job seekers, we've found that many do not understand some services of the career industry, particularly those geared to the older, more experienced professional. You may not be sure what these services do, when you *could* be using them, how you *should* be using them, and for what. This appendix is here to give you some ideas, improve your understanding of these services, and allow you to make better decisions in your search for employment.

Executive Search

Most people are familiar with the slang term *headhunter,* but what do these executive search firms and consultants do, and where do they fit into the job search? You may think of recruiters as organizations and people who work to find candidates for jobs, but that is also what an executive search consultant does. What is the difference? They are both recruiters, but it is the *process* of matching employees to the employer and the type of contract with the client that differentiates them. Marcia Fawcett, a search consultant, explains: "Some recruiters work on contingency, but as an executive search consultant, I work on retainer. This means I receive payments for professional services rendered. Working on contingency means you are paid for your services only if you fill a position for the employer." Fawcett is principal of The Fawcett Group, a retained executive search firm that consults for organizations on the "fit-factor" of people within positions and positions within organizations. Her work includes a very intensive search process on behalf of her clients, the goal being to find the ideal employee for the job, presenting only three candidates—the "best of the best."

The difference in payment terms that Fawcett noted defines the way in which recruiters search for appropriate candidates. According to Marcia, "Contingency recruiters collect large numbers of resumes and hold them in a database so they can identify potential candidates for a client quickly." When a client calls with an opening, the contingency recruiter searches the database, looks over what has been retrieved, checks with the candidates, and refers the best resumes to the client in the hope that one will be a good fit with the position the client has in mind.

The amount of consulting with the client is limited, but the search is probably not exclusive to one agency either. Some companies will have several contingency recruiters working to fill the same position. "Retained search consultants like myself work on an exclusive basis with the client to identify the ideal candidate," says Fawcett. "We research the job requirements and work with the client to clearly identify the specific skills and features they are looking for in the candidate. We even examine the work environment and culture of the client company, as well as the collective and individual personalities of the management team. Our goal is to find the best candidate not just in terms of skills, but also in terms of personality so the match is successful."

Once the search consultant has the candidate specifications prepared, he or she then creates the search strategy and works to identify where these ideal candidates might be reached. He or she collects resumes of those persons identified as candidates and not only examines the references they provide, but tracks down even more references through personal networks of people who have known and worked with the candidate in the past. The search consultant then makes the final decision and forwards the agreed-on number of candidates to the client, generally three or four people, or "the real top choices. It takes more time than searching a database, but the whole idea is the fit of the candidate and the success of the match."

Because of the complexity and cost of the search process, this method of recruiting for an organization is usually reserved for senior management or executive staff employees, hence the term *executive search*. As Fawcett notes, "I am primarily looking for candidates with more than 15 years experience in the field and who are commanding a salary around $100,000 or higher." Very few people, particularly those who have recently graduated from school, have this kind of experience. Entry-level folks are not among the pool in which the retained executive search consultant is looking. These job seekers and those with less than 10 years experience are more in the realm of the contingency recruiter. It isn't worth forwarding your resume to executive search consultants in case something comes up at a later time. Most consultants will glance over it, but if it does not meet any of their current search criteria, it is very unlikely it will be retained.

Perhaps you are someone who meets the broad criteria of the "executive," and you are interested in making a change. How do you get your resume where the executive search firms will find you? You might consider mailing a cover letter and resume to some executive search firms to get your name added to their lists of potential candidates, but don't expect a lot from this. According to Fawcett, "Some executive search firms will retain resumes of select, highly qualified candidates, but the smaller firms don't have the time and money to maintain many records. I do keep resumes of candidates I have identified in the past who have made a positive impression that I might want to approach again."

So, how does someone become a potential candidate? The best way to get your name into the executive search arena is to target search firms that specialize in recruiting for your industry and functional field. You might want to identify a few of the larger firms for contact also. How do you identify the good firms? By recommendation. Ask your friends, colleagues, and former employers about firms they have had contact with. Ask them if they have had any experience with a firm and what the quality of service was. If they actually have the name of someone in a firm, contact him or her directly with a cover letter and resume, and use the name of your mutual contact.

Once you've identified the agencies to which you want to submit your resume, prepare your cover letter carefully. Note your interests, geographic preferences, strengths, and pay scale. This letter must summarize you and your employment interests in order to catch the eye of the search consultant. Enclose your resume, and then go about your usual business.

Don't expect a phone call or a face-to-face meeting, and don't call to ask if the letter and resume were received. Fawcett says, "If you are someone I want to talk to right now, I will contact you. Otherwise, your letter and resume will be filed until I have need for them." Don't call and ask for comments on your resume. That type of request doesn't reflect well on you, and it really isn't the role of the search consultant to advise you unless he or she is contacting you about a specific search. In that case, you may be given pointers to help tighten up your resume to match the job specifications.

At all levels, the resume is a very important tool for your job search. You must have a well-prepared resume that should be tailored to the job position being applied for. Move away from just listing your job responsibilities and list your accomplishments instead, particularly what problems you've solved. Fawcett's advice: "We refer to it as the PAR resume— what *problem* was addressed, what *action* was taken to resolve it, and what was the *result*. Employers are looking for problem solvers, and this gives them the information they want along with some indication of how you could contribute to their organization."

Two terms keep appearing in this discussion, the *client* and the *candidate*. The definitions of these terms may surprise you. The client is the organization that contracts or retains the services of the search firm. The client pays all fees associated with the search. You, the job seeker, are the candidate. As the candidate, should you be paying fees to these recruiting firms? *Never*. The days when you would go into an employment agency, pay a fee, and have the staff find a job for you are really gone. The employers are the ones paying the fees now for both retained and contingency searches.

Additional reading and research on recruiting can help you decide both how to approach these firms and what to expect in response to your approach. *The Directory of Executive Recruiters* from Kennedy Publications is a great source of information on both retained and contingency recruiting. In addition to the listings of agencies, the directory opens with several good articles about executive search, what it is, how to use it, and what to look for. Another book for the executive job seeker is *Rites of Passage at $100,000+* by John Lucht. This unique book is geared for the executive job seeker, offering ideas and strategies to approach the executive job search. *The National Business Employment Weekly* (*http://www.nbew.com*) is also an excellent source of information on all aspects of the executive job search and should be read on a regular basis for informative articles and tips to improve your search. If you read all of these publications, plus others that are recommended by the job and career information services librarian in your local public library, you should have little problem setting up and successfully planning your search.

Outplacement

Unless you have been offered outplacement when dismissed from a job, you are probably not familiar with it. In fact, many who have been offered outplacement still have no idea what it is! *Outplacement* is an assistance service for persons leaving an organization to help prepare them for their job search. This idea began in the 1960s as a benefit for senior executives, but it has gradually spread to lower-level employees.

Dr. Laurence J. Stybel stresses the true role of the outplacement consultant: "Outplacement consultants do not find you a job. We work with you to prepare you for the job search, helping you to develop the edge which will help you compete effectively for new employment." Stybel is president of Stybel Peabody/Lincolnshire of Boston, an outplacement and career management firm assisting corporate clients with their executive transitions. He also points out that the keyword in his statement is *you*. The outplacement consultants will not write your resumes, set up your appointments, nor establish your networking connections. They work with you to help you do this for yourself, offering guidance in making decisions and assistance in establishing your search, contact, and interview techniques. But all of the effort is yours and yours alone.

There are three parts to outplacement services:

1. They provide administrative support in the form of office services and work space. You should have a work area and access to a photocopier, a telephone, and a fax machine. A reference library should be available for your use as a part of your job search.

2. They provide psychological support to help you clarify your values, your goals, and even the direction you want to take at this time. As Stybel notes, "Losing your job is a traumatic experience, not just for you, but for your family. Your outplacement consultant can help you and your spouse work through this period and begin the adjustment to unemployment and the job search."

3. They provide marketing assistance and guidance, helping you to position yourself in a way that distinguishes you from all other candidates and improves your chances of gaining new employment quickly.

According to Stybel, "Different firms are stronger in some of these areas than in others, so you want to see where a firm stacks up and decide what mix of these three pieces will work best for you."

Outplacement firms identify themselves as either corporate sponsored or retail, meaning they work on contract with an organization or they are available for you to contract their services privately. Is one better than the other? If you are given notice of your dismissal, should you elect to receive outplacement through an agency hired by your company, or should you take the money to purchase your own outplacement services? Stybel advises, "Take the corporate-sponsored outplacement services. This actually saves you money. If you take the payment from the company, you will have to pay taxes on it and then purchase your outplacement support. You will not be able to write off the expenses of your job search on your tax forms until they equal 3 percent of your gross income. That is a lot of money, and few of us actually meet that requirement. The quality of the outplacement service offered through the company will probably be better than what you can purchase on your own. Human resources professionals talk to each other, and if an outplacement firm is not doing a good job, the word will get around."

You need to know what level of outplacement is being offered to you, full service or limited. Stybel explains, "Full service outplacement means the agency and the company are committed to providing support to an outcome, usually meaning new employment. Limited service means we are committed for a specific period of time, anywhere from one month to a year, regardless of your situation."

Although the outplacement firms identify themselves as corporate sponsored or retail, you need to be aware that there are also two more classifications for outplacement firms in the market today, those who specialize in consulting and those who specialize in training. "The skills in each firm are different," says Stybel. "The training firms will have well-designed programs which are implemented in a consistent manner. The idea can be easily replicated and is useful for large numbers of displaced employees. The consulting firms work to customize the outplacement process to each individual. One approach may work better for you, so you want to be able to choose between them if you can."

What if your organization doesn't offer you outplacement as a part of your severance package? Stybel advises, "Ask for it. Whom should you ask? Human resources would seem to be the most logical choice, but they are not the right people. They are the champions of corporate policy. Any allowance for you may suggest a precedent in policy. The best person to approach to ask for outplacement is the boss who fired you. He or she will be the most receptive to your request although he or she will be the most difficult person to approach. Why will former bosses be so receptive? Guilt has a lot to do with it. They may even arrange to pay for the outplacement from their own budget. This then sets a precedent in the organization and lets them request outplacement if they should be let go. Former bosses actually may not care about you finding new work, but providing support for you will look good to the remaining employees. It's also a recruiting tool, providing assurance to new employees that they will also be supported if they should be let go."

When you discuss outplacement with your employer, there are certain questions you should ask:

- **"Will you receive limited or full-service outplacement?** If possible, you want to push for full-service outplacement.
- **Can you meet with the expected counselor?** You want to be sure that you can work with this person and that he or she can help you. Ask for a choice of agencies, and then ask your employer or the human resources department to recommend two or three."

Finally, if your needs cannot or will not be met by the contracted service, Stybel says, "rattle the cages. Request a new consultant, a new agency, anything you need to assist you at this time." Even if you have received outplacement in the past, request it again. "Don't evaluate an outplacement firm based on your last experience. If last time you worked with a training firm, try for a consulting firm this time." As with any professional service, this is a very personal decision and only you can say what works and does not work for you.

You have been offered outplacement by your organization, and you are meeting with agencies to select the one you will work with. The place looks good, the administrative services look great, but what else should you be looking for to help you make your final decision?

• If you are meeting with the marketing manager for the agency, all you are probably hearing is how great it is. Get past this person and ask to meet the counselor you will be working with. This is the person you will be relying on, not the marketing agent.
• You've met with the counselor, and he or she has an obsessive reliance on networking. "Be on guard," advised Stybel. "For some people this is the most effective technique to a new job, but it is also the least expensive. If you are shy, it may not work for you at all. It should be only one tool in your job search, not the only tool."
• You're meeting with your counselor, and he or she tells you to sit back, relax, and let him or her search the database with its access to the hidden job market. The job market is not in a database and it is not in the counselor's control. It is in your best interests to avoid falling into this trap of complacency and to maintain control of your job search.

Before you make your final choice of outplacement agencies, request the names of other candidates they are currently working with whose cases are similar to yours. Speak with these people and get their impressions of the agency and how it is supporting them.

Stybel suggests asking if the outplacement firm is a member of the Association of Outplacement Consulting Firms International. "This is not an exclusive association, and it is not a guarantee of quality, but the firms who are members have met a certain set of minimum standards which have been established by the association. If a firm is not a member, then what does this say about their commitment to the profession? Anyone can call himself an outplacement consultant or a career counselor, but membership in the association indicates a certain level of dedication to the profession." Another association that many outplacement consultants and smaller firms belong to is the International Association of Career Management Professionals. The individual members agree to uphold a code of ethics in their work with the client and the candidate.

More information on outplacement is readily available. *The Directory of Outplacement Firms* from Kennedy Publications is a good resource for locating firms and includes general information on the industry as well. *The National Business Employment Weekly* (*http://www.nbew.com*) frequently carries good articles about outplacement services, and the new Careers, Not Just Jobs section of the *Wall Street Journal Interactive* can also be a good source of information (*http://careers.wsj.com*). Stybel and his partner, Maryanne Peabody, have authored several articles on outplacement services and were named the Best Outplacement Firm by *The Massachusetts Lawyers' Weekly* Reader Survey for 1996 and again in 1997. You can read many of their articles free of charge on their corporate webserver at *http://www.stybelpeabody.com,* or the reference librarian at your local public library can assist you in locating these articles and many others.

Career Counseling After College

You may have been lucky enough to have the services of career counselors available to you during your college years. You may even have been smart enough to take advantage of these services! Today, most colleges and universities and many high schools have career counseling services for their students. Perhaps you have reached a point in your life where you are thinking about making a change. This might be the time to go back to those career counselors, or to visit them for the first time. But you are no longer enrolled in high school or college. Where do you turn?

While many private counselors are responding to this need for career counseling after college, a number of colleges and universities are also working to meet this demand. Their alumni are returning and asking for assistance, or the community in which they are located is demanding these services. The School of Continuing Studies at Johns Hopkins University established the Career and Life Planning Center under the direction of Kathleen Bovard to work with adults who have job experience and are contemplating making career changes. This office is separate from the career services offered to traditional-age students of the university and serves the continuing education students, the university alumni, and any other attendee who has registered for credit or noncredit courses and either desires or has been forced by circumstances into a change.

What might you expect from a career counselor, especially as an older job seeker? According to Bovard, "Counseling begins with an initial information-gathering meeting between the client and the counselor. We discuss the client's background, establish a plan of action, and set some goals for each session. Career counseling is a very dynamic process. We want to know where our clients, the job seekers, have been, find out some ideas as to where they might like to move, and set up a plan of action to keep them moving forward with their career planning. Self-assessment is often the first step in the process. Clients may benefit from taking one or more standardized vocational assessment tools, such as the Strong Interest Inventory or the Campbell Interest and Skill Survey, to help them identify different career options based on their skills and interests. Eventually we lead clients to a point where they can make the decisions necessary to move on with their careers or even to change them."

When Johns Hopkins established this separate career center, it acknowledged the fact that the older person entering career counseling has different needs than the traditional-age college student. "Working with an experienced adult client can be much more complex than advising the typical college student," says Bovard. "There are often personal and family factors, as well as financial demands, that have to be considered now. They have a job history and a career, and if they have recently lost their job, their self-esteem may be low and their anxiety high." Many of the clients working with this office are not in search of resume preparation assistance. "While we help clients write resumes and prepare for job interviews, our primary services are the self-assessment and decision-making processes. We help our clients work through these important steps so they can take the next step in their job search, whether it is to continue searching in their chosen field or to make a change and try something new."

In all of this, Bovard is referring to the client as the person she is working with: "The client is the person who has been laid off or is seeking career guidance. Many companies do not provide career counseling for their displaced employees." If you feel you might need the services of a career counselor, where can you begin looking for help? "If you are a college graduate, call the career center at your college and see if they might be able to help you or refer you to reciprocal services at another college or university close to you," suggests Bovard. "Many colleges and universities may be willing to provide assistance at no cost if they have established a reciprocal relation-ship with your alma mater. Otherwise, call your local colleges, community colleges, and universities. Check with their career centers about providing these services. If they don't, ask if they could recommend someone in the area. You might also contact univer-sity continuing education offices with similar questions. Some community organizations may have career counseling services available too. Check your local phone book for more information about these types of services." The yellow pages in your area will have these services listed under "Career and Vocational Counseling," "Counseling," and "Social Services Agencies."

If you decide to work with a private career counselor, your local phone book may list any number of people calling themselves career counselors. Bovard suggests using the following checkpoints as one way to help evaluate their services. "Ask if they have been certified by the National Board for Certified Counselors (NBCC) or by their state licensing board. The NBCC has a specific certification program for career counselors, but the state boards also have certain criteria a counselor must meet before being issued a license to practice. Either credential ensures that your counselor has had a minimum number of years of supervised counseling experience, holds a master's degree in counseling, and has successfully passed a comprehensive written examination. Also ask if they are members of the National Career Development Association (NCDA). While it's not a guarantee of quality, membership does show a commitment to the profession. The NBCC has a website available at *http://www.nbcc.org*, and NCDA can be reached online at *http://ncda.org*. Both provide free information on how to select a good counselor for you and what you can expect from this professional." The NBCC will take your request for a list of board-certified counselors in your region by phone or e-mail, and will return the free list to you via standard mail. You can also call your state licensing or certification board to receive a list of counselors licensed to work in your region. If the number is not listed in your phone book, contact the reference desk at your local public library for help.

In working with a career counselor, Bovard offers one more piece of advice: "Realize that the relationship between you and your career counselor is a personal one. If you are not happy with your counselor, find another one. It may be something simple like you don't like his or her style, but that can be a very big deal."

If you are considering making a career change, the self-assessment and decision-making process can be the most difficult part. To get an idea of the process, read some of the great books available at your local public library. Richard Bolles's book *What Color Is Your Parachute?* is probably the best-known, most highly recommended of these and can help you begin thinking about and working through the next step in searching for a new job or new career, or rediscovering the satisfaction of your current work. Tom Jackson's book *Not Just Another Job,* along with several other titles he has authored, will introduce you to new ideas for mapping your career path and applying your skills to new or alternate employment areas. *The National Business Employment Weekly* (*http://www.nbew.com*) regularly carries articles about changing careers and emerging trends in occupations. Your local public library, as well as nearby college and community career centers, should have all of these publications available, or they can assist you in obtaining them and other good books to assist you.

B

Networking
on the Net

We've mentioned throughout this book, and particularly in Chapter 3, that one of the four pieces to the complete job search is networking, and, yes, the Internet can play a part in that process. Included in this appendix are two articles Margaret Riley Dikel wrote for *The National Business Employment Weekly* on this topic, one discussing how to enhance your career by networking online and the other looking at how to establish a presence online. In addition to these articles, we'd like to recommend the following books and suggest you continue to read any articles you find on networking:

- Baker, Wayne E. *Networking Smart: How to Build Relationships for Personal and Organizational Success.* New York: McGraw-Hill, 1994.
- Richardson, Douglas B. *Networking: A National Business Employment Weekly Premier Guide.* New York: John Wiley & Sons, 1994.

Enhance Your Career Through Online Networking*

Participating in electronic discussions can help you stay visible and influential.

Some job hunters are willing to make hundreds of calls to strangers because they know that networking will lead them to their goal of finding work. But when the same people settle in at their new employers, they often drop the ball on networking.

In today's fast-paced world, this neglect can harm your professional future. By continuing to network while employed, you can meet and talk with influential people, learn new ideas, and sound out your own concepts. You'll also hear about job opportunities before they're announced. In short, you can stay so visible that you may never have to job hunt again.

Indeed, in the changing business environment, career success depends increasingly on how well you build your network, says Wayne E. Baker, a professor at the University of Michigan's School of Business Administration in Ann Arbor and author of *Networking Smart: How to Build Relationships for Personal and Organizations Success* (1994, McGraw Hill).

The good news is that you can reach hundreds more people than you can in person simply by hitting a few computer keys. Instead of just talking with friends, business colleagues, and acquaintances and attending occasional conferences or trade shows, you can embrace the Internet as a new link in your networking chain.

*This article was written by Margaret F. Riley. Reprinted by permission from *The National Business Employment Weekly,* © Dow Jones & Co. Inc. All rights reserved. For subscription information, call 1-800-JOB-HUNT or visit www.nbew.com. This article originally appeared in *The National Business Employment Weekly,* November 3–9, 1996, pp. 21–24.

For many executives, such as William Pucci, president of Performance Consultants, a fire-protection engineering consulting firm in Holland, Mass., the Internet is an effective professional development tool. By joining mailing lists, he builds relationships with people in his field prior to meeting them face to face. This makes him "much more comfortable approaching people at conferences and seminars because, in essence, we've already been introduced," he says.

MEETING A "HOT SHOT"

Since the Internet spans the world and never closes, you can get to know people you'd never meet otherwise. After making a presentation at a national conference, Mr. Pucci says he was approached by a "hot shot" in his field who had read his postings on a mailing list.

"He wanted to talk about my ideas on the subject and commented that he enjoyed my posts," says Mr. Pucci, adding, "this has happened to me more than once."

Phil Hey, a professor of English and writing at Briar Cliff College in Sioux City, Iowa, likens his online activities to traditional networking. "Maybe the best analogy is that it's like meeting people at conferences or trade shows—you can simply listen, or engage and be engaged," he says. "You can pursue opportunities as little or as much as you want."

As with any other communications activity, you must be visible, vocal, polite, and articulate online to generate results. If you're interested in an idea or message you read, you can contact its author directly via electronic mail or send a message to an entire list or newsgroup. Hiding in the background, commonly called "lurking," won't help you become known.

One reason for networking professionally is to establish your presence in a profession, specialty, or industry. If you need advice, assistance, or wish to share a discovery, you can then tap into this group. You also can add to the circle of people you trust to go to for advice.

Mr. Pucci uses his online collegial network to find people who can assist him professionally. After developing a relationship, he may subcontract work to them or ask for advice and referrals to others.

"I've used the mailing lists I participate in to identify expertise in an area where I need assistance and have made the contact online," he says. "I'm much more inclined to contact or contract with someone I already know."

NEWSGROUPS AND MAILING LISTS

Joining mailing lists and newsgroups is the best way to begin networking professionally on the Internet. Both can provide thousands of opportunities to participate in discussions with colleagues worldwide.

The difference between the two vehicles is how they operate. Mailing lists, which use software known as listservs, listprocs, or majordomos, operate through e-mail. To participate in a list, send a request asking to be included to the list controller, usually a computer. Anyone who has an e-mail account with a provider offering access to the Internet can participate in mailing lists.

Many Internet guides explain how to join and participate in mailing lists. One good source, "Discussion Lists: Mail List Manager Commands" by Jim Milles (http://lawlib.slu.edu/training/mailser.htm), describes each mailing list service and the commands necessary to join and control the list or remove your name later.

Newsgroups are accessed through a separate part of the Internet, the Usenet. To participate you need access to this network through your online provider and a newsreader software program. (Newer versions of Netscape include this.) Once you have access, you can learn which groups your provider connects with, then read the messages. Generally, it's wise to discuss your setup and newsgroup access with your help desk.

Several good resources can help you locate relevant mailing lists and newsgroups. The most comprehensive may be the Liszt (www.liszt.com), which includes directories of mailing lists and newsgroups that can be searched by keywords. The mailing list directory, which includes more than 65,000 lists, can be searched immediately after connecting. The newsgroup list can be accessed by clicking on the "Newsgroups" button on the bottom of the page.

Another resource is the "Directory of Scholarly and Professional E-Conferences," or simply, The Kovacs List, after its originator, Diane Kovacs (www.n2h2.com/KOVACS). This directory only includes mailing lists and newsgroups that focus on scholarly or professional discussions, thereby eliminating more informal or local lists. It, too, can be searched by keyword or browsed by subject.

If you don't have access to newsgroups or cannot connect with any that interest you, consider following discussions through the Usenet archiving services available on the World Wide Web. While you can't actively participate, you can view the comments and ideas, then contact the writers by e-mail. AltaVista (*www.altavista.digital.com*) offers a searchable archive (select "Search the Usenet" at the top of the page), as does DejaNews (*www.dejanews.com*). Search by the name of a newsgroup you want to view or a few keywords related to your interests.

DEVELOPING RELATIONSHIPS

When meeting strangers, an electronic message can be a less stressful way to break the ice than calling or personally introducing yourself, says Mr. Baker. However, it's more difficult to develop meaningful relationships by e-mail than by talking personally with someone. And, while you may not realize it, how you behave online can significantly affect your professional reputation, says Mr. Pucci.

"I have seen a number of people lose rather than gain the respect of the mailing list participants through improper or irresponsible postings," he says. "As a result, these people already have a strike against them before they are formally introduced in a face-to-face situation."

When you've identified helpful newsgroups and mailing lists, be sure to stop, look, and listen before joining a discussion:

- Stop to learn the rules of netiquette (network etiquette).
- Look for a list of Frequently Asked Questions (the FAQ).
- "Listen" to the postings on the lists or newsgroups you've joined, perhaps for several weeks.

Don't post boldly where you haven't gone before. Take time to learn the language of the list, the tone of voice and mannerisms of the players, and what's really being discussed. When you're online, as in normal conversations, first impressions count for a lot.

To learn more about acceptable online behavior, review Arlene H. Rinaldi's comprehensive guide, "The Net: User Guidelines and Netiquette" (*www.fau.edu/rinaldi/net/index.html*). A webmaster and senior computer programmer at Florida Atlantic University in Boca Raton, Ms. Rinaldi created the guidelines for users of the university's network. Since then, many organizations have adopted the suggestions, earning her the nickname of "Emily Post of the Internet."

After joining a mailing list, you'll receive an introductory letter which may refer to an archive that you should find and read to learn more about the list. Many newsgroup FAQS can be found in the archives maintained by Ohio State University (*http://www.cis.ohio-state.edu/hypertext/faq/usenet/top.html*).

FOLLOW THE GOLDEN RULE

While communicating via computer is supposedly impersonal, you're still dealing with people and must follow the golden rule of networking: Any interchange must be beneficial to both parties. However, many mailing list participants don't take steps to cultivate professional online relationships, says Gordon Curtis, director of career services and alumni relations for Boston College's Wallace E. Carroll Graduate School of Management.

"I never cease to be amazed at the self-serving nature of many inquiries I see on listservs," says Mr. Curtis. "Most of the inquirers seem to think that other members of the list should be willing to share information or perform tasks solely out of their love for the subject. Rarely do I see an inquiry where there is a genuine willingness or offer to reciprocate."

When seeking information, always offer to return the favor by posting the final results back to the list or sharing findings with contributors. When you're asked for information, answer the requests. Most importantly, thank the list and individual participants for the help you receive.

Mr. Curtis says he's most likely to respond to a survey request if a poster offers to share the results of the poll. "To me, networking must be a true exchange of information, especially on a listserv where we're frequently asking total strangers to give us something for free," he says. "It may mean a lot more work for the networker, but I believe the benefit far outweighs the cost."

Philip E. Agre, assistant professor in the department of communications at the University of California, San Diego, prepared his guide, "Networking on the Network" (*http://communica-tion.ucsd.edu/pagre/network.html*), to help students develop professional relationships online. While it's designed for academics, his advice applies to all professionals: "So long as you have your professional hat on, every message you exchange on the network should be a part of the process of finding, building, and maintaining professional relationships."

Done carefully and conscientiously, professional online networking will complement your personal networking activities. In fact, many people wonder what they did before they had computers and e-mail. They likely agree with Phil Hey. "I got along decently before electronic networking, but now I can hardly imagine my career being so active and productive without it," he says.

Establish a Net Presence*

Share some of your expertise with the online world and you'll receive great career opportunities in return.

If you want to make colleagues and industry bigwigs aware of you and your expertise, old-fashioned networking is a great method. By meeting and staying in touch with contacts via conferences, local meetings, phone calls, letters, e-mail, and even Usenet newsgroups, you'll be remembered when interesting career opportunities arise or you need help with a new business venture or job search. But since you probably network primarily with people in the same field or profession, attracting prospective clients or employers from unrelated areas can be a challenge. The key is to establish a presence that makes you known beyond your network and outside of places where you're usually found. Online, it's called your "net presence."

Net presence is "the state or fact of playing a significant role in enhancing the Internet," according to one definition (*http://arganet.tenagra.com/Tenagra/net-presence.html*). And if you develop such a presence, the resulting good karma is sure to return to you.

Consider Nicholas Corcodilos, who worked for a large company when he first began recruiting in 1979 and now runs his own consulting firm, the North Bridge Group in Lebanon, N.J. Soon after Mr. Corcodilos finished writing a book, *The New Interview Instruction Book* in 1994, he joined a commercial online service. Immediately, he saw the Net as an open world to new ideas and opportunities, and realized it would be a great place to sell the self-published book. But he didn't just put up an online ad and wait for orders to come in.

"I knew direct marketing wouldn't work because it wasn't acceptable to this community, so I tried something different," says Mr. Corcodilos. "I volunteered my services to others, figuring if I gave them something of value at no charge, then eventually I'd receive something back in exchange."

The strategy worked. Mr. Corcodilos now hosts "Ask the Headhunter," a popular job-search forum on America Online hosted by The Motley Fools (available on the Net at *www.fool.com/headhunter.htm*). He writes articles for various electronic and print publications, including newsletters by management gurus Tom Peters and Peter Drucker. His phone rings regularly with requests for his consulting services. What's more, his book was picked up by Penguin for a nice sum of money. "My agent said the advance I received is unprecedented for an unknown business author," he says.

LEND A HAND

Mr. Corcodilos intuitively recognized that establishing a net presence requires undertaking a combination of tasks, including providing quality information others need and actively contributing to online forums such as Internet newsgroups, mailing lists, and the public forums on America Online, CompuServe, or other commercial services.

"I basically started all of this in 1995 by going into a message board on Prodigy and posting an offer to help job hunters," he says. "I introduced myself, gave them all my background, and volunteered my services. Then I sat back and waited to see what would happen."

Soon, job hunters began to write to him, asking questions about their searches and how to work with recruiters. Mr. Corcodilos answered every message. As word of his expertise spread, increasing numbers of candidates contacted him. Before long, he was running an informal forum on the network, which he called "Ask the Headhunter." It became so popular, he tried to convert it into an official Prodigy feature, but without success. Still, he continued his efforts to make the forum a real site, finally contacting America Online and a group called The Motley Fools.

"They welcomed me with open arms, and even began to sell my book online in the FoolsMart," he says. "Now they host a discussion forum which I control, and are moving my work on the Web as a part of their site."

FROM SOAPS TO A JOB

This approach also works for job seekers, even those who aren't seriously looking for work. That's what Sherry Miller, a registered nurse in New Jersey, discovered after she became active in CompuServe's Soap Opera Forum.

"I was home with my baby and got tired of watching TV, so I signed on to catch up on news as well as my soap operas," she says. "I began spending a lot of time online, and since I was familiar with computers from work and home, I'd answer questions from other participants about loading new software, how to find things on the network, and other questions which weren't about the soaps. People really began to look to me for this kind of help."

Within a few months, someone contacted her to say that Entertainment Drive (eDrive), a New York City–based firm that runs the Soap Opera Forum and several others on CompuServe, was looking for technical staff to answer questions online. Ms. Miller followed up and quickly received an offer, which she accepted. She now works a flexible, part-time schedule at home.

ADD VALUE

Always be cautious when promoting your business or self online, and keep in mind that it's not the same as traditional marketing. After all, the routine, free exchange of valuable information is one of the foundations of the Net, and most users still hold to this ideal.

Thus, the custom online is that you'll be allowed to market your services and products only if you return something of genuine worth to the community. The popular term used to describe this return is "value-added," namely what you offer that will benefit visitors to your site or participants in your service.

Mr. Corcodilos fulfilled his "value-added" requirement by sending a personal e-mail message to each person who contacted him during a forum. These notes always contained a chapter from the book he'd written. The information was provided free of charge, with the idea of helping the job seeker. An explanation of how to order his book was placed at the bottom of each message.

"I wasn't sending a blatant marketing brochure; I was providing additional valuable information I thought [job hunters] could use," he says. "People liked what they read, so they ordered the book."

Marketing, yes, but with a focus on benefiting the individual, not selling the product. Combined with the free advice offered in the forum, Mr. Corcodilos's "value-added" was quite high and greatly appreciated.

Ms. Miller began adding value simply by answering questions, helping users, and offering advice as she could. She credits some of her success, however, to the courteous manner in which she answered people.

"I was always friendly and polite, no matter how objectionable the other person was," she says. "I think that's very important."

EXPANDING YOUR PRESENCE

If you're trying to create a net presence to promote your business, you'll need to add another tool to your belt. Once you've created a web page to tout your services, you should register it with the major Internet directories, virtual libraries, and search engines. This is a critical step, since online, it's not who you know, but who you're affiliated with. To begin your registration process, contact Yahoo! (*www.yahoo.com*) and The Galaxy (*galaxy.tradewave.com*) and submit your URL (web page address) for inclusion. Be prepared with a short description of your site and keywords you feel best describe it.

Then contact search engines such as Infoseek (*www.infoseek.com*), Lycos (*www.lycos.com*), and Excite (*www.excite.com*) to try to submit your URL for indexing. Look around the main page for an "Add URL" or "Submit Site" button to find the necessary information.

Once you've registered with the biggies, you may want to contact smaller sites dedicated to the industry, occupation, or service you want to associate with. Review potential sites with a critical eye. If you think you'd like to be allied with a site, contact its owner or webmaster about being included in its resource list. Always offer a reciprocal link back to their page as a courtesy. Mr. Corcodilos will be contacting several sites aimed at job seekers, such as Job-Hunt (*www.job-hunt.org*) and Career Magazine (*www.careermag.com*).

When he first thought of marketing himself online, Mr. Corcodilos says people tried to discourage him. "Friends and associates told me I was nuts to give away advice for free," he says. "But I had faith it would work, and it paid off. The joy of it all is that it was such a grassroots effort. Yes, I worked, but it also worked for me."

Ms. Miller also is pleased with the way her net presence has paid off. "I'm now being paid to run some of the forums, I interact with 35 to 40 eDrive staffers, and it was all because of the baby, the soap operas, and my online activities."

Index of Cited Resources

Chapter 1

Jay Barker's Online Connection
  http://www.barkers.org/online
The List
  http://thelist.internet.com/

Chapter 2

America's Talent Bank
  http://www.atb.org
Career Magazine
  http://www.careermag.com
CareerMosaic
  http://www.careermosaic.com/cm/
E-Span
  http://www.espan.com
misc.jobs.resumes
The MonsterBoard
  http://www.monster.com
Online Career Center
  http://www.occ.com
The Riley Guide
  http://www.dbm.com/jobguide/resumes.html

Chapter 3

AltaVista
  http://www.altavista.digital.com
America's Job Bank
  http://www.ajb.dni.us
Asianet
  http://www.asia-net.com
Careers, Not Just Jobs
  (*Wall Street Journal* Interactive)
  http://careers.wsj.com
CityNet
  http://www.city.net
The Clearinghouse
  http://www.clearinghouse.net
Collection of FAQS
  http://www.cis.ohio.state/edu/hypertext/
    faq/usenet/top.html
ComFind
  http://www.comfind.com
DejaNews
  http://www.dejanews.com
Disability Services Careers Online
  http://desserv3.stu.umn.edu
Discussion Lists: Mail List Manager Commands
  http://lawlib.slu.edu/training/mailser.htm
EDGAR 10K Reports
  http://edgar.stern.nyu.edu
Editor & Publisher Interactive
  http://www.mediainfo.com
Enews
  http://www.enews.com
Excite
  http://www.excite.com
The Galaxy
  http://galaxy.tradewave.com
HotBot
  http://www.hotbot.com
HotMail
  http://www.hotmail.com
Hoovers Online
  http://www.hoovers.com

Info-Mine
  http://www.info-mine.com
InfoSeek
  http://www.infoseek.com
The Liszt
  http://www.liszt.com
Job Hunt
  http://www.job-hunt.org
JobSmart Salary Surveys
  http://jobsmart.org/tools/salary
Juno
  http://www.juno.com
The Kovacs List
  http://www.n2h2.com/KOVACS/
Librarian's Index to the Internet
  http://sunsite.berkeley.edu/InternetIndex/
Looksmart
  http://www.looksmart.com
Lycos
  http://www.lycos.com
Magellan Internet Guide
  http://www.mckinley.com/
The Mining Company
  http://www.miningco.com
National Business Employment Weekly
  http://www.nbew.com
The Net: User Guidelines and Netiquette
  http://www.fau.edu/rinaldi/net/index.html
Net Happenings
  http://scout.cs.wisc.edu/scout/net-hap/
Networking on the Network
  http://communication.ucsd.edu/pagre/
    network.html
NewJour Archive
  http://gort.ucsd.edu/newjour
New Rider's Official World Wide Web Yellow Pages
  http://www.mcp.com/newriders/wwwyp/
    index.html
Newsgroup FAQS
  http://www.cis.ohio-state.edu/hypertext/faq/
    usenet/top.html
Northern Lights
  http://www.nlsearch.com
Online Career Center
  http://www.occ.com
The Riley Guide
  http://www.dbm.com/jobguide/
  http://www.dbm.com/jobguide/resumes.html
  http://www.dbm.com/jobguide/research.html
SaludosWeb
  http://www.saludos.com
Search Insider
  http://www.searchinsider.com
Scholarly Societies Project
  http://www.lib.uwaterloo.ca/society/
    overview.html
The Scout Report
  http://wwwscout.cs.wisc.edu/scout/report
Search.Com
  http://www.search.com
State & Local Government on the Net
  http://www.piperinfo.com/state/states.html
Virtual Library (W30)
  http://vlib.stanford.edu/Overview.html
WebCrawler
  http://webcrawler.com

WebScout
  http://www.webscout.com/
What Color Is Your Parachute?
  http://www.washingtonpost.com/parachute
Yahoo!
  http://www.yahoo.com
Yahoo! Mail
  http://www.yahoo.com
YPN: Your Personal Net
  http://www.ypn.com

Chapter 4

AdOne
  http://www.adone.com
AdSearch
  http://www.adsearch.com
America's Employers
  http://www.americasemployers.com
America's Job Bank
  http://www.ajb.dni.us/
Asianet
  http://www.asia-net.com/
Best Jobs in the USA Today
  http://www.bestjobsusa.com
biz.jobs.offered
The Black Collegian
  http://www.black-collegian.com/
Career Blazers
  http://www.cblazers.com
CareerBuilder
  http://www.careerbuilder.com/
CareerCity
  http://www.careercity.com
Career Expo
  http://www.careerexpo.com
Career Magazine
  http://www.careermag.com
CareerMart
  http://www.careermart.com
CareerMosaic
  http://www.careermosaic.com
CareerNET, Career Resource Center
  http://www.careers.org
Career Paradise
  http://www.emory.edu/CAREER/
CareerPath.com
  http://www.careerpath.com
Careers, Not Just Jobs
  (*Wall Street Journal* Interactive)
  http://careers.wsj.com
The Career Resource Homepage
RPI
  http://www.eng.rpi.edu/dept/cdc/homepage.html
Careersite
  http://www.careersite.com
CareerWeb
  http://www.cweb.com
The Catapult, Career Service Professionals Homepage
  http://www.jobweb.org/catapult/catapult.htm
College Grad Job Hunter
  http://www.collegegrad.com/
College of William and Mary Career Services Center
  http://www.wm.edu/csrv/career/index.html
The Huntington Group's Career Network
  http://www.hgllc.com

Contract Employment Weekly, Jobs Online
http://www.ceweekly.wa.com

The EPages Classifieds
http://ep.com

E-Span, The Interactive Employment Network
http://www.espan.com

Experience on Demand
http://www.experienceondemand.com

4work
http://www.4work.com

HeadHunter.Net
http://www.headhunter.net/

Heart Advertising's Career.com
http://www.career.com

Help Wanted.Com
Yss Inc.
http://www.helpwanted.com/

Hire Quality
http://www.hire-quality.com/

Imcor
http://www.imcor.com

Internet Career Connection
http://www.iccweb.com

JobBank USA
http://www.jobbankusa.com/

JobCenter
http://www.jobcenter.com

JobHunt: A Meta-List of On-line Job Search Resources and Services
http://www.job-hunt.org

The Job Market
http://www.thejobmarket.com

JobSmart
http://jobsmart.org

JobTrak
http://www.jobtrak.com

Home Page of Malachy
http://www.execpc.com/~maltoal/

Manpower
http://www.manpower.com

misc.jobs.offered
misc.jobs.offered.entry
misc.jobs.contract
misc.jobs.resumes
misc.jobs.wanted

The Monster Board
http://www.monster.com/

NationJob Online Job Database
http://www.nationjob.com

Online Career Center
http://www.occ.com

Priority Search.Com
http://prioritysearch.com/career.htm

Purdue University Center for Career Opportunities
http://www.ups.purdue.edu/Student/jobsites.htm

PursuitNet
http://www.tiac.net/users/jobs/index.html

Recruiters OnLine Network
http://www.ipa.com/

Recruitinglinks.Com
http://www.recruiting-links.com/index.html

The Riley Guide: Employment Opportunities and Job Resources on the Internet
http://www.dbm.com/jobguide/index.html

Saludos Web Site
http://www.saludos.com

Topjobs USA
http://www.topjobsusa.com/

The Virtual Job Fair
http://www.http://www.vjf.com

Weddle's Web Guide
http://www.nbew.com/weddle.html

What Color Is Your Parachute: The Net Guide
http://www.washingtonpost.com/parachute/

Work-Web
http://www.work-web.com

The World Wide Web Employment Office
http://www.harbornet.com/biz/office/annex.html

Yahoo's Classifieds
http://classifieds.yahoo.com

Yahoo's Listings of Employment Information
http://www.yahoo.com/Business/Employment

Chapter 5

AAFA—The American Association of Finance and Accounting
http://www.aafa.com

AccountingNet
http://www.accountingnet.com

Advertising Age's Online JobBank
http://adage.com/job_bank/index.html

American Marketing Association
http://www.ama.org

American Society for Quality
http://www.asqc.org/

BeautyVision
http://www.beautyvision.com/

Bloomberg Online: Career Opportunities
http://www.bloomberg.com/fun/jobs.html

Business Job Finder
http://www.cob.ohio-state.edu/dept/fin/osujobs.htm

CareGuide
http://www.careguide.net

CareerMosaic's Accounting and Finance Jobs
http://www.accountingjobs.com/

Champion Personnel System
http://www.championjobs.com

Cross Staffing Services
http://www.snelling.com/cross

Equipment Leasing Association Online
http://www.elaonline.com

FinancialJobs.com
http://www.FINANCIALjobs.com/

Food and Drug Packaging
http://www.fdp.com

FuneralNet
http://www.funeralnet.com

Robert Half
http://www.roberthalf.com/jobsRH/

HR Careers
http://www.tcm.com/hr-careers/career

Instructional Systems Technology Jobs
http://education.indiana.edu/ist/students/jobs/joblink.html

Insurance Career Center
http://www.connectyou.com/talent/

Job Postings for Benefits & HR Professionals
http://www.ifebp.org/jobs/index.html

Management Consulting Online
http://www.cob.ohio-state.edu/~fin/jobs/mco/mco.html

Management Recruiters International
http://www.mrinet.com/

Marketing Classifieds
http://www.marketingjobs.com

MBAJob
http://www.mbajob.com

MIT Sloan School of Management
http://www.mit.edu/cdo/www

National Funeral Directors Association
http://www.nfda.org/

NationJob Network Financial/Accounting/ Insurance Jobs Page
http://www.nationjob.com/financial

NationJob Network Human Resources Jobs Page
http://www.nationjob.com/hr

NationJob Network Marketing and Sales Jobs Page
http://www.nationjob.com/marketing

National Banking Network
http://www.banking-financejobs.com

The Online MBA
http://www.columbia.edu/cu/business/career/links

Packinfo-World
http://www.packinfo-world.com/WPO/

RJ Pascale & Company
http://www.ct-jobs.com/pascale/

Philanthropy Journal Online
http://www.philanthropy-journal.org

RealBank
http://www.realbank.com

Retail JobNet
http://www.retailjobnet.com/cf/main.cm

Rollins Search Group
http://www.rollinssearch.com

Rutgers Accounting Web
http://www.rutgers.edu/Accounting/raw.html

Society for Human Resource Management
http://www.shrm.org/jobs

Chapter 6

Academe This Week
http://chronicle.merit.edu/ads/links.html

AERAJob Openings
http://tikkun.ed.asu.edu/~jobs/joblinks.html

Academic Position Network (APN)
http://www.umn.edu/apn/

AIR-L, Electronic Newsletter of the Association for Institutional Research
http://www.fsu.edu/~air

American Association of Law Libraries Job Placement Hotline
http://www.aallnet.org/services/hotline.html

ALA Library Education and Employment Menu Page
http://www.ala.org/education/

American Psychological Society (APS) Observer Job Listings
http://psych.hanover.edu/APS/job.html

Ann's Place—Library Job Hunting
http://tigger.cc.uic.edu/~aerobin/libjob.html

APA Monitor Classified Advertising
http://apa.org/ads

Archaeological Fieldwork Server
http://www.cincpac.com/afs/testpit.html

ARLIS/NA JobNet
http://afalib.uflib.ufl.edu/arlis/jobs.html

C. Berger and Company: Library Consultants
http://www.cberger.com/

BUBL Employment Bulletin Board
http://bubl.ac.uk

CAUSE Job Posting Service
http://cause-www.colorado.edu/pd/jobpost/jobpost.html

College and Research Libraries News Classified Advertising Archives
http://www.ala.org/acrl/advert3.html

Community Career Center
http://www.nonprofitjobs.org

Council for Advancement and Support of Education (CASE) Job Classifieds
http://www.case.org/

EFLWEB
http://www.u-net.com/eflweb/home.htm

E-JOE
http://maynard.ww.tu-berlin.de/e-joe/

Employment Opportunities in Women's Studies and Feminism
http://www.inform.umd.edu/EdRes/Topic/WomensStudies

The ESL JobCenter
http://www.pacific.net.net/~sperling/jobcenter.html

Good Works
http://www.tripod.com/work/goodworks/search.html

Hieros Gamos Legal Employment Classified
http://www.cgsg.com/hg/employ.html

Impact Online
http://www.impactonline.org

Independent School Management
http://www.isminc.com/mm.html

International Service Agencies
http://www.charity.org

Internet Non-Profit Center: Home to Donors and Volunteers
http://www.nonprofits.org/

JOBPLACE Mailing List
LISTSERV@news.jobweb.org

Jobs in Higher Education—Geographical Listings
http://volvo.gslis.utexas.edu/~acadres/jobs/index.html

Jobs in Linguistics
http://www.linguistlist.org/jobindex.html

JobSearch from library Journal Digital
http://www.bookwire.com/ljdigital/job.htm

JobWire
http://www.jobweb.org/jobwire.htm

JOE-Job Opportunities for Economists
http://www.eco.utexas.edu/joe/

The Legal Employment Search Site
http://www.legalemploy.com/

LIBJOB-L
listserv@ubvm.cc.buffalo.edu

Library and Information Specialists' Jobs
http://www.palinet.org/stecem

Library Job Postings on the Internet
http://www.sils.umich.edu/~nesbeitt/libraryjobs.html

Library Jobs and Employment: A Guide to Internet Resources by Jeff Lee
http://www.zoots.com/libjob/jefflee.htm

LIS-JOBLIST
mailserv@ac.dal.ca

Mental Health Net Joblink: Openings
http://cmhc.com/joblink/

Music Library Association Joblist
http://www.music.indiana.edu/tech_s/mla/joblist/joblist.htm

NASW Jobs Bulletin
http://naswca.org/jobbulletin.html

The National Civic League
http://www.ncl.org/ncl

The National Federation of Paralegal Associations
http://www.paralegals.org/Center/home.html

The Networked Librarian: JobSearch Guide
http://www.netcom.com/~feridun/libjobs.htm

NISS, National Information Services and Systems
http://www.niss.ac.uk/noticeboard/index.html

North Suburban Library System Blue Sheets
http://nsls1.nslsilus.org/SERVICES/BlueSheets/bsinfo.html

Opportunity Nocs
http://www.opnocs.org

Philanthropy Journal Online
http://www.philanthropy-journal.org

Positions in Psychology: The First Worldwide Register
http://psy.anu.edu.au/academia/psy.htm

Psych-Web List of Scholarly Psychology Resources on the Web
http://www.psycho-web.com/resource/bytopic.htm

The Seamless Web Legal Job Center
http://www.seamless.com/jobs/

SLAJOB
listserv@iubvm.ucs.indiana.edu

Socialservice.com
http://socialservice.com

Social Work and Social Services Jobs Online
http://128.252.132.4/jobs/

soc.org.nonprofit

Southern Connecticut State University Library
http://scsu.ctstateu.edu/~jobline

TESLJB-L
listserv@cunyvm.cuny.edu

THESIS: The Times Higher Education Supplement InterView Service
http://www.thesis.co.uk/

TIP: The Industrial and Organizational Psychologist Home Page
http://www.siop.org/positions.html

University of Michigan ILSL Library Job Postings
http://www.lib.umich.edu/libhome/ILSL.lib/ILSLjobs.html

University of Minnesota's College of Education Job Search Bulletin Board
http://www.cis.umn.edu:11119/
gopher://rodent.cis.umn.edu:11119/

Chapter 7

The Airline Employment Assistance Corps
http://www.avjobs.com

Airwaves Job Services
http://www.airwaves.com

The Arts Deadlines List Information
http://www.xensei.com/adl

Arts Wire Current
http://www.artswire.org

Auditions Online
http://www.auditions.com/

Aviation Employee Placement Service
http://www.aeps.com/aeps/aepshm.html

Bakery-Net
http://www.bakery-net.com

The Bookbinders Guild of New York Job Bank
http://www.bbgny.com/guild/jb.html

Cool Works
http://www.coolworks.com/showme

Design Sphere Online Job Hunt
http://www.dsphere.net/b2b/directory.html#browse

Escoffier Online
http://www.escoffier.com/nonscape/index.html

Executive Placement Services
http://www.execplacement.com

Find a Pilot
http://www.findapilot.com

GWeb, An Electronic Trade Journal for Computer Animators
http://www.gweb.org/lists.html

Hospitality Net Virtual Job Exchange
http://www.hospitalitynet.nl/job/

HotWired's Dream Jobs
http://www.hotwired.com/dreamjobs/

The Inkspot: Resources for Writers
http://www.inkspot.com/

Jobs in Philosophy
http://www.sozialwiss.uni-hamburg.de/phil/ag/jobs/main_english.html

Job Openings in Newspaper New Media (and Related Fields)
http://www.media.info.com/ephome/class/classhtm/class.htm

JobXchange
http://www.jobxchange.com

Journalism-Related Job Openings
http://eb.journ.latech.edu/jobs/jobs_home.html

Media Links
http://www.bctv.net/telcom/pub/links/marks.html

Mediaweek Help Wanted: Miscellaneous
http://www.mediaweek.com/classifieds/multi.asp

Museum Employment Resource Center (MERC)
http://199.190.151.4:80/~MERC/

NATCA, the National Air Traffic Controllers Association
http://home.natca.org/natca/default.html

National Diversity Journalism Job Bank
http://www.newsjobs.com/jobs.html

National Writers Union Job Hotline
http://www.nwu.org/nwu/hotline/hotwrite.htm

Newspaper Mania Job Center
http://www.club.innet.be/~year0230/jobs.htm

Online Sports Career center
http://www.onlinesports.com/pages/CareerCenter.html

ORCHESTRALIST
listproc@hubcap.clemson.edu
(message: subscribe orchestralist)

Playbill On-Line
http://www1.playbill.com/playbill/

PressTemps
http://www.presstemps.com

Showbizjobs.com
http://www.showbizjobs.com

SiliconAlley Connections
http://www.salley.com

SportLink
http://www.sportlink.com

3DSite
http://www.3dsite.com

Truckers.com
http://www.truckers.com/

TruckNet
http://www.truck.net

TV Jobs
http://www.tvjobs.com

VideoPro Classifieds
http://www.txdirect.net/videopro/default.html

The Write Jobs from The Writers Write
http://www.writerswrite.com/jobs/jobs.htm

Yahoo! Symphony Orchestra
http://www.yahoo.com/Entertainment/Music/Artists/Orchestras/Symphony_Orchestras/

Chapter 8

AAEA Employment Service, American Agricultural Economic Association
http://www.aaea.org/employment.html

Academic Physician and Scientist
http://www.acphysci.com/

AgriCareers
http://www.agricareers.com

Allied Health Opportunities
http://www.gvpub.com

American Astronomical Society Job Register
http://www.aas.org/JobRegister/aasjobs.html

BioNet Employment Wanted
http://www.bionet:80/hypermail/
EMPLOYMENT-WANTED

BioNet Employment Opportunities
http://www.bionet:80/hypermail/EMPLOYMENT

bionet.jobs.offered

bionet.jobs.wanted

Call24 Online
http://www.call24online.com

Career Resources in Agronomy
http://www.agronomy.org/career/career.html

Career Services, American Institute of Physics
http://www.aps.org/industry.html

Cell Press Online
http://www.cellpress.com

Chemistry and Industry
http://chemistry.mond.org

College of Food, Agricultural, and Environmental
Sciences Career Information, Ohio State University
http://hortwww-2.ag.ohio-state.edu/faes/
career/career.html

Ecological Society of America NewSource
http://www.sdsc.edu/~esa/newspage.htm

EE-Link: The Environmental Education Web Server
http://www.nceet.snre.umich.edu/jobs.html

Employment Opportunities in Water Resources
http://www.uwin.siu.edu/announce/jobs/

Ensign Bickford Industries
http://pages.prodigy.com/CT/aspire/

Environmental Careers Organization
http://www.eco.org/

Environmental Careers World
http://environmental-jobs.com/

Environmental Sites on the Internet
http://www.lib.kth.se/~lg/envsite.htm

Experimental Medicine Job Listings
http://www.medcor.mcgill.ca/
EXPMED/DOCS/jobs.html

GEOSCI—Jobs Mailing List Archives
http://www.eskimo.com/~tcsmith/
mail/geoscij.html

GeoWeb
http://www.ggrweb.com/job.html

GIS Jobs Clearinghouse
http://www.gis.umn.edu/rsgisinfo/jobs.html

Global Health Network
http://info.pitt.edu/HOME/GHNet/GHNet.html

Health Careers Online
http://www.healthcareers-online.com

Interim Services
http://www.interim.com

International Agribusiness Internship Center
http://www.usu.edu/~iaic/

Job.com
http://www.job.com/main.html

JobLinks
http://cip.physik.uni-wuerzburg.de/Job/job.html

JobSpan
http://www.jobspan.com

Mental Health Net
http://www.cmhc.com

MET—Jobs Mailing List Archives
http://www.eskimo.com/~tcsmith/
mail/met-jobs.html

National Network for HealthCare Professionals
http://www.treknet.net/hcroaz/

Nightingale
http://nightingale.con.utk.edu

ORES—Online Resources for Earth Scientists
http://www.calweb.com/~tcsmith/ores/

Physician Recruitment Ads from JAMA, the Journal
of the American Medical Association
http://www.ama-assn.org/sci-pubs/
md_recr/md_recr.htm

Physicians Employment
http://www.fairfield.com/physemp/

Physics Job Announcements by Thread
http://XXX.lanl.gov/Announce/
Jobs/date.html#end

Physics Jobs On-Line
http://www.tp.umu.se/TIPTOP/FORUM/JOBS/

Professional Information from the American College
of Nurse-Midwives
http://www.midwife.org/prof/

RehabJobs
http://www.rehabjobs.com

Science Professional Network
http://recruit.sciencemag.org/

sci.research.careers

sci.research.postdoc

Soil and Water Conservation Society Jobs Database

WeedJobs, Positions in Weed Science
http://www.nrcan.gc.ca/~bcampbel/

Chapter 9

ACM SIGMOD's Database Jobs Listings
http://www1.acm.org.81/sigmod

The Ada Project (TAP)
http://www.cs.yale.edu/HTML/YALE/CS/
HyPlans/tap/positions.html

AD&A Software Jobs Home Page
http://www.softwarejob.com

AECT Placement Center
http://www.aect.org/Employment/
Employment.htm

AeroJobs
http://www.aerojobs.com

Aeronautics/Aviation Career Search Resources
http://24.1.77.43/career.html

AIA Online
http://www.aia.org

Alpha Systems
http://www.jobbs.com

American Gas Association
http://www.aga.com

American Mathematical Society
http://www.ams.org/employment

American Public Works Association
http://www.pubworks.org

ASMENET, the American Society
of Mechanical Engineers
http://www.asme.org/index.html

Association for Facilities Engineers CareerNet
http://www.afe.org/jobs.shtml

At-Sea Processors Association
http://www.atsea.org/employ.html

Automotive Employment Connection
http://www.autocareers.com

The Beardsley Group
http://www.beardsleygroup.com

Career Information from the ACM
http://www.acm.org/member_services/career

Chancellor & Chancellor
http://www.chancellor.com

CIVENG-JOBS
http://www.eskimo.com/~ltcsmith/
mail/civengj.html

Comforce Corporation
http://www.comforce.com

Communications Week Classifieds
http://techweb.cmp.com/cw/ccareers

comp.jobs.offered

Computer Jobs
http://www.computerjobs.com

Computer-Aided Three-Dimensional Interactive
Application (CATIA) Job Network
http://www.catjn.com

ComputerWorld Careers
http://careers.computerworld.com

ComputerWorld's CareerAgent
http://careeragent.computerworld.com

Computing and Technology Companies Online
http://www.cmpcmm.com/cc/companies.html

Computing Research Association
http://cra.org/jobs

Contract Labor Pool
http://www.clp.com

Contractor Net
http://www.contractornet.com

D.I.C.E, Data Processing Independent
Consultant's Exchange
http://www.dice.com

Daley Consulting & Search and
Daley Technical Search
http://www.dpsearch.com

Discover a New World of Opportunity . . .
http://www.4chipjobs.com/index.html

e-Mine
http://www.rci.co.uk

Edmonds Personnel Inc.
http://www.edmondspersonnel.com

EE Times Jobs Online
http://jobs.hodes.com/j2/owa/
j2.dyna.page?iid=1001

Electric Power NewsLink
http://www.powermag.com/employ.html

Electrical World
http://www.electricalworld.com/employ.html

The Electronic Blue Book
http://www.thebluebook.com

Electronic News Classifieds On_Line
http://www.sumnet.com/enews/
class/clas_ol.html

Employment Opportunities from The Mechanic
http://www.the-mechanic.com/jobs.html

Engineering Job Source
http://www.engineerjobs.com

Engineering News Record
http://www.enr.com

EngineeringJobs.com
http://www.engineeringjobs.com

FacilitiesNet Forums
http://www.facilitiesnet.com/forums/
cgi/get/jobs.html

Fargo Enterprise Gateway to the Camera
Repair Industry
http://www.fargo-ent.com/index.html

FishJobs
http://www.fishjobs.com

Food Processing Machinery and Supplies
Association
http://www.fpmsa.org

Hardhats Online
http://www.hardhatsonline.com

HotJobs!
http://www.hotjobs.com

IDEAS Job Network
http://www.ideasjn.com

IEEE Job Bank
http://www.ieee.org/jobs.html

IndustryNet
http://www.monster.com/inet/inet.srch.html

The Information Professional's Career Page
http://www.brint.com/jobs.htm

Info-Mine
http://www.info-mine.com/

Job Hunting in Planning, Architecture, and
Landscape Architecture
http://www.lib.berkeley.edu/ENVI/jobs.html

Kolak Enterprises
http://www.mindspring.com/~jkolok

MacTemps
http://www.mactemps.com

Manufacturing Marketplace
http://www.manufacturing.net/resources/
jobs/default.htm

Mechanical Engineering Magazine
http://www.memagazine.org/contents/
current/jobs/jobs.html

Medical Device Link
http://www.devicelink.com/index.html

MedSearch
http://www.medsearch.com

Medzilla/FSG Online
http://www.chemistry.com/

Mindsource Software
http://www.mindsrc.com

MineNet Job Mart
http://www.microserve.net/~ldoug/
jobmart.html

Mining USA
http://www.miningusa.com/

Mooney Aircraft Corporation Employment
Opportunities
http://www.mooney.com/EMPLOY.HTM

NACCB Online Job Board & Resume Bank
http://www.computerwork.com

National Society of Professional Engineers
http://www.nspe.org

New Dimensions in Technology, Inc.
http://www.ndt.com

Offshore Guides
http://OffshoreGuides.com/

Olsten Professional Technical Services
http://www.olstenpts.com

Optics.org
http://optics.org/employment

PMA Job Site
http://www.intr.net/pma/pmajobs.htm

Pro/E Job Network
http://www.pejn.com

Provident Search Group
http://www.dpjobs.com

Right of Way
http://www.rightofway.com/

Rollins Search Group
http://www.rollinssearch.com

Rothrock Associates, Inc. (RAI)
http://www.raijobs.com

Sanford Rose Associates
http://www.sanfordrose.com

Seek Consulting
http://www.seek-consulting.com/

Semi/Sematech
http://www.sematech.org/semi-sematech

Space Jobs
http://www.spacejobs.com

Superior Group of Companies
http://www.supdes.com

Telecom Publishing Group
http://www.telecommunications.com

Transaction Information Systems
http://www.tkointl.com/

UG Job Network
http://www.ugjn.com

Utility Newslink
http://www.itforutilities.com/employ.html

Virtual Job Fair
http://www.vjf.com

Volt Services Group
http://www.volteast.com

Winter, Wyman, and Co.
http://www.winterwyman.com

Women in Technology International (WITI)
http://www.witi.com/

Chapter 10

Alabama
http://204.29.92.2/alapers/index.htm

Alaska
http://www.state.ak.us/local/jobs.htm

Arizona
http://www.adc.state.az.us:81/ADCweb/hrd2.htm

Brookings Institute
http://www.brook.edu/

California
http://www.spb.ca/gov/
http://www.statejobs.com/ca.html

Career Opportunities and Information
from DefenseLink
http://www.defenselink.mil/other_info/
careers.html

Colorado
http://www.state.co.us/gov_dir/interns/
http://www.statejobs.com/co.html

Connecticut
http://www.statejobs.com/ct.html

Delaware
http://www.state.de.us/spo/empsvc.htm

Department of Justice
http://www.usdoj.gov/careers/careers.html

Department of the Interior Automated Vacancy
Announcement System (AVADS)
http://info.er.usgs.gov/doi/avads/index.html

District of Columbia, Metro-Washington Council
of Governments
http://www.mwcog.org/geninfo/jobs.html
http://www.statejobs.com/va.html

dod.jobs

Federal Computer Week
http://fcw.com/

Federal Government Job Hotlines
http://www.unl.edu/careers/jobs/fedhotl.htm

Federal Jobs Digest
http://www.jobsfed.com/

FEDIX/MOLIS
http://www.RAMS-FIE.COM/

FEDWORLD JOBS, LABOR, AND MANAGEMENT
WEB PAGE
http://www.fedworld.gov/jobs/jobsearch.html

Florida
http://www.fcn.state.fl.us/fcn/centers/job_center/
http://www.statejobs.com/fl.html

Florida State Career Center Job Openings and
Placement Administration Help
http://www.fsu.edu/spap/job_intern/jobs/
job_listings.html

Georgia
http://www.state.ga.us/GMS/
http://www.statejob.com/ga.html

Government JOBS Central
http://members.aol.com/govjobs/index.htm

Hawaii
http://www.state.hi.us/hrd

The Heritage Foundation
http://www.heritage.org/

Idaho
http://www.ips.state.id.us/

Illinois
http://www.statejobs.com/il.html

Indiana
http://www.state.in.us/acin/personnel/index.html

International Monetary Fund
http://www.imf.org

The Internet Job Source at statejob.com
http://www.statejobs.com/

Iowa
http://www.state.ia.us/jobs/index.htm

Jobs Database from NACE
http://www.jobweb.org/search/jobs/

Jobs In Government
http://www.JobsInGovernment.com/

Kansas
http://www.ink.org/public/perssvcs/

Kentucky
http://www.state.ky.us/agencies/personnel/
jobspage.htm

Library of Congress
http://lcweb.loc.gov/homepage/
about.html#working
gopher://marvel.loc.gov/11/employee/employ/

Local Government Institute/Local Government
Job Net
http://www.lgi.org

Louisiana
http://www.dscs.state.la.us/csjobopp.htm

Maine
http://www.state.me.us/bhr/career/career.htm

The Few. The Proud. The Marines.
http://www.usmc.mil/wwwmcrc/mcrc.htm

Maryland
http://www.statejobs.com/md.html

Massachusetts
http://www.magnet.state.ma.us/refshelf.htm#jobs
http://www.statejobs.com/ma.html

Michigan
http://www.mdcs.state.mi.us/Employ/
Emp_info.htm

Michigan
http://www.statejobs.com/mi.html

Minnesota
http://www.doer.state.mn.us/
http://www.statejobs.com/mn.html

Mississippi
http://www.spb.state.ms.us/

Missouri
http://www.state.mo.us/oa/stjobs.htm

Montana
http://161.7.163.2/state/state.htm

National Fire Protection Association
http://www.nfpa.org/

National Science Foundation
http://www.nsf.gov/home/chart/work.htm

Navy Opportunities
http://www.navyjobs.com/

Nebraska
http://www.das.state.ne.us/das_cop/index.html

Nevada
http://www.state.nv.us/nvjobs.htm

New Hampshire
http://www.statejobs.com/nh.html

New Jersey
http://www.state.nj.us/personnel/vacancy/
vacancy.htm

New Jersey
http://www.statejobs.com/nj.html

New Mexico
http://www.state.nm.us/spo/

New York
http://www.cs.state.ny.us/
http://www.statejobs.com/ny.html

North Carolina
http://www.osp.state.nc.us/OSP/

North Dakota
http://www.state.nd.us/www/jobs.html

Ohio
http://www.state.oh.us/das/dhr/emprec.html
http://www.statejobs.com/oh.html
gopher://gizmo.freenet.columbus.oh.us/
11/governmentcenter/stateofohio/
State%20Government%20Job%20Opportunities

Oklahoma
http://www.state.ok.us/_opm/

Oregon
http://www.dashr.state.or.us/

Pennsylvania
http://www.state.pa.us/jobpost.html
http://www.statejobs.com/pa.html

Planning Your Future: A Federal Employee's Survival Guide
http://safetynet.doleta.gove/

The Police Officer's International Directory
http://www.officer.com/

Private Sector Federal Job Information Sites
http://www.govexec.com/careers/privinfo.htm

Rand
http://www.rand.org/

South Carolina
http://www.state.sc.us/jobs/esc/

South Dakota
http://www.state.sd.us/state/executive/bop/listings/openings.htm

Tennessee
http://www.state.tn.us/personnel

Texas
http://www.statejobs.com/tx.html
http://www.tws.state.tx.us/joblists/gvjb.html

United States Army Recruiting Home Page
http://www.goarmy.com/

United States Department of Justice
http://www.usdjo.gov/careers/careers.html

USAJobs
http://www.usajobs.opm.gov/

Utah
http://www.dhrm.state.us.us/

Vermont
http://www.state.vt.us/pers/employ.htm

Virginia
http://www.state.va.us/~dpt/menu
http://www.statejobs.com/va.html

Washington
http://www.statejobs.com/wa.html

Washington
http://www.wa.gov/dop/employ.html

Welcome to the Air Force
http://www.airforce.com/

West Virginia
http://www.state.wv.us/admin/personnel

Wisconsin
http://badger.state.wi.us/agencies/der/empopp.htm
gopher://badger.state.wi.us:70/11/agencies/der

Wyoming
http://personnel.state.wy.us/stjobs

The X-118 Qualification Standards for Federal Jobs
http://safety.net.doleta.gov/text/require.htm

Chapter 11

America's Job Bank
http://www.ajb.dni.us

AmeriCorps
http://www.cns.gov/americorps.htm

AmeriCorps*VISTA
http://www.libertynet.org/~zelson/vweb.html

California Polytechnic State University
http://www.careerservices.calpoly.edu/

Career Center Internship Index
http://www.carleton.edu/cgi-bin/intern/internwais.pl

Case Western Reserve University
http://www.cwru.edu/CWRU/Admin/cpp/summer.html

The Catapult, Career Service Professionals Homepage
http://www.jobweb.com/catapult/catapult.htm

College Grad Job Hunter
http://www.collegegrad.com/

CollegeConnection
http://www.careermosaic.com/cm/cc/

CollegePro Painters
http://wanda.phl.pond.com/mall/collegepro/

Cool Works
http://www.coolworks.com/

The Entry Level Job Seeker Assistant
http://andromedia.einet.net/galaxy/Community/Workplace/joseph-schmalhofer/jobs.html

1st Steps in the Hunt
http://www.interbiz.net.com/hunt

Intern-NET
http://www.vicon.net/~internnet/

International Agribusiness Internship Center
http://www.usu.edu/~iaic/

Internship and Fieldwork Listings Nationwide
http://www.virginia.edu/~career/intern.html

Jobnet Internships
http://www.westga.edu/~coop/internships.html

JobTrak
http://www.jobtrak.com

JobWeb, The National Association of Colleges and Employers
http://www.jobweb.org

The Mighty Internship Review
http://www.daily.umn.edu/~mckinney/

New England Board of Higher Education Opportunities for Minority Students
http://www.nebhe.org/minority_intro.html

Office for Special Learning Opportunities (OSLO)
http://oslo.umn.edu/

Peace Corps
http://www.peacecorps.gov/

Peterson's Guides
http://www.petersons.com/career/

Princeton Review
http://www.review.com/careers/

Project America Home Page
http://project.org/

Project Vote Smart
http://www.vote-smart.org/

Russian and Eastern European Internship Opportunities
http://www.indiana.edu/~reeiweb/indemp.html

StudentCenter.com
http://www.studentcenter.com

studyabroad.com
http://www.studyabroad.com/

Summer Jobs
http://www.summerjobs.com/

Teach for America
http://www.teachforamerica.org/

UCLA YES
http://www.yes.ucla.edu/voices/intern.html

University of California, Berkeley's Work Study Home Page
http://workstudy.berkely.edu/

VISTA Link
http://bcn.boulder.co.us/community/vistalink/

VISTA-L, VISTA On-Line
listserv@american.edu (message: subscribe vista-l yourfirstname yourlastname)

Washington Intern Foundation
http://interns.org/

The White House Fellowships
http://www.whitehouse.gov/WH_Fellows/

Youth Resource Network of Canada
http://www.youth.gc.ca

Chapter 12

ABQjournal: Albuquerque Journal Online
http://www.abqjournal.com

Access Indiana
http://www.ai.org/index.html
http://www.state.in.us/

ACLIN (Access Colorado Library & Information Network)
http://www.aclin.org/

Addison County Independent
http://www.addisonindependent.com/

Alabama State Employment Service Job Search
http://al.jobsearch.org/

Alaska Job Resources
http://www.state.ak.us/local/akpages/LABOR/esd_alaska_jobs/ak_resor.htm

Alaska Jobs Center
http://www.juneau.com/alaskajobs/

Alaska's Job Bank
http://labor-aix.state.ak.us/cgi-bin/jobs

AlaWeb
http://www.state.al.us

America's Job Bank
http://www.ajb.dni.us/

Anchorage Daily News
http://www.adn.com/

ArizonaCareers Online
http://www.diversecity.com/jobs.html

Arizona Central
http://www.azcentral.com/class/employsearch.html

Arizona's Job Bank
http://az.jobsearch.org/

Arkansas Employment Register
http://www.arjobs.com/

Arkansas Job Bank
http://ar.jobsearch.org/

Arkansas Online
http://www.ardemgaz.com/class/clo5.htm

atl.jobs

Atlanta Classifieds
http://www.atlantaclassifieds.com/

Atlanta Web Guide
http://www.webguide.com/

Atlanta's Computer Job Store
http://www.atlanta.computerjobs.com/

Austin City Links
http://www.austinlinks.com/

austin.jobs

Austin360: The City Site for Austin
http://www.austin360.com/

az.jobs

ba.jobs

ba.jobs.contract

ba.jobs.misc

ba.jobs.offered

ba.jobs.resumes

balt.jobs

The Baton Rouge Advocate
http://www.theadvocate.com/classifieds/employ.htm

Bay Area Jobs Home
http://www.sonic.net/cory/ba_jobs.html

Blacksburg Electronic Village
http://www.bev.net/mall/index.html#employ

Boston Online
http://ftp.std.com/www/NE/boseconomy.html

Boston.Com, the Boston Globe Online
http://careers.boston.com/
http://www.boston.com/

Boulder Community Network
http://bcn.boulder.co.us/

Boulder County Government
http://www.boco.co.gov/jobs.html

Brooklyn Public Library Education, Job and Computer Center
http://www.brooklynpubliclibrary.org/central/ejcc.htm

California Career and Employment Center
http://www.webcom.com/-career/

California State Government
http://www.ca.gov/

California's Job Bank
http://ca.jobsearch.org/

The Capitol Online
http://192.41.44.21

CareerPath
http://www.careerpath.com

Carnegie Library of Pittsburgh
http://www.clpgh.org/

Carolina Career Center
http://www.webcom.com/nccareer/

Carolina ComputerJobs Store
http://www.carolina.computerjobs.com/

CascadeLink
http://www.region.portland.or.us/

Central Vermont Home Page
http://www.central-vt.com/

Champaign-Urbana News Gazette
http://www.news-gazette.com/

Charleston Gazette Online
http://www.wvgazette.com

Charleston.Net Home Page
http://www.charleston.net/

Charlotte.com: The Charlotte Observer Online
http://charlotte.com/

Charlotte's Web
http://www.charweb.org/

chi.jobs

Chicago Newspaper Network
http://www.chicago-news.com/classified/
Employment.html

Chicago Sun-Times
http://www.suntimes.com/classified/
Employment.html

Chicago Tribune
http://www.chicago.tribune.com/

Chicago WorksMart: Directory of City Services
http://www.ci.chi.il.us/WorksMart/

ChicagoJobs.org: the Definitive Chicago Area Job
and Career Guide
http://www.chicagojobs.org/

cinci.jobs

Cincinnati Enquirer
http://enquirer.com/

Cincinnati Post
http://www.cincypost.com/

City of Atlanta Jobs
http://www.atlanta.org/employ/employ.htm

City of Cambridge Employment Opportunities
http://www.ci.cambridge.ma.us/
employment.html

City of Madison
http://www.ci.madison.wi.us/

City of Oklahoma City Hall
http://www.okc-cityhall.org/

cle.jobs

cmh.jobs

Colorado Jobs Information
http://www.state.co.us/jobinfo.html

Colorado's Job Bank
http://co.jobsearch.org/

Columbus Dispatch
http://www.dispatch.com/

Commonwealth of Kentucky Workforce
Development Cabinet
http://www.state.ky.us/agencies/wforce/
des/des.htm

Connect Oklahoma
http://www.connectok.com/

Connecticut Works
http://www.ctdol.state.ct.us/

Connecticut's Job Bank
http://ct.jobsearch.org/

Dallas Examiner
http://www.dallasexaminer.com/

dc.jobs

Del-AWARE
http://www.lib.de.us/business/
jobs_and_careers.html

Delaware's Job Bank
http://de.jobsearch.org/

The Denver Post Online
http://www.denverpost.com/jobs/jobs.htm

Deseret News
http://www.desnews.com/

dfw.jobs

Digital City Chicago
http://chicago.digitalcity.com

District of Columbia's Job Bank
http://dc.jobsearch.org

Dominion Post Online
http://www.dominionpost.com/

Employment Development Department
http://wwwedd.cahwnet.gov/

Employment Hotlines for Minnesota
http://www.disserv.stu.umn.edu/TC/
Grants/COL/hotline.html

Employment Hotlines for Omaha, NE
http://www.unl.edu/careers/jobs/omaha.htm

Employment Security Commission of North
Carolina (NCESC)
http://www.esc.state.nc.us/

Express-News Online
http://www.express-news.net/

Finding Work in Alaska
http://www.state.ak.us/local/akpages/LABOR/
esd_alaska_jobs/ak_over.htm

fl.jobs

Florida Communities Network (FCN)
http://www.state.fl.us/

Frequently Asked Questions About Nebraska
http://www.state.ne.us/faq/faq.html

Fulton County Employment & Job Opportunities
http://www.co.fulton.ga.us/employ.htm

Galveston County Daily News
http://www.galvnews.com/

The Gate: The Bay Area's Home Page
http://www.sfgate.com/

Gateway Virginia
http://www.gateway-va.com

Georgia's Job Bank
http://www.dol.state.ga.us/eshtml/eshtml02.htm

git.ohr.jobs.digest

Go Cincinnati!
http://gocinci.net/

Go Cincinnati!
http://www.gocinci.com/

GoCinci.Net Careerfinder
http://careerfinder.gocinci.net

Guam Chamber of Commerce Directory of Members
http://www.guamchamber.com/directory/

Guam's Job Bank
http://gu.jobsearch.org/

Hartford Courant Newspaper
http://news.courant.com/class.stm

Hawaii Department of Labor and Industrial Relations
http://www.aloha.net/~edpso/

Hawaii Home Page
http://www.hawaii.net/

Hawaii JobPage
http://www.lava.net/hijobs/

Hawaii's Job Bank
http://hi.jobsearch.org/

Heartland Regional Network, the Community Network
for Central Illinois
http://hrn.bradley.edu/heart.htm

Herald Extra
http://www.daily-herald.com

Home Page Washington
http://www.state.wa.us/

HoosierNet
http://www.bloomington.in.us/

Houston Chronicle Interactive
http://www.chron.com/

houston.jobs

houston.jobs.offered

houston.jobs.wanted

hsv.jobs

Idaho Works
http://www.doe.state.id.us/

Idaho Works Job Bank
http://www.doe.state.id.us/pubjs/jsmain.asp

Illinois Department of Commerce and
Community Affairs
http://www.commerce.state.il.us/dcca/
menus/wfjt.htm

Illinois Job Bank
http://il.jobsearch.org/

IN Jersey
http://www.injersey.com/

in.jobs

Indiana Workforce Development
http://www.bloomington.in.us/employment

Indiana's Job Bank
http://in.jobsearch.org/

Indianapolis Online
http://www.indianapolis.in.us/

InfoMine Reference Links
http://www.wvlc.wvnet.edu/commish/ref.html

Inside Denver: Colorado Jobs
http://InsideDenver.com/jobs/

Iowa Jobs
http://www.state.ia.us/jobs/

Iowa Jobs Hotline
http://www.unl.edu/careers/jobs/iowahotl.htm

Iowa Workforce Development
http://www.state.ia.us/iwd

IowAccess
http://www.state.ia.us/government/iitt/
iowaccess/index.htm

IR Online
http://www.intelligencer-record.com/

Jefferson County Personnel Board (Birmingham)
http://www.bham.net/pbjc/index.html

Job Board
http://www.fsu.edu/Jobs.html

Job Hotlines for Washington
http://www.gspa.washington.edu/Career/
hotlines.html

Job Hunt (formerly Webdog's Job Hunt)
http://csueb.sfsu.edu/jobs.html

Job Opportunities in North Dakota
http://www.tradecorridor.com/jobs.htm

Job Opportunities in South Carolina
http://www.state.sc.us/jobopps.html

Job Service North Dakota
http://www.state.nd.us/jsnd

Jobfind.com
http://www.jobfind.com

JobNET
http://www.jobnet.com/

Jobs Jobs Jobs
http://www.jobsjobsjobs.com/

JobSmart
http://jobsmart.org
JobSmart: California Job Search Guide
http://www.jobsmart.org
Juneau Empire Classifieds
http://juneauempire.com/Classified/classc.htm
Kansas City Star
http://www.kcstar.com/
Kansas City, Missouri
http://www.kcmo.org/
Kansas Department of Human Resources
http://www.hr.state.ks.us/
Kansas Job Bank
http://www.ink.org/public/kdhr/jobbank.html
Kentucky's Job Bank
http://ky.jobsearch.org/
Knoxville News-Sentinel Online
http://www.knoxnews.com/
La Plaza Telecommunity
http://www.laplaza.org/
la.jobs
Las Vegas Review-Journal
http://www.lvrj.com/
li.jobs
LibertyNet: Linking People and Information in the
Philadelphia Region
Library of Congress Information on State and
Local Governments
http://lcweb.loc.gov/global/state/stategov.html
Locating Government Job Opportunities in Florida
http://www.state.fl.us/fcn/centers/
job_center/vacancy/
Los Angeles Times
http://www.latimes.com/HOME/CLASS/EMPLOY/
lou.lft.jobs
Louisiana Department of Labor (DOL)
http://www.ldol.state.la.us/homepage.htm
Louisiana's Job Bank
http://www.ldol.state.la.us/JIS/JISMAINC.HTML
Louisville Courier-Journal
http://classifieds.courier-journal.com/cv3/lville
http://www.courier-journal.com/
Madison Daily Leader
http://www.madisondailyleader.com/
madison.com
http://www.madison.com/
Mail Tribune
http://www.mailtribune.com/main.htm
Maine State Government
http://www.state.me.us/
Maine's Job Bank
http://mejobsearch.org/
Maryland's CareerNet
http://www.careernet.state.md.us/
Maryland's Job Bank
http://md.jobsearch.org/search.html
Massachusetts Job Bank
http://ma.jobsearch.org
Maui Web Directory
http://www.mauimapp.com/
MEL: Michigan Electronic Library
http://mel.lib.mi.us
Memphis Commercial Appeal
http://www.gomemphis.com/
Memphis.employment
METRONET
http://www.metronet.lib.mn.us/
Metropolitan Government of Nashville and
Davidson County
http://janis.nashville.org/
mi.jobs
Michigan Government Internet Sites
http://www.state.mi.us/

Michigan Jobs Commission
http://www.mjc.state.mi.us/mjc/index.htm
milw.jobs
Milwaukee Journal Sentinel
http://www.jsonline.com/
Minnesota's Job Bank & SkillsNet
http://www.des.state.mn.us/
Mississippi Employment Security Commission
http://www.mesc.state.ms.us/
Mississippi's Job Bank
http://ms.jobsearch.org/
Missouri Department of Labor and Industrial
Relations
http://www.dolir.state.mo.us/
Missouri State Government Web
http://www.state.mo.us/
Missouri Works! Job Bank
http://www.works.state.mo.us/search/
index.htm
Montana Vacancies in Education
http://jsd.dli.mt.gov/state/edu.htm
Montana's Job Bank
http://jsd.dli.mt.gov/
NASIRE (National Association of State Information
Resource Executives)
http://www.nasire.org/
ne.jobs
ne.jobs.contract
Nebraska Department of Labor
http://www.dol.state.ne.us/
Nebraska State Government
http://www.state.ne.us
Nebraska Web
http://www.neb.web.com/
Nebraska World Wide Web Registry
http://www.novia.net/~rfulk/web
Nebraska's Job Bank
http://ne.jobsearch.org/
NebraskaLink
http://www.neblink.com/
Nevada's Job Bank
http://nvjobsearch.org/index.html
NevadaNet
http://www.nevadanet.com/
New Hampshire's Job Bank
http://www.nhworks.state.nh.us/
New Jersey Home Page
http://www.state.nj.us/
New Jersey News.com: Your One-Stop for Garden
State News
http://www.newjerseynews.com/
New Jersey Online
http://www.njjobs.com/
New Jersey's Job Bank
http://nj.jobsearch.org/
New Mexico Department of Labor
http://www.state.nm.us/dol
New Mexico's Job Bank
http://nm.jobsearch.org
The News and Observer Classifieds
http://www.nando.net/classads/employment
http://www.news-observer.com/classads/
employment/
New York City Reference
http://www.panix.com/clay/nyc
New York State Department of Labor
http://www.labor.state.ny.us/
New York Times on the Web
http://www.nytimes.com/
New York's Job Bank
http://www.labor.state.ny.us/doleemp.htm
Newsday.com
http://www.newsday.com/

nm.jobs
North Carolina Information Server
http://www.state.nc.us/
North Carolina's Job & Career Navigator
http://www.exc.state.nc.us/NCJC/
North Carolina's Job Bank
http://www.exc.state.nc.us/jis/
North Dakota State Government
http://www.state.nd.us/
North Dakota's Job Bank
http://www.nd.jobsearch.org/
North Star: Minnesota Government Information
and Services
http://www.state.mn.us/
Northscape
http://www.gfherald.com/
Northwest Source: The Seattle Times Company
http://www.seatimes.com/
NYC Employment, Career & Job Resources
http://www.allny.com/jobs.html
NYC LINK: the Official New York City World Wide
Web Site
http://www.ci.nyc.ny.us/
nyc.jobs
nyc.jobs.contract
nyc.jobs.misc
nyc.jobs.offered
nyc.jobs.wanted
OBES: Ohio's Job Bank
http://www.state.oh.us/obes/
Ocean State Free-Net (OSFN)
http://osfn.rhilinet.gov/
telnet://osfn.org
Oklahoma City and Related Links
http://okccvb.org/okclinks.html
Oklahoma Employment Security Commission
http://www.oexc.state.ok.us/
Oklahoma's Job Bank
http://www.oesc.state.ok.us/jobnet
The Oklahoman Online
http://www.oklahoman.net/opub
Omaha CareerLink
http://www.careerlink.org/index.htm
http://www.omaha.org/careerlink.html
Oregon Live
http://www.oregonian.com/
Oregon OnLine
http://www.state.or.us/
Oregon's Essential Links
http://www.el.com/To/Oregon
Oregon's Job Bank
http://www.emp.state.or.us/empmtsvcs/
osu.jobs
Palo Alto Online
http://www.PaloAltoOnline.com/
Palo Alto Weekly Online Edition
http://www.service.com/PAW/home.html
PA-Today: the Best of Pennsylvania's
Newspapers Online
http://www.pa-today.com/
pdaxs.jobs.construction
pdaxs.jobs.engineering
pdaxs.jobs.management
pdaxs.jobs.misc
pdaxs.jobs.resumes
pdaxs.jobs.sale
pdaxs.jobs.temporary
pdaxs.jobs.wanted
PDXJOBS Home Page
http://www.pdxjobs.com/
Pennsylvania's Job Bank
http://pa.jobsearch.org/

Peoria Journal Star
http://www.adquest.com/local/pjstar/employ.asp

pgh.jobs wanted

pgh.jobs.offered

PHILA.GOV
http://www.phila.gov/

Philadelphia Online/Philly Jobs
http://www.phillynews.com/programs/
ads/SUNHLP

Philanthropy Journal of North Carolina
http://www.philanthropy-journal.org/
http://www.pj.org/

Phillyworks
http://www.slipps.com/phillyworks/

phl.jobs.offered

phl.jobs.wanted

Pierre Home Page
http://www.pierre.org

Pilot Online
http://www.pilotonline.com/

Portland Press Herald/Maine Sunday Telegram
http://www.maineclassified.com/
http://www.portland.com/

POSTnet
http://www.stlnet.com/

Projo.com
http://www.projo.com/

Providence RI Home Page
http://www.providenceri.com/

Raleigh Online
http://www.webs4you.com/raleigh/ral2.htm#jobs

The Red Guide to Temp Agencies
http://www.panix.com/~grvsmth/redguide/

Rhode Island's Job Bank
http://ri.jobsearch.org/

RIDLT: Rhode Island Department of Labor
and Training
http://www.det.state.ri.us/

The Sacramento Bee
http://www.sacbee.com/classads/ads/today/
employment_index.html

Sailor: Maryland's Online Public Information Network
http://sailor.lib.md.us/sailor/

San Bernardino County Employment Opportunities
http://www.co.san-bernardino.ca.us/ht/jobs/
mainjobs.htm

San Diego Jobs
http://www.sandiegojobs.com/

San Francisco Bay Area Volunteer Information Center
http://www.meer.net/users/taylor/

San Francisco Cityspan Information Center
http://www.ci.sf.ca.us/infoemp.htm

San Jose Mercury
http://spyglass.sjmercury.com/class/help/
index.htm

San Mateo Times, and . . .
http://www.newschoice.com/default.asp

SCIway . . . Gateway to Online South Carolina
http://www.sciway.net/jobs/index.html

sdnet.jobs

Seattle Community Network
http://www.scn.org/

Seattle Online
http://www.pan.ci.seattle.wa.us/

seattle.jobs

seattle.jobs.offered

seattle.jobs.wanted

Sioux Falls
http://www.siouxfalls.org/

SLED: Alaska's Statewide Library Electronic Doorway
http://sled.alaska.edu/

SmartUtah
http://www.smartutah.org/

The SofTech Jobs Board
http://www.northbay.com/softech/index.html

South Carolina Employment Security Commission
http://scjob.sces.org/

South Carolina's Job Bank
http://sc.jobsearch.org/

South Dakota Department of Labor
http://www.state.sd.us/state/executive/dol

South Dakota Popular Internet Places
http://sodapop.dsu.edu

South Dakota's Job Bank
http://sd.jobsearch.org

St. Louis Employment Links
http://members.tripod.com/~Jablon/assess.html

Star/News Online
http://www.starnews.com/

StarNet Electrifieds
http://www.azstarnet.com/public/electrifieds/

State and Local Government on the Net
http://www.piperinfo.com/state/states.html

State of Alaska Jobs and Job Services
http://www.state.ak.us/local/jobs.htm

State of Mississippi # http://www.state.ms.us/

State of Ohio Government Information and Services
http://www.ohio.gov/ohio/index.htm

State of Oklahoma Government Information Server
http://www.state.ok.us/

State of Rhode Island Home Page
http://www.state.ri.us/

State of South Carolina Public Information
Home Page
http://www.state.sc.us/

State of Texas Government Information
http://www.state.tx.us/
http://www.texas.gov/

State of Utah: Employment
http://www.state.ut.us/html/employment.htm

State of Vermont Home Page
http://www.state.vt.us

State of West Virginia Home Page
http://www.state.wv.us/

State of Wisconsin Department
of Workforce Development
http://www.dwd.state.wi.us/

State of Wisconsin Information Server
http://www.state.wi.us/

Statejobs.com
http://www.statejobs.com

stl.jobs

su.jobs.

Syracuse Online
http://www.syracuse.com/

Tallahassee Free-net
http://www.freenet.tlh.fl.us/Employ.html

Tango! Telegram and Gazette
http://www.telegram.com/

The Telegraph on the Web
http://www.nashuatelegraph.com

Tennessee Department of Employment Security
http://www.state.tn.us/employsecurity/

Tennessee's Job Bank
http://tn.jobsearch.org

Texas ComputerJobs Store
http://www.texas.computerjobs.com/

Texas Job Bank
http://www.tec.state.tx.us/twc.html
telnet://hi-tec.tec.state.tx.us/
telnet://twcdirect.twc.state.tx.us/
(login: jobs)

Texas One
http://www.texas-one.org

Three Rivers Free-Net
http://trfn.clpgh.org/

Times Daily Classified
http://www.timesdaily.com/classified/classif2.htm

Topeka Capital-Journal Classifieds
http://voyager.stauffergold.com/clbrowse/
clbrowse.dll

Town Online
http://www.townonline.com/working

triangle.jobs

trib.com
http://www.trib.com/

TRIBnet
http://www.tribnet.com/

Twin Cities Free-Net
http://freenet.msp.mn.us/

tx.jobs

ucb.jobs

ucd.cs.jobs

ucd.jobs

uiuc.cs.jobs

umich.jobs

umn.cs.jobs

umn.general.jobs

umn.itlab.jobs

ut.jobs

Utah Department of Workforce Services
http://dwsa.state.ut.us/

utah.jobs

Utah's Job Bank
http://ut.jobsearch.org/

utcs.jobs

Vermont Department of Employment and Training
http://www.det.state.vt.us/

Virginia Department of Personnel and Training
http://www.state.va.us/~dpt/

Virginia Employment Commission
http://www.state.va.us/vec

Virginia's Job Bank
http://va.jobsearch.org

Washington Online Reemployment Kiosk
http://www.wa.gov/esd/employment.html

The Washington Post
http://204.246.47.74/search.html

Washington's Job Bank
http://wa.jobsearch.org/

WE CAN Job Search
http://www.onestop.org/jbsearch.htm

WEBSTER: the New Hampshire State Government
Online Information Center
http://www.state.nh.us/

West Bend Community Career Network
http://www.careernet.com/

West Virginia Bureau of Employment Programs
http://www.state.wv.us/bep/

West Virginia Online
http://www.wvonline.com/

West Virginia's Job Bank
http://wv.jobsearch.org

Western New York Jobs
http://www.wnyjobs.com/

Wichita Area Chamber of Commerce
http://www.wacc.org/index.html

Wisconsin JobNet
http://167.218.251.8/jobnet/

WorkAvenue.com
http://www.startribune.com/mcu/workave/
stonline/content/workave/work_main1.shtml

WorkBase
http://www.workbase.com/

Workforce Florida
http://www.floridajobs.org/

Workforce New Jersey Public Information Network
http://www.wnjpin.state.nj.us/

Working in Nevada
http://www.state.nv.us/detr/index.html

Work-Web
http://www.work-web.com

Wyoming Department of Employment
http://wydoe.state.wy.us/

Wyoming's Job Bank
http://wyjobs.state.wy.us/region.htm

Yahoo! Atlanta
http://atlanta.yahoo.com

Yahoo! Austin
http://austin.yahoo.com

Yahoo! Boston
http://boston.yahoo.com

Yahoo! Chicago
http://chi.yahoo.com

Yahoo! Dallas/Fort Worth
http://dfw.yahoo.com

Yahoo! Los Angeles
http://la.yahoo.com

Yahoo! Miami
http://miami.yahoo.com

Yahoo! New York
http://ny.yahoo.com

Yahoo! San Francisco Bay Area
http://sfbay.yahoo.com

Yahoo! Seattle
http://seattle.yahoo.com

Yahoo! Twin Cities
http://minn.yahoo.com

Yahoo! Washington D.C.
http://dc.yahoo.com

Chapter 13

AACI Israel Jobnet
http://192.116.74.141/images/weleng.htm

ActiJob
http://www.activeemploi.com/tp_menu.html

AK Jobnet, Austin Knight Company
http://www.ak.com.au/akjobnet.html

Alliance-China Online
http://www.alliance-china.com

Asia Online!
http://www.asiadragons.com/asia/asiawork/
asiawork.htm

Asianet
http://www.asia-net.com

Association Bernard Gregory
http://abg.grenet.fr./abg/

at.jobs

Aupair JobMatch
http://www.aupairs.co.uk

aus.ads.jobs

aus.jobs

Australia Department of Employment, Education,
Training and Youth Affairs
http://www.deetya.gov.au/

BC Ministry of Employment and Investment
http://www.ei.gov.bc.ca/

BizLINKS Resources
http://sunflower.singnet.com.sb/~g6615000

bln.jobs

Blue Sky Community Networks
http://www.freenet.mb.ca

Breitbach & Partner
http://www.breitbach.com/

Bridge Information Technology Inc.
http://www.bridgerecruit.com/index.cfm

British Council
http://www.britcoun.org/eis/

Calgary Free-Net
http://www.freenet.calgary.ab.ca/home.shtml

can.jobs

Canada WorkInfoNet
http://www.workinfonet.ca

Canada WorkInfoNet: Alberta
http://www.edsg.com:80/canwin

Canada WorkInfoNet: British Columbia
http://workinfonet.bc.ca/

Canada WorkInfoNet: New Brunswick
http://www.gov.nb.ca/ael/.mab/
cwnhome.htm

Canada WorkInfoNet: Northwest Territory
http://siksik.learnnet.nt.ca/career

Canada WorkInfoNet: Quebec
http://www.workinfonet.ca/cwn/english/quebec

Canada WorkInfoNet: Saskatchewan
http://www.sasked.gov.sk.ca/careers

Career and Placement Services (CAPS)
http://www.ualberta.ca/~caps/homepage.htm

Career China
http://www.globalvillager.com/villager/CC.html

CareerMosaic Asia
http://www.careerasia.com.sg/index.html

CareerMosaic Australia
http://employment.com.au/index.html
http://www.careermosaic.jobs.com.au/
cmaust.html

CareerMosaic Canada
http://canada.careermosaic.com/

CareerMosaic France
http://www.careermosaic.tm.fr/

CareerMosaic Hong Kong
http://www.careermosaic.com.hk/

CareerMosaic International Gateway
http://www.careermosaic.com/cm/gateway/
gateway1.html

CareerMosaic Japan
http://www.careermosaic.or.jp/

CareerMosaic Korea
http://www.careermosaickorea.com/

CareerMosaic UK
http://www.careermosaic-uk.co.uk

CareerPlace
http://www.careerplace.com/

Careers Online Australia
http://www.careersonline.com.au

China Gold
http://www.chinagold.com/

Creyf's
http://www.creyfs.be/

de Marchel von Bakker Inskip, Ltd.
http://www.dmvbi.com/index.html

de.markt.jobs

dk.jobs

Eastern and Central European Job Bank
http://www.ecejobbank.com

Edmonton FreeNet
http://freenet.edmonton.ab.ca/

Electronic Labour Exchange
http://ele.ingenia.com/

EMAP Media Web
http://main.emap.com/media/

employment.net.au
http://www.employment.net.au/

Expat Forum
http://www.expatforum.com/

FDAssociates
http://www.pratique.fr/pro/FDAssociates/

fr.jobs.d

fr.jobs.demandes

fr.jobs.off-res

FROGJOBS-Employment in France
listproc@cren.org
(message: subscribe frogjobs yourname)

Gaijin Gleaner
http://kyushu.com/kcentral

Gemini Personnel Group
http://www.gemini.com.hk/

GlobalNet Markets
http://www.bolsadetrabajo.com/main.htm

Government of Alberta Home Page
http://www.gov.ab.ca

Greater Victoria Chamber of Commerce
http://www.chamber.victoria.bc.ca/chamber

Halinet (formerly Halton Community Network)
http://www.hhpl.on.ca/

Hampton Consultancy
http://www.hampton.co.za/

Headhunters
http://www.xs4all.nl/~avotek

Human Resources Development Canada
http://www.hrde-drhc.gc.ca/

ICEN-L International Career and Employment
Network (NAFSA)
listserv@IUBVM.UCS.INDIANA.EDU (message:
subscribe icen-l yourfirstname yourlastname)

ie.jobs

InfoTech Weekly Online JobNet NZ
http://www.jobnetnz.co.nz/

International Academic Job Market
http://www.camrev.com.au/share/jobs.html

International Herald Tribune Recruitment Ads
http://www.washingtonpost.com/wp-adv/
classifieds/careerpost.iht.htm

International Job Search Resources
http://www.overseasjobs.com/resources/
jobs_main.html

International Organizations with Job Openings
on the Internet
http://www.psc.cfp.gc.ca/intpgm/epb6.htm

International Rescue Committee
http://www.intrescom.org/toc.html

Internet Employment Café
http://cafe.sde.uwo.ca/low/iecmain.html

Internet Job Links
http://www.the-beaches.com/empl.html

Irish Jobs Page
http://www.exp.ie/

israel.jobs.misc

israel.jobs.offered

israel.jobs.resumes

Job Market China
http://www.jobchina.net

Job.net
http://www2.vnu.co.uk/jobnet/

JobSAT
http://www.jobsat.com

JobServe
http://www.demon.co.uk/jobserve/

kingston.jobs

kw.jobs

Les Pages Emploi
http://emploi.hrnet.fr/

M & M Recruitment Limited
http://www.mmstaff.co.uk/

Manitoba Government Home Page
http://www.gov.mb.ca

National Graduate Register
http://ngr.schoolnet.ca/engine/

Naukri
http://www.naukri.com/

Nexus Job Index
http://www.nexus.ch/

Niagara's Electronic Village
http://www.npiec.on.ca/

Niagara's Electronic Village
telnet://freenet.npiec.on.ca (login: guest)

NISS, National Information Services and Systems
http://www.niss.ac.uk/noticeboard/index.html

O-Hayo Sensei, The Newsletter of (English) Teaching
Jobs in Japan
http://www.ohayosensei.com/

Online Career Center Africa#
http://www.occ.com/occ/Africa.html

Online Career Center Asia
http://www.occ.com/Asia.html

Online Career Center Australia
http://www.occ.com/occ/Australia.html

Online Career Center Canada
http://www.occ.com/occ/Canada.html

Online Career Center Central America
http://www.occ.com/occ/CentralAmerica.html

Online Career Center Europe
http://www.occ.com/occ/Europe.html

Online Career Center International
http://www.occ.com/occ/international.html

Online Career Center Mexico (in English)
http://www.occ.com/occ/Mexico.html

Online Career Center Mexico (in Spanish)
http://www.occ.com/mx/

Online Career Center Middle East
http://www.occ.com/occ/MiddleEast.html

Online Career Center Scandinavia
http://www.occ.com/occ/Scandinavia

Online Career Center South America
http://www.occ.com/occ/SouthAmerica.html

ont.jobs

ott.jobs

Overseas Job Web
http://www.overseasjobs.com/index.html

The Parksville-Qualicum Career Centre
http://www.island.net/~careers/

People Bank
http://www.peoplebank.com.au

The Personnel Concept
http://www.web.co/za/p-concept

Positionwatch Information Technology
Employment Network
http://www.positionwatch.com/

Price Jamieson Online
http://www.pricejam.com/

Prince George Free-Net
telnet://frodo.pgfn.bc.ca (login: guest)

Professionals On-Line
http://www.webcom.com/wordimg/pro/

Prospective Management Overseas (PMO)
http://www.pmo.be/home.htm

Public Service Commission of Canada
http://www.psc-cfp.gc.ca

qc.jobs

Reed Personnel Services
http://www.reed.co.uk/

relcom.commerce.jobs

Reseau Europeen pour l'Emploi
http://www.reseau.org/emploi

Russian and East European Institute Employment
Opportunities
http://www.indiana.edu/~reeiweb/indemp.html

The Russian Word, Inc.
http://www.russianword.com

SASIS, Inc.
http://www.sasia.com/main.htm

Sheridan College Career Centre Online!
http://www.sheridan.on.ca/career/home.htm

Strategis
http://strategis.ic.gc.ca/

SwissWebJobs
http://www.swisswebjobs.ch

swnet.jobs

Sympatico
http://www.sympatico.ca/

taps.com
http://www.taps.co.uk

Telejob
http://www.telejob.ethz.ch

THESIS: The Times Higher Education Supplement
InterView Service
http://www.thesis.co.uk

TKO Personnel Inc.
http://www.tkointl.com/

tor.jobs

Toronto Free-Net, Inc.
http://www.freenet.toronto.on.ca/

Vancouver CommunityNet
http://www.vcn.bc.ca

Victoria Telecommunity Network
http://freenet.victoria.bc.ca

Ward and Associates
http://www.ward-associates.com/

Work MadeEasy
http://work.madeeasy.com/

WorkWeb: Canada's On-Line Campus Career Centre
http://www.cacee.com/

Yahoo!
http://www.yahoo.com

Yahoo! Asia
http://www.yahoo.com.sg

Yahoo! Australia & NewZealand
http://www.yahoo.com.au/

Yahoo! Canada
http://www.yahoo.ca/

Yahoo! France
http://www.yahoo.fr

Youth Resource Network of Canada
http://www.youth.gc.ca/

za.ads.jobs

Chapter 14

AAA Resume Service
http://www.infi.net/~resume/

About Work
http://www.aboutwork.com

Acorn Career Counseling and Resume Writing
http://www.acornresume.com

Alt.Psychology.Personality.Archives
http://sunsite.unc.edu/personality/

America's Career InfoNet
http://www.acinet.org

Business Researcher's Interests
http://www.brint.com/interests.html

Career Interests Game
http://www.missouri.edu/~cppcwww/
holland.html

Career Magazine: Career-Related Links
http://www.careermag.com/db/cmag_careerlinks

Career Resource Center
http://www.careers.org/

Careers On-Line at the University of Minnesota
http://disserv3.stu.umn.edu/COL/

Catapult, Career Service Professionals Homepage
http://www.jobweb.org/catapult/catapult.html

Chamber of Commerce International Directory
http://chamber-of-commerce.com

CityNet
http://www.city.net

CompanyLink
http://www.companylink.com

Comprehensive College Financing Information
http://www.infi.net/collegemoney/

Definitive Guide to Internet Career Resources
http://phoenix.placement.oakland.edu/
career/Guide.htm

Employment Directory of American Markets
http://www.careermosaic.com/cm/directory/
edl.html

E-Span Career Briefcase—AssessmentTools
http://espan2.espan.com/career/p1/dir/
care/asse.htm

FinAid, The Financial Aid Information Page
http://www.finaid.org

Find Your Career: USNews
http://www4.usnews.com/usnews/edu/
beyond/bccguide.htm

1st Steps in the Hunt
http://interbiznet.net/hunt/assist.html

Forty Plus of Northern California
http://www.fortyplus.org

Getting Past Go: A Survival Guide
for College Graduates
http://www.mongen.com/getgo

Getworking
http://www.getworking.msn.com/getworking/
toc/default.htm

Graduate Horizons, Career Information
http://www.gold.net/arcadia/horizons/

Hoover's Online
http://www.hoovers.com

International Association of Career
Management Professionals
http://www.iacmp.org

IQ Tests, Personality Tests, and Entrepreneurial
Tests on the WWW
http://www.2h.com

JobSmart
http://www.jobsmart.org

JobWeb
http://www.jobweb.org

Keirsey Temperament Web Site
http://www.keirsey.com/

National Board of Certified Counselors
http://www.nbcc.org

National Career Development Association
http://www.ncda.org

1998-99 Occupational Outlook Handbook
http://stats.bls.gov/ocohome.htm

OWL-Online Writing Lab, Purdue University
http://owl.trc.purdue.edu/

Personality and IQ Tests
http://www.davideck.com

Peterson's Education Center
http://www.petersons.com

Platinum Rule-Personality Style Quiz
http://www.platinumrule.com/

Presidents Committee on Employment of People
with Disabilities
http://www.pcebd.gov

Princeton Review-So You Want to Get a Career
http://www.review.com/career/index.cfm

Quinetessential Career and Job-Hunting
Resources Guide
http://stetson.edu/~rhansen/careers.html

Rebecca Smith's eResumes & Resources
http://www.eresumes.com/

Resources for Persons with Disabilities
from The Catapult
http://www.jobweb.org/catapult/DISABLED.htm

Resumania On-Line
http://www.umn.edu/ohr/ecep/resume

Resumix
http://www.resumix.com

State and Local Government on the Net
http://www.piperinfo.com/state/states.html

State Occupational Projections, 1994–2005
http://udesc.state.ut.us/almis/stateproj/

Tripod
http://www.tripod.com

University of California, Berkeley Career
Exploration Links
http://www.berkeley.edu/CareerLibrary/links/
careerme.htm

University of Waterloo Career Services—Career
Development Manual
http://www.adm.uwaterloo.ca/infocecs/CRC/
manual-home.html

What Color Is Your Parachute: Job Hunting Online
http://www.washingtonpost.com/parachute.

Women's Wire
http://www.women.com

Working and Living Overseas
http://www.magi.com/~issi

WWWomen
http://www.wwwomen.com

Appendix A

Careers, Not Just Jobs: Wall Street
Journal Interactive
http://careers.wsj.com

National Board for Certified Counselors
http://www.nbcc.org

National Business Employment Weekly
http://www.nbew.com

National Career Development Association (NCDA)
http://ncda.org

Stybel & Peabody
http://www.stybelpeabody.com

Appendix B

AltaVista
http://www.altavista.digital.com

Ask the Headhunter
http://www.fool.com/headhunter.htm

Career Magazine
http://www.careermag.com

DejaNews
http://www.dejanews.com

Discussion Lists: Mail List Manager Commands
http://lawlib.slu.edu/training/mailser.htm

Excite
http://www.excite.com

Galaxy
http://galaxy.tradewave.com

Infoseek
http://www.infoseek.com

Job-Hunt
http://www.job-hunt.org

Kovacs LIst
http://www.n2h2.com/KOVACS

Liszt
http://www.liszt.com

Lycos
http://www.lycos.com

The Net: User Guidelines and Netiquette
http://www.fau.edu/rinaldi/net/
index.html Net Presence
http://arganet.tenagra.com/Tenagra/
net-presence.html

Networking on the Network
http://communication.ucsd.edu/pagre/
network.html

Newsgroup FAQs
http://www.cis.ohio-state.edu/hypertext/
faq/usenet/top.html

Yahoo!
http://www.yahoo.com

Index

Accounting and finance, 50–52
Acting and entertainment jobs, 72
Ada Project, 96
Adams Publishing, 38
AdOne, 37
AdSearch, 37
Advertising Age, 55
AdWeek, 75
Aeronautics/aviation, 93–94
Africa and the Middle East, 226–28
Agre, Phil, 29
Agriculture and forestry, 82
ALA Library Education and Employment Menu
    Page, 63
Alabama, 115, 136
AlaWeb, 136
Alaska, 116, 136–38
AltaVista, 20, 23, 33
America Online, 7, 102
America's Employers, 37
American Association of Finance and Accounting, 50
American Economics Association, 58–59
American Educational Research Association, 59
American Library Association, 63
American Marketing Association, 54
American Mathematical Society, 105
American Psychological Association Monitor, 67
America's Job Bank, 19, 25, 32, 37, 135
America's Talent Bank, 16
Annual report, 24
Anspach, Spencer, 64
AOL. *See* America Online
Application. *See* Job application
Archaeology, 58
Architecture, 94
Arizona, 116, 138–39
Arkansas, 139–40
Art Libraries Society of North America, 65
ASCII text, 12
Asia and Pacific Rim, 228–32
Asianet, 26, 38
Association of College and Research Libraries, 63
Astronomy, 83
Attachments, 12
Automotive, 94

Baud rates, 5, 8
Beckman, Roger, 64
Berger, Carol, 63
Best Jobs in the USA Today, 38
Biology/biotechnology/physiology, 83–84
Biomedicine/biotechnology, 95
Bits per second (bps), 5
Black Collegian, 38
Bloomberg Online: Career Opportunities, 51
Blue Book of Building and Construction, 101
Bookbinders Guild of New York Job Bank, 78
Bolles, Richard Nelson, 33, 48
Brandweek, 75
Brookings Institute, 120
Browsers, 6
Browsing, 19, 22
BSA Advertising, 39
Business, 49–55
Business Job Finder, 50

California, 116, 140–44
Camera repair, 95
Canada, 212–19
Career counseling, 234, 252–54
Career counseling job sites, 58
Career counselors, 19
Career exploration and selection, 235
Career Expo, 39

Career Fitness guide, 40
Career Magazine, 14, 39
Career Paradise, 46
Career Resource Homepage, 46
Career Resources Online, 233–43
CareerCity, 38
CareerMosaic, 14, 16, 39, 102
CareerNET, Career Resource Center, 46
CareerPath.com, 39
Careers, Not Just Jobs, 33, 39–40
CareerWeb, 40
*CareerXroads: The 1998 Directory to the 500 Best
    Job, Resume, and Career Management Sites
    on the World Wide Web,* 33
Chancellor and Chancellor, 97
Charette, Leo, 46, 47
Charitable contributions, 6
Chemistry, 84
Child and elder care, 56
CityNet, 25
Civil engineering, 95
Clearinghouse, 23
College Grad Job Hunter, 47
Colorado, 116, 144–46
Commercial services, 55–56
ComFind, 33
Communication programs, 5
Community freenets, 7
Computer-aided design, 96
Computer-aided engineering, 96
Computer-aided manufacturing, 96
Computer Currents, 9
Computing and technology, 96–100
Confidentiality, 4, 15, 30
Connecticut, 116, 146
Construction and public works, 101–102
Contract Employment Weekly, Jobs Online, 40
Co-ops, 123–31
Corcodilos, Nick, 102
Cover letter, 12–13
Career Builder, 38
Criscito, Pat, 33
Crispin, Gerry, 33
Culinary and baking arts, 73
Cybercafes, 7

Dalhousie University 64
Delaware, 116, 146–47
Dept. of the Interior Automated Vacancy
    Announcement System, 115
Dept. of Justice, U.S., 62, 114, 121
Dial-in numbers, local, 8
Dial-up program, 5
Dikel, Margaret Riley, 29, 46
Disability Services Careers Online, 26
Discussion Lists: Mail List Manager Commands, 26
District of Columbia, 147
DOS text, 12

Eastern Europe, 225–26
Economics, 58
EDGAR 10K Reports, 25
Education and academe, 59–61
EFL. *See* English as a second or foreign language
Electric and other utilities, 102
Electrical engineering, 102
Electronic Blue Book, 101
Electronic journals/newspapers, 2, 23
Electronic mail, 5, 7, 8, 27
Ellsworth, Jill, 9
E-mail. *See* Electronic mail
Employer profiles, 31
Employment services Web sites, 26
Enews, 23

Engineering, 91–107
English as a second or foreign language, 61–62
Entry-level employment, 123–31
Environment/geographic information systems/earth
    sciences, 84–86
Equipment leasing, 56
ESL. *See* English as a second or foreign language
ESL Job Center, 62
Etiquette, online, 28
Excite, 23, 33
Executive search, 246–48
Experience on Demand, 41
Experienced job seekers, services for, 245–54

Facilities maintenance, 103–4
FAQ. *See* Frequently Asked Questions
Federal government, 110–13
Federal Government Job Hotlines, 110
FedWorld: The United States Government Bulletin
    Board, 111
Flaming, 29, 36
Florida, 116
Food and drug packaging, 56
Food processing, 104
4Work, 41
Free trial period, 9
Frequently Asked Questions, 21, 28
Fund-raising jobs, 52
Funeral directors, 56

Galaxy, The, 20, 22
Georgia, 116, 149–50
*Get Wired, You're Hired: The Canadian Guide to Job
    Hunting Online,* 33
Gilster, Paul, 9
Good Works, 66
Government, federal, 109–21
Government, state and local, 25, 133–208
Graphic arts, 73–74
Graphical browser, 6
Graphics, viewing, 6
Grimes, Galen A., 9
Guam, 150–51

Hahn, Harley, 9
Hard drive, 5
Harley Hahn's Internet and Web Yellow Pages 1997, 9
Hawaii, 116, 151
Health, 81–89
Health care, 86–87
Home page, employer's, 24
Hoover's Online, 20, 23, 33
HotBot, 23
Hospitality, 71–79
HotJobs!, 97
HotMail, 27
How to Get Your Dream Job Using the Web, 33
HR Careers, 53
Human resources and training, 52, 53
Humanities, 71–79

Idaho, 116, 152
Illinois, 117, 152–55
Imcor, 42
Indiana, 117, 155–56
Info-Mine, 26
InfoSeek, 20, 23
Institute of Electrical and Electronic Engineers, 102
Insurance jobs sites, 53
International Monetary Fund, 120
International opportunities, 209–32
Internships, 123–31
Inquiring, 19, 20
Internet access, 6–9
Internet basics, 4–10

Internet Career Connection, 42
Internet for Dummies, 9
Internet 1997 Unleashed, 9
Internet resume, 14
Internet service providers (ISPs), 7–9
Internet World, 10
Iowa, 117
ISPs. *See* Internet service providers

Jay Barker's Online Connection, 8
Job application, Internet, 11–16
Job banks, 25
Job Hunting on the Internet, 33
Job listing sites, 35–48
Job numbers, 13
Job search criteria, 18–19
JobBank USA, 43
JobCenter, 43
JobHunt: A Meta-List of Online Job Search
    Resources and Services, 47
JobSmart, 47
JobSmart Salary Surveys, 25
Job Trak, 43, 126
JobWire, 58
Journalism and broadcast media, 74–76
Juno, 27

Kansas, 117, 157–58
Karl, Arthur, 33
Karl, Shannon, 33
Kentucky, 117, 158
Keyword list, 19
Kovacs List, 27

Landmark Communications, 40
Latin America and South America, 219–20
Lauber, Daniel, 33
Law, 62
Law enforcement and protective services, 121
Levine, John R., 9
Librarian's Index to the Internet, 22
Library and information sciences, 63–65
Library Journal, 65
Library of Congress, 65, 114
Linguistics, 66
List, The (of ISPs), 8
Listproc, 26, 27
Listserv, 26, 27
Liszt, The (mailing list), 27
Looksmart, 22
Louisiana, 117, 158–59
Lycos, 23, 33

MacTemps, 98
Magellan Internet Guide, 22
Mail resume, 13
Mailers (software programs), 5, 8
Mailing lists, 2, 21, 25, 26–27
Maine, 117, 159–60
Majordomo, 26, 27
Manpower, 43
Manufacturing, 104
Marketing, 49–55
Maryland, 117, 160–61
Massachusetts, 117, 161–63
Master List of Servers, 59
Mathematics, 91–107
Mechanical engineering, 105
Medicine, 81–89
Megaherz (MHz), 5
Mehler, Mark, 33
Memory, as criteria for computer choice, 6
Mental Health, 87
Michigan, 117, 163
Midwives, 87
Military, 113
Milles, Jim, 26
Mining Company, 22
Mining/drilling/offshore, 106
Minnesota, 117, 164–65
Mission statements, 24
Mississippi, 117, 165–66
Missouri, 118, 166–67
Modem, 5

Modem-to-user ratio, 8
Monitor, 6
Monster Board, 2, 16, 44, 55, 92
Montana, 118, 167
Museums and archives, 76
Music job sites, 77

National Business Employment Weekly, 29, 33,
    39–40, 47
Nebraska, 118, 168–69
Net Happenings, 22
NetGuide, 10
Netiquette, 28
Networking, 2, 26–29, 255–64
Networking on the Network, 29
Nevada, 118, 169–70
New graduates, resources for, 124–25
New Hampshire, 118, 170–71
New Jersey, 118, 171–73
New Mexico, 118, 173
New York, 118, 174–76
New York Times, 39
Newsgroup FAQs, 28
Newsfeed, 26
"Newsgroup Knowhow," 29
Newsgroups. *See* Usenet newsgroups
Newsreaders, 5, 8, 26
Nonprofits, 66–69
North America, 212–19
North Carolina, 118, 177–79
North Dakota, 118, 179–80
Northern Lights, 23
Notepad, 14
Nursing, 87

Office of Personnel Management, 112
Ohio, 118, 180–82
Oklahoma, 119, 182–84
Olsten Professional Technical Services, 93
Online Career Center, 16, 19, 25, 32, 44
Online Guides to the Job Hunt, 36, 46–48
Online journals and newspapers, 25
Online recruiting sites/services, 2, 36, 37–45
Online resource guides, 2, 20, 21, 22, 23, 26, 31
Opler, Tim, 53
Optical engineering, 107
Oregon, 119, 184–86
Outplacement, 248–52

Packaging job sites, 56
Peace Corps, 129
Pennsylvania, 119, 186–88
Personal care, 55
Personal services, 55–56
Petersons (directory), 59, 127
Philosophy, 77
Physical and occupational therapy, 88
Physicians, 88
Physics, 88
Pitch, monitor, 6
Plain text resume, 12, 13–14
Political internships, 128–29
Printing and bookbinding, 77–78
Professional's Job Finder: 1997–2000, 33
Protocols, 4
Psychology, 67
Public administration, 121
Public policy/service, 109–21

Quality control, 55

Real estate, 54
Recreation, 71–79
Recruiting sites, 25, 31
Relocating, 241–42
Resolution, monitor, 6
Resources for reaching potential employers, 241
Resume databases, 2
Resumes, 12–16, 29–30, 36, 239–40
*Resumes in Cyberspace: Your Complete Guide
    to a Computerized Job Search,* 33
Returning to school, information on, 240–41
Rhode Island, 188–90
Riley Guide, The, 16, 20, 23, 25, 32, 46

Rinaldi, Arlene H., 28
Russian and Eastern European internship
    opportunities, 127

Sales and marketing, 54–55
Saludos Web site, 26, 45
Scandinavia, 226
Scholarly societies project, 23
Science, 81–89
Search engines, 2, 20, 31, 33
Searching, 19, 20, 22
Self-assessment tests, 238–39
Semiconductor industry, 107
Set-up fee, 8
Skill set, 15
Small, Lori, 64
Social sciences, 57–66
Social work, 68
South Carolina, 119, 190–91
South Dakota, 119, 191–93
Special Libraries Association, 64
Speed, as criteria for computer choice, 5
Sports and recreation, 78
State and local resources, United States, 25,
    133–208
Strategic plan, 24
Summer employment, 123–31
Support groups, 242–43
Swartz, Mark, 33

Technical support, 9
Technology, 91–107
Telecommunications, 107
*10-Minute Guide to the Internet and the World
    Wide Web,* 9
Tennessee, 119, 193–94
Texas, 119, 194–97
Text editor, 14
Time management, 30–31
Times Higher Education Supplement, 60
Transportation, 71–79

Uniform resource locator, 21
URL. *See* Uniform resource locator
Usage fee, 8
USAJobs, 112
Usenet archives, 27–28
Usenet newsgroups, 2, 5, 7, 8, 21, 25, 26, 27,
    33, 36–37
Utah, 119, 197–98

Vermont, 119, 199–200
Video production, 79
Virginia, 119, 200–202
Virtual Job Fair, 45, 99
Virtual libraries, 20, 22, 26, 31, 32, 33, 59
Volunteer resources, 128–29

Wall Street Interactive, 33
Wall Street Journal, 39–40
Washington, 119, 202–203
Washington Intern Foundation, 129
Web browsers, 5, 7
Web Navigator, 9
WebCrawler, 23
WebScout, 22
Weddle's Web Guide, 47
West Virginia, 120, 204–5
Western Europe, 220–25
What Color Is Your Parachute?, 19
Wisconsin, 120, 205–7
Work-Web, 45
World Wide Web, 5, 7, 8
World Wide Web Employment Office, 45
Women in Technology, Int'l., 100
Women's studies, 69
Wyoming, 120, 207–8

X-118 Qualification Standards for Federal Jobs, 113

Yahoo!, 20, 22
Yahoo! Mail, 27
Yahoo's Classifieds, 45
Yahoo's Listings of Employment Information, 48
YPN: Your Personal Net, 22